St. Louis Community College

Library

5801 Wilson Avenue
St. Louis, Missouri 63110

Slavery and Freedom
in the Age of
the American Revolution

BLACKS IN THE NEW WORLD
August Meier, Series Editor

A list of books in the series appears at the end of the book.

Slavery and Freedom
in the Age of
the American Revolution

Edited by
IRA BERLIN
and
RONALD HOFFMAN

Published for the

UNITED STATES CAPITOL HISTORICAL SOCIETY

BY THE UNIVERSITY OF ILLINOIS PRESS

Urbana and Chicago

An Illini Book from the University of Illinois Press, 1986

© 1983 by the Rector and Visitors of the University of Virginia

Published for the United States Capitol Historical
Society by arrangement with the University Press of
Virginia. A list of other publications sponsored by
the Society appears at the end of the book.

Manufactured in the United States of America
P 5 4 3 2 1

This book is printed on acid-free paper.

Library of Congress Cataloging-in-Publication Data

Slavery and freedom in the age of the American
  Revolution

  (Blacks in the New World)

  Reprint. Originally published: Charlottesville:
Published for the United States Capitol Historical
Society by the University Press of Virginia, 1983.
  Includes bibliographies and index.
  1. Slavery—United States—History—18th century.
2. Slavery—America—History—18th century. 3. United
States—History—Revolution, 1775–1783—Influence.
4. Afro-Americans—History—To 1863. 5. Blacks—
America—History. I. Berlin, Ira, 1941–
II. Hoffman, Ronald, 1941–   . III. United States
Capitol Historical Society. IV. Series.
E446.S62   1986   305.8'96073'073   86–11232
ISBN 0–252–01363–8 (alk. paper)

Dedicated to

WILLIAM COOPER NELL (1816–74)

GEORGE WASHINGTON WILLIAMS (1849–91)

LUTHER PORTER JACKSON (1892–1950)

BENJAMIN QUARLES (1904–   )

Contents

Preface

At the concluding session of the United States Capitol Historical Society's 1979 symposium, I had the privilege of introducing one of the great historians of the American Revolution, Professor Merrill Jensen of the University of Wisconsin. That was a wonderful moment for me since Merrill was my professor and I will always be his student. What none of us knew that evening was that Merrill's paper—since published in the second volume of this series—would be his last original composition. Merrill Jensen died on January 30, 1980. The end of his days was typical of the man. As expressed by the poet Dylan Thomas, Merrill Jensen did not "go gentle into that good night," but made his exit with the same dignity and gruff independence that were characteristic of his life.

In his broad-ranging talk Merrill discussed the political dilemma which slavery and the slave trade posed for the Continental Congress. He noted that in 1782, when the bitter sectional crisis over the form of government for the new nation had been temporarily resolved by ratification of the Articles of Confederation, a New England preacher expressed the lingering fears and distrust with which many citizens regarded the fragile union their leaders had forged. The South, asserted the clergyman, would actually prefer empire, for the "Southern gentry," he observed, were "habituated to despotism by being the sovereigns of slaves." It was only "accident or interest," he warned ominously, that had "made the body of them the temporary sons of liberty."

The observation was a prophetic one, for within the next eighty years the union born of the Revolution was shattered, and Americans went to war with each other to determine whether it could be remade. The answer to that great question demanded a resolution of the contradiction between the reality of chattel slavery and the rhetoric of liberty and equality upon which the nation had been founded. One of the

ix

most eloquent invocations of this dimension of the Civil War is contained in Michael Shaara's fine novel about the battle of Gettysburg, *The Killer Angels*. In an early chapter, Shaara recreates a dramatic moment. It is the day before the battle. Joshua Lawrence Chamberlain, a former professor at Bowdoin College and now colonel of the 20th Maine, an infantry regiment composed of volunteers, is faced with a hundred and twenty mutineers. Before he must speak to this group of desperate and disillusioned men, Chamberlain tries to sort out in his mind his deepest convictions about America and the cause for which he is fighting. In Shaara's words, these are Chamberlain's thoughts:

> The faith itself was simple: he believed in the dignity of man. His ancestors were Huguenots, refugees of a chained and bloody Europe. He had learned their stories in the cradle. He had grown up believing in America and the individual and it was a stronger faith than his faith in God. This was the land where no man had to bow. In this place at last a man could stand up free of the past, free of tradition and blood ties and the curse of royalty and become what he wished to become. This was the first place on earth where man mattered more than the state. True freedom had begun here and it would spread eventually over all the earth. But it had begun *here*. The fact of slavery upon this incredibly beautiful new clean earth was appalling, but even more than that was the horror of old Europe, the curse of nobility, which the South was transplanting to new soil. They were forming a new aristocracy, a new breed of glittering men, and Chamberlain had come to crush it. But he was fighting for the dignity of man and in that way he was fighting for himself. If men were equal in America, all these former Poles and English and Czechs and blacks, then they were equal everywhere, and there was really no such thing as a foreigner; there were only free men and slaves. And so it was not even patriotism, but a new faith. The Frenchman may fight for France, but the American fights for mankind, for freedom; for the people, not the land.

As much as I admire this quotation, I am aware that there is a danger in using it in this context. The very nobility of such sentiments expressed in that moment of acknowledged national crisis tends to suggest that because the contradiction of slavery in the age of the American Revolution was not resolved in the 1770s and 1780s, its philosophical and moral implications were neither recognized nor understood by the pragmatic creators of the new Republic. John Adams and his contemporaries knew better. Jefferson's proposal to condemn the slave trade which was contained in the original draft of the Declaration of Independence, precipitated, according to Adams, the most violent and divisive debate of the Continental Congress's proceedings. In the end Jefferson's condemnation was expunged and, in the name of unity and necessity, the gentlemen of the Congress discreetly compromised the issue by agreeing to ignore it.

Whether the exigencies of the times justified or even required such a decision may be argued endlessly. The canons of responsible historiography are, however, less debatable, and therefore, the failure of scholars until recently to focus attention on the black experience and the seminal role of slavery during the formative period of the American nation is difficult to explain. But one thing is clear—for too many years, historians were parties to the compromise of the founding fathers.

Four historians, however, set out early to rectify this situation by examining the historic experience of their people enslaved in a nation founded upon the proposition that all men by virtue of their creation are intrinsically equal and equally entitled to liberty. The first of these was William C. Nell, who published in 1855 a book entitled *The Colored Patriots of the American Revolution*. George Washington Williams's *History of the Negro Race in America* followed in 1883, and then after almost sixty years Luther P. Jackson's study *Virginia Negro Soldiers and Seamen in the Revolutionary War* appeared in 1944. The fourth of these scholars—Dr. Benjamin Quarles, Professor Emeritus of Morgan State University, is the author of *The Negro in the American Revolution*, published in 1961. His essay provides the epilogue to this volume.

The debt the scholarship contained in this volume owes to these four historians transcends the rich information their work purveys. Within the painful racial history of this country, they had the courage and integrity to ask questions and the dedication and tenacity to pursue answers in a climate that was characteristically inhospitable to their efforts. It is to honor these men—prophets in their own country—that this book is dedicated.

RONALD HOFFMAN

Acknowledgments

In preparing this volume, the editors have accumulated a number of debts which they take pleasure in acknowledging. First and foremost, we thank the United States Capitol Historical Society and its president, Fred Schwengel, for their generous support for both the symposium and the publication series of which this volume is a part. A grant from the National Endowment for the Humanities enabled the editors to expand the format of the symposium to meet the demands of a subject as large as slavery and freedom in the Age of Revolution. During the conference, the presentation by Peter Wood and the critical commentaries by Barbara J. Fields, Michael Mullin, and Armstead Robinson enlivened the sessions and broadened the perspective of all in attendance. Their criticism subsequently provided important guidance for the editors and many of the contributors. The sharp editorial eye of Leslie S. Rowland improved the volume in numerous ways, and Peter J. Albert saw the volume through publication. The steady typing of Susan Bailey speeded this work toward completion.

Introduction

The history of black people in the United States pivots around some half-dozen seminal events: enslavement in the 1660s, emancipation in the midst of Civil War, the Great Migration and the formation of the ghetto in the early years of the twentieth century, and the Civil Rights Revolution of the 1960s, to name just the most obvious. Equal in importance to these watersheds of black life but rarely accorded the same standing is the American Revolution. Coming at the confluence of the cultural transformation of Africans into Afro-Americans and the creation of an independent American nation, the Revolution allowed large numbers of black people to secure their freedom and to identify their liberty with the establishment of American nationality. That coincidence made the Revolution, as Benjamin Quarles observes, a black declaration of independence in the deepest sense.

But the Revolution was not only a stride forward in the expansion of black liberty. American independence also allowed slaveholders to legitimate their claims of property in man and it provided them with new mechanisms to defend their peculiar institution. The Revolution strengthened the plantation regime and slavery grew as never before, spreading across a continent. Thus, if the Revolution marked a new birth of freedom, it also launched a great expansion of slavery.

The contradictory character of the American Revolution had a profound impact on the structure of black society and race relations in the mainland British colonies that became the United States. The diverse effects of the Revolution pushed American society in many directions so that the new racial order that took shape in the course of the Age of Revolution did not emerge at once or uniformly in all parts of the North American mainland. Instead, it developed unevenly, sometimes epitomizing those principles that the leaders of the American Revolution liked most to celebrate: the general expansion of human liberty; sometimes representing those practices the leaders of the Revolution liked most to denounce: the continued domination of the many by the few. Some blacks gained their freedom and moved quickly to establish their independence as a free people while others become more deeply mired in bondage. Similarly, relations between blacks and whites in some places approached a new measure of mutual respect and occasionally even camaraderie, while elsewhere the old pattern of subordination and superordination continued with renewed force. Indeed, changes initiated by the Revolution introduced new tensions and hostilities in relations between black and white peoples.

The particular chronology of the American struggle for independence and the complex, contradictory nature of a slaveholder's rebellion for liberty account for much of this diversity. But Afro-American society and race relations on mainland British North America had already developed in distinctive ways by the eve of the Revolution. During the seventeenth and first half of the eighteenth centuries, at least three slave systems had evolved on mainland North America: a nonplantation system in the northern colonies and two plantation systems in the southern, one around the Chesapeake and the other in the Carolina and Georgia lowcountry. Still others had begun to take shape in the Virginia and Carolina backcountry and elsewhere on the frontier. Since black culture and race relations had developed differently in each region, the events of the Revolutionary era naturally gained a different meaning in the North, the Chesapeake, and the lowcountry and on the new western frontier. The forces unleashed by the Revolution, whether libertarian or repressive, did not simply have a different impact in each of these regions; they assumed a different meaning in each.

Such basic differences in the terms of historical change operated not only between the regions of mainland North America but also within these regions as well. A close examination of black life in Boston and Philadelphia, the lower and upper Chesapeake, or Charleston and its environs uncovers intraregional differences equaling or surpassing regional ones. By exposing black life more fully and by questioning existing standards of race relations more openly, the Revolution provides scholars with an opportunity to gain a more complete understanding of Afro-American society on mainland North America. Yet the impact of the Revolution was more than the sum of Afro-American cultural diversity. Viewed from the perspective of the Caribbean and Europe, the larger themes of the American Revolution become evident: the egalitarian impulse, the restraining presence of slavery, and the ubiquity of racial division.

The essays that follow weigh how the events of the American Revolution reshaped the structure of Afro-American society and American race relations as they had developed over the previous two centuries. In doing so, these essays illuminate both the continued diversity of black life and the growing unity of Afro-American society. For if Afro-American life in the North, Chesapeake, and lowcountry continued to develop in distinctive ways and if entirely new slave societies took shape on the frontier, a single Afro-American society also began to emerge. Similarly, if the formal division between free and slave states that followed the Revolution fragmented American race relations along regional lines, a common American racial ideology and practice was more evident at the end of the era than at the beginning. Indeed, in increasing both racial unity and diversity within the mainland United States and in stimulating the development of similar patterns elsewhere in the world, the American Revolution revealed its full force.

Nowhere did the events and ideas of the American Revolution have a greater impact than in the nonplantation slave system that had developed in the northern colonies. The forces unleashed by the Revolution smashed slavery, if not at once—for northern slave masters valued their property and resisted emancipation—at least forever. By 1804, abolitionists had induced every northern state either to free its slaves or to adopt some plan of gradual emancipation. Slavery dwindled thereafter and, by the 1820s, had for all practical purposes disappeared. The northern colonies had become the free states.

Once emancipated, black people began to remake their lives as free men and women. While the story of the destruction of northern slavery has been told many times, Gary B. Nash breaks new ground in exploring the reconstruction of black life in freedom. Nash reveals not only the enthusiasm with which black people grasped liberty in a society where slavery was notable for its mildness but also the difficulties they had in separating themselves from bondage in a society where slavery survived on the margins of the dominant free labor system. By counterpointing the reconstruction of black society in three centers of northern Afro-American life—Boston, where slavery died almost simultaneously with American independence; New York, where slavery lingered on well into the nineteenth century; and Philadelphia, where the timing of abolition (like the commitment to slavery) fell between the two extremes—Nash explicates the process by which black people secured their freedom.

Nash's study of the common processes of black liberation in these three seaports exposes both the emerging unity and the continued diversity of Afro-American society in the North. Everywhere black people took new names and new residences to escape the stigma of bondage, created new institutions and communities to assert their independence as a free people, and rebuilt their family life to guarantee the liberty of their posterity. Similarly, blacks everywhere met whites desirous of constraining their economic ambitions, limiting their rights as citizens, and threatening their newly won liberty. But if the dynamics of emancipation followed a similar course in Boston, New York, and Philadelphia, freedom unfolded in different ways. The names black people adopted, the pace at which their familial independence emerged, the character of the institutions they created, as well as patterns of black occupations, leadership, and resistance, differed from place to place depending on the nature of Afro-American life during slavery, the character of the various urban economies, and the timing of emancipation.

While freedom pressed successfully against slavery in the North, the events of the Revolution had the opposite effect in lowcountry Carolina and Georgia. For although the Revolution greatly disrupted lowcountry society, it never seriously threatened slavery, and many more blacks entered bondage than escaped it. Philip D. Morgan, in a close examination of the development of Afro-American life in South

Carolina documents the enormous expansion of lowcountry slavery during the Age of Revolution. However, he also notes that even as racial slavery grew in power and sophistication, lowland slaves gained greater independence from their masters and a more complete dominion over their own lives.

The simultaneous expansion of black bondage and black autonomy provides a central theme for understanding Afro-American life in the Revolutionary lowcountry. This paradox in some measure had little to do with the American Revolution and instead reflected the continuation of long-term regional developments. The introduction of large-scale rice cultivation in the early years of the eighteenth century, bringing with it dependence on African imports and an omnipresent black majority, gave lowcountry slavery its peculiar character. The urban-based (and therefore quasi-absentee) planter class, the consequent reliance on black drivers and on the task system of labor, and the prevalence of a local provision economy that rested upon the slaves' possession of their own garden plots all allowed black people considerable independence even as the slave economy expanded.

The dislocations that accompanied the Revolutionary War permitted lowcountry slaves to enlarge the independence they had already achieved. Belligerents on both sides—not to mention marauders who knew allegiance to no flag—ravaged the countryside, destroying estates and disrupting plantation life. The war left masters stranded in Charleston and slaves homeless in the countryside. Many blacks died in this wartime tumult, but others used the confusion of war to flee bondage. Thousands of slaves took refuge with the Indians to the west and the Spanish to the south; still others left with the British at war's end. As a result of these wartime changes, the slave population of the lowcountry declined precipitously. But many more slaves remained on the old estates working their provision grounds and protecting *their* property without the semblance of white supervision while patriots, loyalists, and "Tories" battled for control of the countryside. Under the direction of black drivers, these slaves reconstituted the plantation order in ways more to their own liking.

Despite the growth of black independence, massive wartime losses, and even the occasional inroads of Revolutionary egalitarianism, the patriot triumph allowed planters to reassert their authority at war's end. Before long, South Carolina and Georgia reopened the international slave trade, and African slaves poured into the region until the federal prohibition went into effect in 1808.

But the new order was not simply a carbon copy of the old. Subtle differences in the structure and style of lowcountry life transformed black society. Some of these changes had to do with long-term demographic trends, technological innovations, and the introduction of new crops, but the new pattern of black life also grew directly out of the Revolutionary experience. The wartime absence of slaveholders allowed blacks to bolster the traditional supports of slave autonomy in the lowcountry: the presence of black drivers, the task organization of production, and the practice of slaves cultivating their own provisioning grounds, marketing their surplus, and accumulating property. Drivers gained in authority, and slave property holdings appear to have grown larger than ever. Having governed themselves with little pretense of white direction during the war, blacks resisted the imposition of the old controls. The arrival of Africans in large numbers, widening the cultural gulf between master and slave, doubtless reinforced both the independence of black people and the willingness of planters to leave their slaves alone. Planters regained their hegemony, but they did so only by conceding an unprecedented measure of autonomy to their slaves. While the growth of slavery and black independence drew on established lowcountry traditions, it owed much to the Revolutionary experience.

Befitting its geographic position between the North, where freedom overwhelmed slavery, and the lowcountry, where black independence grew even as slavery expanded, the Chesapeake region partook in both of these developments. With the Revolution, Maryland and Virginia legislators rewrote manumission laws, and masters—driven by a combination of Revolutionary libertarianism, evangelical egalitarianism, and economic necessity—freed their slaves in large numbers. The free black population in the region grew rapidly, and by 1790 more than a third of the black freepeople in the nation resided around the Chesapeake. But the upward surge in the number of black free men and women stopped considerably short of abolition. Free blacks remained a minority throughout the Chesapeake region, while the number of slaves, the number of masters, and the commitment to slavery increased.

With the growth of freedom and slavery in the Chesapeake came the combination of the social developments that characterized black life in the Revolutionary North and in the lowcountry. As in the North, freed blacks moved quickly to give meaning to their newly won status. They took new names and residences, reconstructed their families, and established institutions that secured their independence and proclaimed their standing as a free people. Free black life in the Chesapeake ultimately came to differ from that in the North because of the distinctive pattern of manumission and the continued presence of slavery, but the emergence of black freedom generally followed the same course in the Chesapeake as it did in the northern states. At the same time, the expansion of slavery permitted Chesapeake slaves to claim a good deal more independence. As in the lowcountry, larger plantation units and a thicker network of settlement allowed slaves to knit kinship and friendship into community solidarity. Slave life in the Chesapeake continued to differ from that in the lowcountry because of the nature of agricultural production and a variety of demographic factors, but the expansion of slavery in the Chesapeake had many of the same effects it had in the lowcountry.

Focusing on demographic patterns in the Chesapeake, Richard S. Dunn explores the complexities of the simultaneous expansion of freedom and slavery and registers its meaning. The central development, as Dunn views it, was the destruction of the Chesapeake as a single region and its division into the lower Chesapeake, where slavery became more entrenched, and the upper Chesapeake, where freedom prospered. The impact of this division reached beyond the continued growth of the slave and free black populations. It shaped new patterns of black and white migration, spurred the emergence of large-scale slave hiring in Virginia, and hastened the growth of free black tenancy in Maryland. But

INTRODUCTION

the largest implication lay in the future. For the division of
the Chesapeake that began in the Age of Revolution continued in the decades that followed. When the nation resorted
to arms to resolve the question of slavery, Maryland stood
with the Union and Virginia with the Confederacy.

While the three principal colonial slave societies continued
to evolve in their own distinctive ways during the Age of Revolution, a single Afro-American society also began to emerge
in the wake of American independence. The growing irrel-
evance of the distinction between Africans and creoles provided the surest sign of the coalescence of Afro-American
life. During the colonial era this cultural cleavage had served
as the most important social measure within Afro-American
society. But with the international slave trade closed or closing, its importance dwindled. Even in the lowcountry, the site
of the great influx of Africans, creoles composed the majority of the post-Revolutionary black population. As the creole-
African distinction lost its force, a new social standard rose
to unite and divide black people. Partial emancipation created, for the first time, a large number of black free men and
women, and their experiences increasingly diverged from
those of blacks remaining in bondage. Slowly differences between free and slave became the dominant division within
black society. Often the relationship between freemen and
bondsmen paralleled that between creoles and Africans, in
some measure because creoles had won their liberty in disproportionate numbers. And, as in the colonial period, this
new social order acquired a different form in the North, the
Chesapeake, and the lowcountry. Still, a social system that
turned on matters of status—free and slave—rather than degree of acculturation—creole and African—gave a striking
new shape to black society.

The forces unleashed by the Revolution also gave rise to a
new slave order on the frontier. Anglo-Americans had been
drifting west since the beginnings of settlement, frequently
taking their slaves with them. But the removal of British restraints on westward expansion turned this slow trickle of
slaves into a stream. Within a generation, the emergence of
cotton as a major staple crop turned the stream into a flood.

By the second decade of the nineteenth century, the new frontier was fast becoming the center of plantation slavery in the United States.

How this new slave system evolved in the Southwest is a question with which scholars have only begun to wrestle. Frontier life required different skills and attributes of slave migrants just as it did of free ones, and the demands of cotton production in the Southwest differed sharply from those of urban bondage in the seaport cities, tobacco and mixed farming around the Chesapeake, and rice culture in the lowcountry. The migration from the seaboard not only separated slaves from family and friends but also cut them off from the traditions that mitigated the harshest aspects of chattel bondage. The slave's right to labor by the task, to cultivate provisioning grounds, and to market extra produce had little meaning to masters struck by the dream of making a fortune in cotton and unrestrained by customary practices and established community standards. In addition, many slaves entering the frontier from Louisiana or the West Indies had no knowledge of Anglo-American culture. Still others, recruited directly from Africa, knew nothing of bondage. Yet within a generation these black men and women molded their diverse traditions into a distinctive way of life.

Surveying the westward movement of black people in the Age of Revolution, Allan Kulikoff lays the foundation for comprehending the growth of Afro-American society in the Southwest by outlining who went where, when, and how. His description of the migratory patterns of black people provides scholars with a starting point for determining what kinds of beliefs and institutions blacks carried to the frontier. Joined together with knowledge of the transit of Anglo-American society and frontier demography and economics, Kulikoff's essay offers the first step toward understanding the evolution of Afro-American culture in the cotton South.

Collectively, these studies of the development of Afro-American society in the northern seaports, the Chesapeake, the lowcountry, and the western frontier provide the fullest available portrait of Afro-American life in the Age of Revolution. Exploring two of the most important black institutions—the family and the church—as they developed throughout British mainland North America offers still another view of the same terrain. Mary Beth Norton, Herbert G. Gutman, and Ira Berlin examine the growth of black domestic life during the eighteenth century from the perspective of the great plantations of the Chesapeake and the lowcountry. Their work in reconstructing the family life of the slaves on the Jefferson, Carroll, and Pinckney plantations as well as other slave estates reveals how rapidly black kin ties evolved, despite the constraints of bondage. It also suggests the social process by which Afro-Americans transferred their emerging culture along generational lines and the methods by which they protected their cultural independence. That independence—whether manifested in naming practices, the transfer of trades from parent to child, or the network of extended kinship that linked slaves together within plantations and between plantations—served black people well in the Revolutionary era. It allowed many to weather the trauma of the war and forced migration, and it provided still others with the means of escaping bondage.

Like the black family, the Afro-American church also guided the black response to the Revolution. The events of the Age of Revolution—particularly the evangelical awakenings that accompanied American independence—spurred the growth of the black church and the emergence of an Afro-American Christianity. The evangelical revivals initiated a widespread questioning of the morality of slavery and allowed blacks to enter fully into American religious life. Although the power of slavery quickly overwhelmed the nascent antislavery sentiment, blacks and whites continued to worship together within evangelical churches in ways that induced these churches to protect slave members against some of the harshest aspects of bondage. The evangelical awakenings also allowed some blacks, many of whom had gained their liberty as a result of the Revolution, to establish their own independent religious organizations. "African" churches, scattered between Savannah and Boston, became the institutional hub of black religious life, and their theological practices and polity dominated Afro-American religion for the next century or more. In a sweeping evaluation of the evolution of black religion during the Age of Revolution, Albert J. Raboteau unravels the events in which blacks wrestled the exclusive claim to Christianity away from whites, at once establishing their own distinctive religious practice and transforming American religious life generally. By the end of the era, blacks had ceased to be a "missioned" people and had begun to sponsor missions of their own.

Just as the Revolution transformed Afro-American society, it had a formative influence on American racial ideology and racial policies. This large subject has attracted considerable attention during the last two decades, and a substantial literature has developed. Drawing on that literature, Duncan J. MacLeod proposes a new chronology for the development of black life and race relations on British mainland North America. During the first period, the years between the arrival of black people in the seventeenth century and the third decade of the eighteenth century, MacLeod finds a common pattern in the growth of Afro-American life on the North American mainland. Although the proportion of Afro-Americans within the northern, Chesapeake, and lowcountry colonies differed, the black population throughout the British mainland grew at a similar rate, driven by the common demands of the Atlantic economy. The second period, roughly the middle decades of the eighteenth century, witnessed the transformation of the Chesapeake and lowcountry from societies with slaves to slave societies, while northern bondage became an increasingly marginal institution. But even in these slave societies, Anglo-Americans did not yet rationalize slavery in racial terms, and no concept of blacks as a "minority"—in terms of power, not numbers—developed. The Revolution changed all that. By declaring all men free and equal, the men who made the Revolution could explain and, increasingly, justify the status of black people only by declaring them a lesser class: lazy, larcenous, and licentious. This new rationale for the status of black people grew in importance and coherence as the successful Revolutionaries debated the future of slavery and the spread of their own principles. The growth of the free Negro caste, ending the coincidence between color and status commonplace throughout the colonial era, made it all the more imperative to observe racial distinctions among freepeople. Thus the Revolution established a new mode of racial thought and set in motion the development of a pattern of thinking and acting that shaped American racial relations into the twentieth century.

The forces that remade Afro-American society and racial ideology on the North American mainland soon reverberated through the Atlantic world, and it did not take long for other slave societies to feel the effects. In a carefully hewn essay, Franklin W. Knight demonstrates how the changes initiated by the American Revolution set Caribbean slavery on the road to extinction, not so much by the power of Revolutionary example but by jarring the foundation of the imperial system upon which Caribbean slave societies rested. Once the foundation stones of that imperial order had been knocked off center, the entire edifice of West Indian slavery began to shake. Knight traces the effects of these tremors first as they disrupted imperial ties by altering international patterns of trade, then as they created new relations between masters and slaves by changing the internal economies of the islands, and finally as they set the stage for the great rebellion on Saint-Domingue. As on the mainland, these changes did not affect all Caribbean slave societies in the same way, for the repercussions of the American Revolution resonated differently within different imperial systems on islands at different stages of development. Caribbean slavery survived the American Revolution as it would survive the French and Haitian ones, but it would never be the same.

David Brion Davis also carries the implications of the American Revolution beyond the boundaries of the American Republic by exploring still more broadly the global connections between the Revolution and the fate of slavery. Asking "what if" within the tight framework of known historical events, Davis weaves a counterfactual "fantasy" to examine subsequent events in the absence of an independent North American Republic. His survey of the development of slavery and abolition on both sides of the Atlantic reveals how much of the history of the Atlantic world rests on the chain of events set in motion by the American Revolution. As on the North American mainland, the Revolution retarded the development of slavery in some places while speeding its growth in others. But no matter what the vector of change or its velocity, the presence of an independent United States shaped both the defense of chattel bondage and the assaults upon it. By positing the failure of the Revolution, Davis documents its pivotal importance to the history of slavery and slavery's demise.

No one understood this more fully than those black men and women who gained their liberty as a result of the Revolution. The principles that propelled them from slavery to freedom became central to their lives and those of their children. While others might ignore the egalitarian legacy of the Revolution or reshape it in an exclusivist manner, these blacks seized the ideas of the Declaration of Independence and made them the cornerstone of their own political identity. Benjamin Quarles explores the implications of this coincidence of racial and national identity and places it in the context of Afro-American history. He demonstrates that by identifying fully with the egalitarian aspects of the American Revolution and calling upon those principles to expand black liberty in the century to come, blacks helped to transform the legacy of the Revolution from one in which slaveholders secured their right to property in man to one in which all men held property in their own person. In so doing, blacks laid the foundation for universal emancipation and shaped the nation's destiny.

IRA BERLIN

I

The Transformation of Afro-American Society in the Age of Revolution

GARY B. NASH

Forging Freedom
The Emancipation Experience in
the Northern Seaport Cities
1775–1820

ON THE EVE of the American Revolution some 4,000 slaves and a few hundred free blacks lived in Boston, New York, and Philadelphia, the northern seaport capitals of colonial society. Fifty years later nearly 22,000 free blacks and about 500 slaves resided in these same cities, most of the latter in New York. In two generations a large majority of the northern Afro-American population made the transition from bondage to freedom. Although northern slavemasters had neither constructed a strong moral justification for holding slaves nor manifested a powerful economic need for bonded labor, blacks did not scale the barrier between slavery and freedom easily. Instead, they constructed the economic, institutional, and social scaffolding of freedom slowly, usually in the face of open white hostility.[1] Moreover, the transit from slavery to freedom proceeded unevenly, depending on the nature of slavery and the timing of emancipation, as well as the specific economic and demographic conditions of urban

The author is indebted to Cynthia Shelton for research assistance and criticism in the preparation of this essay.

[1]This inquiry is not directed at how whites treated blacks in the northern cities after the Revolution, a dismal subject that has been comprehensively treated elsewhere. See, for example, Leon F. Litwack, *North of Slavery: The Negro in the Free States, 1790–1860* (Chicago, 1961); see also Winthrop D. Jordan, *White over Black: American Attitudes toward the Negro, 1550–1812* (Chapel Hill, N.C., 1968), pp. 406–26.

life. But everywhere the coming of freedom marked the transformation of black life, the emergence of new institutions, and the development of a new consciousness.

Once the exhilaration of freedom had been savored, one brute necessity stood above all others for black Americans of the Revolutionary era: finding a livelihood. During the years of actual fighting some blacks solved the problem of maintenance by military service, either with the American or, more typically, the British armies. At war's end, the necessities of life could no longer be procured through membership in a large, white-directed organization; now every freedman was on his own. Standing alone, freed blacks, both men and women, looked to the coastal towns for economic survival.[2] The urban migration that ensued swelled the black population in Boston, New York, and Philadelphia fourfold between the Revolution and 1820 (table 1).

Rapid postemancipation urbanization increased the urban bias already characteristic of black life in the colonial period. The intensive capitalization of a few industries, demand for laborers by artisans, and the desire of status-conscious gentlefolk for black servants had combined to make pre-Revolutionary bondage a disproportionately urban phenomenon.[3] Thus, New York City, which contained 13 percent of the colony's white population in 1771, was the home of 16 percent of the slave population. Boston, with 6 percent of the white population of Massachusetts in 1765, contained 15 percent of the colony's slaves. Slaves in Pennsylvania were

[2]W. E. B. Du Bois first noted this movement to the cities in his classic study *The Philadelphia Negro: A Social Study* (1899; reprint ed., New York, 1967), p. 17. Ira Berlin also draws attention to this phenomenon in "The Structure of the Free Negro Caste in the Antebellum United States," *Journal of Social History* 9 (1976):300.

[3]Parts of southern New York were exceptions. In Ulster, Westchester, Queens, and especially Kings counties the percentage of blacks in the population at the end of the colonial period exceeded that of New York City. See the 1771 census in Evarts B. Greene and Virginia D. Harrington, *American Population before the Federal Census of 1790* (1932; reprint ed., Gloucester, Mass., 1966), p. 102.

4

Table 1: Black population in three northern cities

Year	Boston				New York				Philadelphia			
	Slave	Free	Total	Decadal increase	Slave	Free	Total	Decadal increase	Slave	Free	Total	Decadal increase
Pre-Revolutionary*	751	60	811	—	3,037	100	3,137	—	672	200	872	—
1790	0	766	766	—	2,369	1,101	3,470	—	273	1,805	2,078	—
1800	0	1,174	1,174	53.3%	2,868	3,499	6,367	83.5%	55	6,379	6,434	209.6%
1810	0	1,484	1,484	26.4%	1,686	8,137	9,823	54.3%	3	9,675	9,678	50.4%
1820	0	1,726	1,726	16.3%	518	10,368	10,886	10.8%	0	10,758	10,758	11.2%

SOURCES: Boston (1765): J. H. Benton, *Early Census Making in Massachusetts* (Boston, 1905), following p. 71; New York (1771): Evarts B. Greene and Virginia D. Harrington, *American Population before the Federal Census of 1790* (1932; reprint ed., Gloucester, Mass., 1966), p. 102; Philadelphia (1775): Gary B. Nash, "Slaves and Slaveowners in Colonial Philadelphia," *William and Mary Quarterly*, 3d ser. 30 (1973): 237. The number of free blacks in each city has been estimated. Population data for 1790 to 1820 taken from the published federal censuses.

*Boston, 1765; New York, 1771; Philadelphia, 1775.

twice as likely to live in Philadelphia as were the colony's white inhabitants in the 1760s (table 2).

Most urban slaves apparently remained in the cities after gaining their liberty. They were joined there by hundreds of former bondspeople from the countryside who, like their urban counterparts, concluded that the cities offered the best chance for widening their economic opportunities and enriching their social life. In particular they headed for the maritime towns, for black men had long been important on the coasting vessels and overseas ships of colonial commerce, and black women could hope for domestic service in the homes of an increasingly affluent urban upper class. By taking out of the hands of the master class decisions about where blacks lived, emancipation permanently altered the geography of northern black life.

This urban migration was especially pronounced in the first two decades after the Revolution (table 1), when a large proportion of northern slaves received their freedom. The percentage of Massachusetts free blacks who lived in Boston rose only slowly in this period, but in both New York and Pennsylvania the proportion of the black populace living in the capital city doubled between the early 1770s and 1800 (table 2).[4] By 1820 Massachusetts blacks were three times as likely to live in Boston as were Massachusetts whites; in New York and Pennsylvania, Afro-Americans were four times as likely as whites to live in the seaport capital (table 2).

[4] The move to the metropolis from the towns around Boston can be seen in the population changes between 1765 and 1820. In the former year Boston had 848 slaves and the surrounding towns 404. By 1790, 766 free blacks lived in Boston and only 189 in outlying towns. Thirty years later, in 1820, Boston's black population stood at 1,484, while 239 blacks lived in the adjacent towns. Thus Boston's share of the regional black population rose from 68 percent in 1765 to 87 percent in 1820 (Oscar Handlin, *Boston's Immigrants* [1941; reprint ed., New York, 1968], p. 249, table 12. I have changed Handlin's figure for the black population of Boston in 1820 to correspond with the 1820 census). The growth of Boston's black population may have been slowed by the city's efforts to discourage immigrating freedpeople, as, for example, in 1800, when the selectmen ordered the expulsion of 235 wayfarers (Arthur O. White, "The Black Leadership Class and Education in Antebellum Boston," *Journal of Negro Education* 42 [1973]:507).

6

Table 2: Percentage of state population living in capital city

Year	Boston		New York		Philadelphia*	
	Black	White	Black	White	Black —%	White —%
Pre-Revolutionary†	14.7%	6.2%	15.8%	12.5%	—%	—%
1790	14.2	4.6	23.5	9.5	20.3	9.5
1800	18.2	5.7	33.6	9.7	43.8	10.9
1810	22.0	7.1	32.1	9.4	41.7‡	10.6
1820	25.6	8.2	35.4	8.5	36.6	9.1

SOURCES: Boston (1765): J. H. Benton, *Early Census Making in Massachusetts* (Boston, 1905), following p. 71; New York (1771): Evarts B. Greene and Virginia D. Harrington, *American Population before the Federal Census of 1790* (1932; reprint ed., Gloucester, Mass., 1966), p. 102; Philadelphia (1775): Gary B. Nash, "Slaves and Slaveowners in Colonial Philadelphia," *William and Mary Quarterly*, 3d ser. 30 (1973): 237. The number of free blacks in each city has been estimated. Population data for 1790 to 1820 taken from the published federal censuses.

*Including Southwark, Moyamensing, Passyunk, and Northern Liberties.

†Boston, 1765; New York, 1771.

‡After correcting for apparent error in west Southwark; the census figure of 1,100 has been reduced to 800.

Immigrants from the South augmented the expansion of urban black life in the North. Between the Revolution and 1800 Delaware, Maryland, and Virginia masters manumitted thousands of slaves, many of whom, along with hundreds of fugitive bondspeople, headed northward. For the first time the North Star came to symbolize freedom. As the center of American abolitionism, Philadelphia especially became the destination for a generation of southern blacks, mostly from the upper South. Because it adjoined three slaves states, Pennsylvania "afforded an asylum for their free blacks and runaway slaves."[5] Indeed, by 1800 the Afro-American population of Philadelphia overtook that of New York City, although on the eve of the Revolution it had been less than a quarter as large (table 1).

For freedmen the possibility of maritime work, either on ships at sea or as stevedores along the wharves, provided a large part of the urban pull. Federal protection certificates, issued to merchant seamen beginning in 1796, indicate that by the beginning of the nineteenth century free blacks composed at least one-fifth of some 2,000 merchant seamen in Philadelphia, making this the city's single most important job opportunity for black freemen.[6] Because they indicate the birthplace of each mariner, these certificates can be used to

[5]Visiting Committee to Acting Committee, Jan. 8, 1821, Pennsylvania Prison Society Records, 2, Part A, Historical Society of Pennsylvania, Philadelphia. For the growth of the free black population in the upper South, see Ira Berlin, *Slaves without Masters: The Free Negro in the Antebellum South* (New York, 1974), pp. 29–35.

[6]The proportion of blacks in Philadelphia's maritime labor force can be estimated from the ships' crew lists in the National Archives. In a sample of thirty-seven ships leaving Philadelphia in 1803, 24 percent of the mariners were black; on twenty-five ships sailing in 1805, 21 percent (Ships' Crew Lists, Record Group 36, National Archives). This information has been provided by Billy G. Smith). The estimate of 2,000 mariners in 1800 is based on the following. In the 1770s the number of ship captains belonging to the Society for the Relief of Poor and Distressed Masters of Ships averaged about 200 in Philadelphia. Ships averaged at least six crew members, so Philadelphia probably had about 1,000–1,200 merchant seamen on the eve of the Revolution. The Philadelphia Customs House records for 1770–71 show that 71,164 pence of Greenwich Hospital money were collected from Philadelphia sailors between July 1, 1770, and July 1,

trace migration into the seaport centers from both the rural North and the upper South.[7] James Phillips, a free black mariner, received his certificate in 1798. Born outside Philadelphia in 1771 to a free black mother and a white father, he had come to the Delaware River port to make a living at sea. Alexander Giles, another free black Philadelphia seaman, had been born in 1777 in nearby Kent County, Delaware. The son of a black freeman, he too migrated to the Pennsylvania capital. Randall Shepherd, the son of a free black laborer in Nansemond County, Virginia, had trekked north and taken up life as a merchant seaman in Philadelphia, where he obtained a certificate in 1798. Henry Bray had been born in Boston in the year of the Massacre. Like his father, he went to sea to make a living but had resettled in Philadelphia in the 1790s. George Gray had tried all three major maritime capitals. Born in New York City, he moved to Boston and then to Philadelphia. Of the fifteen black mariners who shipped out of Philadelphia in 1798 and applied for certificates, only two had been born in that city. Six had migrated from the upper South, four from the Philadelphia hinterland, two from New England, and one had been born in Africa.[8]

1771. At sixpence per month of wages, this would indicate a total of 1,078 seamen, assuming that each sailor drew eleven months' wages during the year. Corroborating this estimate is a remark from the Customs House Officer, Nov. 15, 1770, that "there are not less than a thousand Seamen here at this time" (Customs House Papers, vol. 10, Hist. Soc. of Pa. The Greenwich Hospital money is recorded in vol. 11, p. 1409). Since Philadelphia more than doubled in size between 1770 and 1800 and since the number of ships clearing the port also more than doubled during these years, it seems safe to assume that there were at least 2,000 sailors in the population at the end of the century. (I am indebted to Billy G. Smith for the data for these estimates.)

[7] The origin of the certificates and the information included in them are described by Ira Dye, "Early American Merchant Seafarers," *Proceedings of the American Philosophical Society* 120 (1976):331–34.

[8] Seamen's Protective Certificate Applications to the Collector of Customs for the Port of Philadelphia, R.G. 36, Nat. Arch. (I am grateful to Billy G. Smith for providing this information.) Of 137 black seamen applying for protection certificates from 1812 to 1815 in Philadelphia, only 15 percent had been born in the city (Dye, "Early American Merchant Seafarers," p. 351, table 6).

Crew lists also reveal the lure of maritime jobs. From a random selection of thirty-seven ships departing Philadelphia in 1803, the place of birth of forty-one black merchant seamen can be ascertained. Only two of these had been born in Philadelphia. Four black seamen came from elsewhere in Pennsylvania and eight from adjoining areas in New Jersey and Delaware. Three were from New York; four claimed New England birthplaces; thirteen hailed from Maryland, Virginia, or South Carolina; four came from Saint-Domingue; and one each had been born elsewhere in the West Indies, in Guinea, and in Portugal.[9] Young black men freed in the hinterlands after the Revolution could have had only faint hope of carving out a life for themselves as independent farmers and landholders. Facing strong racial prejudice and lacking capital to buy land, tools, and livestock, life in the countryside meant becoming one of a growing number of rural transients or hiring out as a day laborer to farmers, ironmasters, or small-town shopkeepers.[10] More and more black men seized the opportunities available in the maritime centers, where they became part of a literally floating proletariat.

The appeal of the city was not solely economic. Alongside greater opportunities for employment stood the many attractions of black community life. In rural areas freed Afro-Americans lived in relative isolation from other black people and therefore were relatively defenseless against white hostility. But in the cities the concentration of free blacks provided some security against a hostile world and meant greater chances to find an acceptable marriage partner, to establish a

[9]Ships' Crew Lists, R.G. 36, Nat. Arch. (This information has also been provided by Billy G. Smith.) A study of crew lists and protection certificates for New York and Boston would probably reveal a similar pattern. The free blacks of Massachusetts, wrote an early historian of the period, "have generally . . . left the country and resorted to the maritime towns" ("Judge Tucker's Queries respecting Slavery, with Doctor Belknap's Answers," Massachusetts Historical Society *Collections*, 1st ser. 4 [1795]:206).

[10]For an evocative study of the immiserization of free blacks who tried their luck in Chester and Lancaster counties, west of Philadelphia, see Carl D. Oblinger, "Alms for Oblivion: The Making of a Black Underclass in Southeastern Pennsylvania, 1780–1869," in John E. Bodnar, ed., *The Ethnic Experience in Pennsylvania* (Lewisburg, Pa., 1973), pp. 94–119.

family, and to participate in the activities of black churches, schools, fraternal societies, and benevolent organizations. The strength of this urban attraction cannot be quantified, but the possibility of developing a black community doubtless made the city even more appealing to black migrants. Every Afro-American in the post-Revolutionary generation faced the fact that the abolition of slavery tended to augment rather than dissolve white racial hostility, and the animus was no less virulent in the cities than in rural areas.[11] But the dense network of urban black institutions and a rich community life made it easier to confront racism in the cities than in the countryside.

The timing of emancipation shaped the pattern of the black urban migration. Boston reported no slaves in the first federal census, and in Philadelphia, where a gradual abolition law had been in effect for ten years, enumerators counted only 273 bondspeople. By the turn of the century both cities had become havens for free Afro-Americans. New York, on the other hand, did not pass an abolition law until 1799, and this measure offered no immediate freedom; instead it liberated slaveborn children only when they reached the age of twenty-five if female, twenty-eight if male. Consequently, the slave population of New York City continued to increase steadily from the end of the Revolution until about 1800. Indeed, as late as 1790 New York had more slaves than any city in the nation except Charleston, South Carolina. As the remaining center of northern slavery in the early nineteenth century, New York at first attracted less than its share of freedpeople. Although that city's slaveowners released or sold their slaves far faster than their rural counterparts in the rest of the state, the free black population nevertheless grew less rapidly in New York City than in Philadelphia from 1780 to 1800.[12] Migrating blacks found "free" cities more attractive than "slave" ones.

Black migration to the cities after the Revolution was dis-

[11]Jordan, *White over Black*, pp. 403–26.

[12]For the persistence of slavery in one New York county, see Carl Nordstrom, "Slavery in a New York County: Rockland County, 1686–1827," *Afro-Americans in New York Life and History* 1 (1977):145–66. In 1800, when 55

proportionately female, a fact with important ramifications for every aspect of urban black life. It reversed the sexual imbalance of the colonial urban black population, which had usually numbered about three males for every two females.[13] Although the failure of the federal census to distinguish blacks by gender before 1820 makes this development difficult to chart, in that year females represented 55 percent of Boston's black population, 57 percent of Philadelphia's, and 60 percent of New York's (table 3). The deficit of males in 1820 applied to all age categories but was particularly pronounced among young adults between fourteen and twenty-five years old (table 3).[14] This shortage can be explained partially by

---

percent of New York City's black population was free, nearly three-quarters of the 24,920 blacks elsewhere in the state remained in slavery. In some counties more than 90 percent of the black population was still in bondage. For the number of slaves and free blacks in each county, see *Return of the Whole Number of Persons within the Several Districts of the United States* (Washington, D.C., 1801), p. 32.

[13]In Boston in 1765 there were 510 male and 301 female slaves (J. H. Benton, *Early Census Making in Massachusetts* [Boston, 1905], following p. 71). In Philadelphia constables' reports for 1775, male slaves in two wards outnumbered female slaves 33 to 22 (Constables' Reports, 1775, City Archives, City Hall Annex, Philadelphia). New York may have been the exception. In 1771 there were 1,500 male slaves and 1,637 female slaves (Greene and Harrington, *American Population*, p. 102). By 1786 New York contained 896 male and 1,207 female slaves (ibid., p. 104). This female predominance may reflect the disproportionately large number of male slaves who gained their freedom fighting with the British during the Revolution and were evacuated in 1783 to Nova Scotia.

[14]This male deficit has led Robert W. Fogel and Stanley L. Engerman to argue that in New York between 1810 and 1820, hundreds of owners sold young male slaves south, thus "cashing in on capital gains" and avoiding the emancipation of their slaves ("Philanthropy at Bargain Prices: Notes on the Economics of Gradual Emancipation," *Journal of Legal Studies* 3 [1974]:393). There are several difficulties with this explanation. First, the skewed New York sex ratio among blacks aged fourteen to twenty-five was virtually the same in Boston and Philadelphia, where there were no slaves to sell south (table 3). Second, in rural Massachusetts and New York black males and females in the fourteen to twenty-five age category were nearly balanced, and in Pennsylvania the number of males slightly exceeded the number of females. It seems unlikely that the selling of male slaves would be specific to one city. Thus the urban imbalance needs an alternative ex-

Table 3: Population in 1820 by race, age, and sex

Age	Boston		Other Mass.		New York City		Other N.Y.		Philadelphia		Other Pa.	
	Male	Female	Male	Female	Male	Female	Male	Female	Male	Female	Male	Female
Free black												
0–13	190	222	895	747	1,281	1,491	3,916	3,851	1,607	1,635	4,059	3,830
14–25	81	168	599	610	920	1,851	2,091	2,344	866	1,670	2,482	2,393
26–44	344	368	552	536	1,387	1,998	1,960	2,188	1,610	2,026	2,280	2,047
45+	159	194	488	587	606	834	1,297	1,324	538	758	1,362	1,039
Total	774	952	2,534	2,480	4,194	6,174	9,264	9,707	4,621	6,089	10,183	9,309
% of Total	44.8	55.2	50.5	49.5	40.5	59.5	49.0	51.0	43.1	56.9	52.2	47.8
White												
0–9	5,371	5,468	65,622	63,792	15,898	15,983	206,710	200,530	12,947	12,605	162,434	154,105
10–15	2,460	3,008	36,113	35,300	7,066	8,335	97,231	93,569	5,577	6,605	71,443	71,820
16–25	3,619	4,590	56,807	48,215	11,017	13,120	151,334	119,372	11,070	10,885	117,381	90,619
26–44	7,438	6,044	46,916	51,677	14,872	13,701	123,762	116,198	10,574	11,940	81,570	82,405
45+	1,542	2,624	37,126	43,547	6,459	6,369	74,800	66,016	4,506	5,938	59,987	53,654
Total	20,430	21,734	242,584	242,531	55,312	57,508	653,837	595,685	44,674	47,973	492,815	452,603
% of Total	48.4	51.6	50.0	50.0	49.0	51.0	52.3	47.7	48.2	51.8	52.1	47.9

SOURCE: *Census for 1820* (Washington, D.C., 1821).

forced sales of young slaves to the South[15] and partially by kidnapping, a constant danger in all northern cities.[16] In addition, census takers and other enumerators exaggerated this sexual imbalance by ignoring large numbers of young male transients and mariners who spent much of their time at sea.[17] Still, the deficit of young men cannot be denied. More than eighty years ago W. E. B. Du Bois offered perhaps the most important explanation for this sexual imbalance in the urban black population: "The industrial opportunities of Negro women in cities have been far greater than those of men, through their large employment in domestic service. At the same time the restriction of employments open to Negroes, which perhaps reached a climax in 1830–1840, . . . has served to limit the number of men."[18] Corroboration for his analysis

planation. Third, an unbalanced sex ratio for *whites* in the ten to fifteen and sixteen to twenty-five age categories, while not so distorted as for blacks, was pronounced (table 3), suggesting that the demographic imbalance stemmed from a factor affecting both whites and blacks.

[15]The reported data for New York are particularly puzzling. After growing 21 percent between 1790 and 1800 and 29 percent between 1800 and 1810, the black population of the state of New York fell 2 percent between 1810 and 1820. If the average decadal rate of growth from 1790 to 1810 had continued between 1810 and 1820, New York's black population would have been 50,397 in the latter year instead of the 39,367 recorded in the census. There is no satisfactory explanation for this sharp demographic change in New York, but it should be noted that the rate of population increase slowed elsewhere in the North and also in the South. See the data on decadal rates of increase from 1790 to 1820 in Fogel and Engerman, "Philanthropy," p. 392.

[16]For kidnapping in Pennsylvania see Edward R. Turner, *The Negro in Pennsylvania* (1910; reprint ed., New York, 1969), pp. 115–16; for New York see Rhoda G. Freeman, "The Free Negro in New York City in the Era before the Civil War," Ph.D. diss., Columbia University, 1966, pp. 65–97; for Boston see Lorenzo J. Greene, "Prince Hall: Massachusetts Leader in Crisis," *Freedomways* 1 (1961):238.

[17]John B. Sharpless and Ray M. Shortridge, "Biased Underenumeration in Census Manuscripts: Methodological Implications," *Journal of Urban History* 1 (1974–75):409–39.

[18]Du Bois, *Philadelphia Negro*, p. 55. Theodore Hershberg also notes this for a somewhat later period in Philadelphia ("Free Blacks in Antebellum Philadelphia: A Study of Ex-Slaves, Freeborn, and Socioeconomic Decline," *Journal of Social History* 5 [1971–72]:190).

can be found in the sex ratios of free blacks in the rural areas surrounding the port cities. In many such counties in 1820, males outnumbered females in the fourteen to twenty-five age category.[19]

The possibility of maritime work for men and domestic employment for women lay at the root of the free black migration to the cities. But former slaves also availed themselves of a variety of other occupational opportunities. Historians have customarily assumed a degradation of black skills in the emancipation period, as former slave artisans, lacking a master's protection and patronage, were forced as freemen into menial labor.[20] But loss of skill may not in fact have been extensive, since fewer colonial slaves possessed artisan training than historians have sometimes supposed.[21] In any case, it would be a mistake to analyze only the changing occupational status of black men, for the labor of black women was equally important to the survival of black households. Far more than among whites, the black family was an economic

[19]For example, in Delaware, Chester, Montgomery, and Bucks counties, surrounding Philadelphia, there were 794 males and 665 females aged fourteen to twenty-five and 788 males and 628 females aged twenty-six to forty-four in 1820 (*Census for 1820* [Washington, D.C., 1821], pp. 18–18*).

[20]Du Bois, *Philadelphia Negro*, pp. 141–42; Litwack, *North of Slavery*, pp. 153–86. The period after 1820, when Irish immigrants began to flood the northern cities, marked a tragic new era in the black struggle for an economic base.

[21]Ira Berlin, "Time, Space, and the Evolution of Afro-American Society on British Mainland North America," *American Historical Review* 85 (1980):46–49. Only in Philadelphia are tax lists available for the late colonial period that indicate the occupations of slaveowners. About half the slaves owned in the city in 1767 belonged to artisans, mariners, or tavernkeepers, but since some of these were slave women working as domestic servants and some of the male slaves owned by artisans were not necessarily trained as craftsmen, it is impossible to know precisely the proportion of male slaves who possessed artisan skills. My guess, based on information in tax lists and inventories of estate for Boston and Philadelphia, is about one-quarter. See Gary B. Nash, "Slaves and Slaveowners in Colonial Philadelphia," *William and Mary Quarterly*, 3d ser. 30 (1973):249–52, and Merle G. Brouwer, "The Negro as a Slave and as a Free Black in Colonial Pennsylvania," Ph.D. diss., Wayne State University, 1973, pp. 51–68.

partnership in which both husband and wife earned wages in the marketplace economy.

Some indications of the occupational structure of the first generation of free blacks can be derived from the 1795 Philadelphia directory, the first in any of the port cities to designate black heads of household. The directory lists only 105 blacks, 83 men and 22 women, which is only one-sixth as many heads of households as might be expected, given Philadelphia's total black population of about 4,000.[22] Of the men, 41 percent worked in unskilled positions as laborers, sweepers, sawyers, and whitewashers. Those employed in domestic or personal service, mostly as waitingmen and coachmen, composed another 12 percent. Nearly 10 percent were mariners, and this figure should probably be doubled, given what other sources reveal about black participation in the seagoing labor force and the traditional underenumeration of seafarers. But a significant number (table 4) worked as professionals (5 percent) and artisans (12 percent) or were engaged in retailing or other proprietorial roles as hucksters, carters, bakers, fruiterers, and grocers (21 percent).[23] Among the 22 women, more than a third were retailers and boardinghouse keepers, and half labored as washerwomen. In 1797 a Philadelphia editor confirmed this evidence that a large number of Afro-Americans had found profitable employment and made a satisfactory adjustment to freedom; he found "the most afflictive and accumulated distress amongst the *Irish Emigrants* and the *French Negroes*."[24]

Twenty-one years after the 1795 enumeration another Philadelphia directory that designated free blacks provided

[22]Edmund Hogan, *The Prospect of Philadelphia and Check on the Next Directory* . . . (Philadelphia, 1795). The directory does not include Southwark, Moyamensing, or the Northern Liberties, where many blacks resided.

[23]In the same year the directory was issued, the Pennsylvania Abolition Society reported that "some of the men follow Mechanick trades and a number of them are mariners, but the greatest part are employed as Day labourers" (quoted in Litwack, *North of Slavery*, p. 154).

[24]*Gale's Independent Gazetteer*, Jan. 3, 1797, quoted in John K. Alexander, *Render Them Submissive: Responses to Poverty in Philadelphia, 1760–1800* (Amherst, Mass., 1980), p. 78.

Table 4: Occupations of free blacks in Philadelphia and Boston

| | Philadelphia (1795) | | | | Philadelphia (1816) | | | | Boston (1829) | |
| | Male | | Female | | Male | | Female | | Male | |
	No.	%	No.	%	No.	%	No.	%	No.	%
Professional	4	4.8	1	4.5	10	1.2	1	3.1	2	1.1
Retail & proprietorial	17	20.5	8	36.4	180	21.6	8	25.0	55	29.4
Artisan	10	12.0	1	4.5	105	12.6	1	3.1	10	5.3
Mariners	8	9.6	0		82	9.8	0		36	19.3
Unskilled	34	41.0	0		327	39.2	3	9.4	62	33.2
Domestic & personal service	10	12.0	12	54.5	130	15.6	19	59.4	22	11.8
Total	83		22		834		32		187	

SOURCES: Edmund Hogan, *The Prospect of Philadelphia and Check on the Next Directory* . . . (Philadelphia, 1795); *The Philadelphia Directory for 1816* . . . (Philadelphia, 1816); John Daniels, *In Freedom's Birthplace: A Study of the Boston Negroes* (Boston, 1914), pp. 17–19.

a second snapshot of black occupational structure.[25] The 1816 directory listed nearly 900 blacks with occupations. The male occupations indicate remarkable stability over two decades. There was a slight drift toward retail and proprietorial roles and toward domestic and personal service, and an erosion of professional positions. But mariners and artisans held their own and even increased slightly their proportions among free blacks (table 4).

While more than half of Philadelphia's black men held positions as laborers, bootblacks, coachmen, sweep masters, wood sawyers, or waiters, many former slaves had found their way into more remunerative and independent occupations. One in five was a small retailer or proprietor, or, in a few cases, a professional. Philadelphia's forty-five black oystermen dominated that business; fifty other blacks were traders, grocers, shopkeepers, fruiterers, victuallers, and milkmen. One in ten listed in the directory worked as a mariner and another one of every eight as a craftsman. Thirty-two black artisans labored in the building trades, eleven in metal crafts, twenty-seven in leather trades, twelve in shipbuilding, and a dozen more in miscellaneous crafts. The transition from slavery to freedom does not appear to have altered dramatically the occupational structure of black society, and most freedpeople continued to work as day laborers and domestic servants. Still, some improved themselves considerably by plying artisan trades or keeping small shops of their own.

Many black men found employment within the fast-growing black neighborhoods of Philadelphia. To even the least skilled worker this must have provided a satisfaction of its own. And even among those who were no longer permitted to practice an artisan skill acquired under slavery, a life of semiskilled or unskilled work for white employers at least left the black waterman, well digger, or whitewasher free to retire each night to his own residence, free to form a family, free to change his residence, free to worship where he chose, and free to seek the company of his brethren.

In analyzing the occupations of black women, whose wages were indispensable to the household budget, city directories

---

[25]*The Philadelphia Directory for 1816* . . . (Philadelphia, 1816).

and federal census returns are of little use, for they usually reported only those women who were widowed heads of household. But investigations into black life by the Pennsylvania Abolition Society partially fill the void. In 1795 the Society reported that "the Women generally, both married and single, wash clothes for a living."[26] Half a century later, a far more extensive survey of black households showed that of 4,249 adult women, all but 290 (7 percent) were employed. The vast majority performed domestic labor, mostly for white families, as washerwomen, seamstresses, and "dayworkers"; others were cooks, tradeswomen, ragpickers, and proprietors. In total, employed black women outnumbered employed black men by 3,959 to 3,358, which corresponds roughly to the female-male ratio reported in the 1850 census.[27]

The Society's reports make it evident that a large majority of free black women performed domestic wage labor for white households throughout the early nineteenth century. For the black family this provided the additional income necessary for survival. The laboring experience of the black woman had changed little since bondage, for under slavery she had also worked in the homes of the white upper and middle classes. Emancipation did not lessen white demand for black domestic servants but merely converted slave labor into domestic wage labor. But some black women, perhaps one in twenty, now occupied roles formerly held by no slave woman: shopkeeper, fruiterer, baker, boardinghouse keeper, schoolmistress, huckster. If emancipation degraded the work roles of some black men while raising those of others, it elevated the occupations of a few black women, leaving the labor of the vast majority unaltered.[28]

[26]Quoted in Litwack, *North of Slavery*, p. 154.

[27]Du Bois, *Philadelphia Negro*, pp. 142–43. Family income was also supplemented by children's labor. The Pennsylvania Abolition Society survey in 1848 found that 911 children were employed and another 230 were apprentices (ibid., p. 143).

[28]No occupational data are available for this period for New York or Boston, but later data that roughly correspond with Philadelphia's indicate that the situation in the three cities did not vary markedly. For a rough occupational breakdown in Boston in 1829, see John Daniels, *In Freedom's*

For newly freed blacks, moving to the city was a logical way to prepare for the future and find work, but changing one's name was the most personal and one of the most satisfying aspects of the transition from bondage to freedom. "A new name," writes Ira Berlin, "was both a symbol of personal liberation and an act of political defiance; it reversed the enslavement process and confirmed the free Negro's newly won liberty, just as the loss of an African name had earlier symbolized enslavement."[29]

By analyzing the forenames and surnames of slaves and freed Afro-Americans in the northern cities, two stages in the process of cultural transformation can be observed: first, the creation of a creole culture; second, the symbolic obliteration of the slave past. A generation before the Revolution, when slave importations into northern ports were at an all-time high, African names or Anglicized versions of African names were common. Twenty-two of the 155 slaves indicted for conspiracy in New York in 1741 had African day names—Cuffee, Cajoe, Quash, Quack, and the like—signifying the day of the week on which they were born. A slightly larger number bore classical names—Pompey, Caesar, and Cato were the most popular—and 28 carried place-names, such as London, York, Hanover, Hereford, and Jamaica. Anglo-American names, usually in a shortened form, were the most

---

Birthplace: A Study of the Boston Negroes (Boston, 1914), pp. 17–19. For the occupations of New York City's free blacks in 1855, see Freeman, "The Free Negro in New York City," pp. 444–45.

[29]Berlin, *Slaves without Masters*, pp. 51–52. On the importance of names in studying consciousness I have been guided by Wilbur Zelinsky, "Cultural Variation in Personal Name Patterns in the Eastern United States," *Annals of the Association of American Geographers* 60 (1970):743–69, and Richard Price and Sally Price, "Saramaka Onomastics: An Afro-American Naming System," *Ethnology* 11 (1972):342–67. A number of historians of the slave experience have lately ventured into what the Prices call "the art of naming," but their work primarily concerns the plantation South. See, for example, Berlin, *Slaves without Masters*, pp. 51–52; Eugene D. Genovese, *Roll, Jordan, Roll: The World the Slaves Made* (New York, 1974), pp. 443–50; Peter H. Wood, *Black Majority: Negroes in Colonial South Carolina from 1670 through the Stono Rebellion* (New York, 1974), pp. 181–85; and, for the most elaborate discussion of naming practices, Herbert G. Gutman, *The Black Family in Slavery and Freedom, 1750–1925* (New York, 1976), pp. 185–256.

common, with 47 slaves named Dick, John, Tom, Toby, or Will.[30] What is striking in this mix of cognomens is the frequency of African names and the relative absence of biblical names, which were attached to only 4 percent of the indicted slaves (table 5).

As slaves adjusted to life in the northern cities, formed conjugal relationships, and bore children, they rapidly adopted Anglo-American cultural ways, especially in comparison to slaves in the southern colonies.[31] On large plantations blacks found the preservation of African customs far easier, because the slave quarters furnished Africans with an arena for cultural autonomy. The urban slave, in contrast, almost always lived amidst a white family, and, while a few other slaves sometimes resided in the same domicile, urban blacks constantly intermingled with whites. Strong evidence of rapid northern acculturation before the Revolution can be found in the forenames given to slave children as they were brought before the Anglican church in Philadelphia for baptism.[32] African, geographical, and classical names were far less common than among the New York slave conspirators of 1741, and biblical and English names appeared far more frequently (table 5). No scholar has been able to determine precisely how these forenames were assigned, but historians have presumed that while the master may have had some role in naming slave children, the parents bore most of the responsibility. To the extent that slaves assumed the right to name their own children, the infrequency of classical and geographical names represented their desire to rid themselves

---

[30]Daniel Horsmanden, *The New York Slave Conspiracy*, ed. Thomas J. Davis (Boston, 1971), pp. 468–73. Nine of the slaves bore Spanish names and another ten were given what may be called fanciful names—Brash, Braveboy, Fortune, Sterling, Tickle, and Venture, for example. In classifying names I have followed Newbell Niles Puckett's pioneering "Names of American Negro Slaves," in George P. Murdock, ed., *Studies in the Science of Society* (New Haven, Conn., 1937), pp. 471–94.

[31]Berlin, "Time, Space, and the Evolution of Afro-American Society," pp. 44–78.

[32]Register Books of Christ Church: Marriages, Christenings, and Burials: 1 (Jan. 1, 1719, to Mar. 1750), 2 (Mar. 1750 to Dec. 1762), 3 (1763–1810), Hist. Soc. of Pa.

of absurd invocations of the classical past and of names that connoted where the master was from or where he traded. By the same token, the increasing frequency of biblical and English names provides evidence of adaptation to the culture into which their children were being born and would presumably spend their lives. Philadelphia's slaves often passed their own names along to their children if their names were Elizabeth, Sarah, Benjamin, Richard, or John. But they rarely perpetuated such names as London, Toss, Sharp, Cato, Othello, and Dirander; and such African names as Quasheba, Quam, and Cuffee also disappeared (table 5).

Upon gaining freedom, Atro-Americans took complete possession of the naming process. Aggregate statistics on forenames, compiled from city directories, manumission records, and census returns, demonstrate the psychological importance that blacks attached to affirming freedom and wiping away reminders of the slave past by taking a new name or adding to an old one. Of all the free black men listed in the Philadelphia directory of 1795, only one had retained a place-name (Dublin), and none carried derisive names (such as Mistake, Moody, and Fortune) that had been hung on them by former owners. The frequency of biblical names increased. The same was true of English names but with one significant difference. The diminutive forms that had earlier been so common had been traded in for the full English cognomen: Ben became Benjamin, Will became William, Tom became Thomas.

Within a generation of emancipation the classically derived Cato, Scipio, Caesar, and Pompey had all but disappeared among Philadelphia's free blacks, as had geographical names and names connoting qualities, virtuous or otherwise. African forenames were also rare by 1795, with only an occasional Cuffe or Cuff remaining from the list of old day names. But biblical names were on the rise among blacks who in many cases had been born free: Abraham, Isaac, Jacob, Daniel, David, and Joseph were common, and black men named Absalom, Aaron, Elijah, Ishmael, or Solomon were scattered throughout the city. However, the most common male forenames in the 1795 listing were John, James, William, and Thomas, and English forenames accounted for three-quar-

Table 5: Forenames of slaves and free blacks, 1741–1820

	N.Y. (1741) Men	Phila. parents (1747–74) Men & women	Phila. children (1747–1774) Boys & girls	Phila. (1795) Men	N.Y. former slaves (1790–1810) Men & women	Phila. (1816) Men	N.Y. (1820) Men & Women	Boston (1820) Men & women
African	14.2%	10.4%	1.9%	0	1.8%	0.4%	0.4%	1.0%
Biblical	3.9	16.6	19.0	17.1	7.8	20.7	11.1	8.4
Classical	16.1	18.5	2.5	7.3	10.3	2.1	2.5	5.4
Geographical	18.1	2.4	1.9	1.2	0.7	0.5	0.8	1.0
English	30.3	42.7	66.5	70.7	72.5	76.2	80.2	81.7
Qualities	6.5	5.2	1.9	0	1.4	0	0.4	0
Other	11.0	4.3	6.3	3.7	5.5	0	4.5	2.5
Number	155	211	158	82	437	752	243	202

SOURCES: New York (1741): Daniel Horsmanden, *The New York Slave Conspiracy*, ed. Thomas J. Davis (Boston, 1971), pp. 468–73; Philadelphia Parents and Children (1747–74): Register Books of Christ Church: Marriages, Christenings, and Burials: 1 (Jan. 1, 1719, to Mar. 1750), 2 (Mar. 1750 to Dec. 1762), 3 (1763–1810), Historical Society of Pennsylvania: Philadelphia (1795): Edmund Hogan, *The Prospect of Philadelphia and Check on the Next Directory . . .* (Philadelphia, 1795): New York Former Slaves (1790–1810): Harry B. Yoshpe, "Record of Slave Manumissions in New York during the Colonial and Early National Period," *Journal of Negro History* 26 (1941): 78–104; Philadelphia (1816): *The Philadelphia Directory for 1816 . . . .* (Philadelphia, 1816); New York and Boston (1820): Population Schedules of the Fourth Census of the United States, 1820 (microfilm at Federal Archives and Records Center, Laguna Niguel, Calif.).

NOTE: The names for 1820 are taken from the manuscript federal census for that year.

ters of all the names of black men in the 1816 directory—
striking evidence of the degree of acculturation that had occurred since slave days. In Boston and New York the trend
was the same. Slaves freed in New York after the Revolution
divested themselves of comical and geographical forenames,
African day names died out rapidly, classical names waned,
and English and biblical names were increasingly common
(table 5).

Surnames also provide important evidence of how emancipated Afro-Americans extended the boundaries of psychological space as they pursued a new life in the port cities. In
slavery most blacks had no surnames or carried the surname
of a master. In freedom they took new surnames or chose
one for the first time. In this selection process there was a
pronounced effort to make complete the break with the former master. Few of the free blacks listed in the Philadelphia
directory of 1795 bore the names of their former owners.[33]
The same is true in New York, where the surnames of Dutch
slaveowners in manumission records were in use only rarely
by 1830.[34] Cognomens such as Alburtus, Brinkerhoff, De-
Peyster, Schermerhorn, Van der Water, and Van Zandt held
no appeal for New York's free blacks, who traded them in for
names that bore no reminders of the days of bondage.

Many freed Afro-Americans used the choice of a new name
to make manifest their transition from slavery to freedom.
Freemans, Newmans, Somersets, and Armsteads were scattered through the census returns of all northern cities. Freeman appears with much greater frequency in New York than
in Boston or Philadelphia, which may indicate that since New

[33]Black surnames in the 1795 directory have been checked against the
surnames of slaveowners in the 1772 Provincial Tax Assessment lists, City
Arch., City Hall An., Philadelphia.

[34]The Dutch surnames of forty slaveowners who freed 105 slaves in
New York City between 1800 and 1816 were attached to only 11 of more
than 2,000 free black householders in 1830. The Dutch surnames were
taken from Harry B. Yoshpe, "Record of Slave Manumissions in New York
during the Colonial and Early National Period," *Journal of Negro History* 26
(1941):78–104. They have been checked against the surnames of free blacks
in 1830 as listed in Carter G. Woodson, *Free Negro Heads of Families in the
United States in 1830* (Washington, D.C., 1925), pp. 91–100.

York's free blacks lived in a society where slavery continued for so long after the Revolution, a number of them wanted to declare their liberation unmistakably through a name announcing their new status. Names suggesting artisan skills were also fairly common—Cooper, Mason, and Carpenter, for example—although sometimes this may have been coincidental. Occasionally a former slave would celebrate freedom with etymological flourish, as did Francis Drake and Hudson Rivers in New York and Julius Caesar in Philadelphia. Others took names commemorating turning points or moments of high drama in their lives. The previous name of the slaveborn West Indian sailor who turned up in Philadelphia during the Revolution and signed aboard John Paul Jones's *Bonhomme Richard* remains unknown. But this Afro-American mariner fought lustily in the epic battle against the *Serapis*, losing a leg during the sanguinary fray, and sometime thereafter renamed himself Paul Jones.[35]

But freed Afro-Americans overwhelmingly chose the most common English surnames, such as Johnson, Brown, Smith, Morris, Williams, Jackson, Thompson, and Thomas.[36] The plainest of English names took an uncommon hold on the black consciousness during the renaming process, to an extent that makes it possible to speak of a homogenization of black surnames during the first and second generations of freedom. Of the 910 surnames of blacks in the 1816 Phila-

[35]The story of the black Paul Jones is given in the Alms House Census for 1810, Surgical Ward, Records of the Guardians of the Poor, City Arch., City Hall An., Philadelphia. The historic figure that we know as John Paul Jones was actually named John Paul but had taken the name Paul Jones when, in great difficulties, he fled from England to America before the Revolution.

[36]It is not clear whether the name Brown was popular because of its color significance. If this was the case, then the fact that Black was seldom chosen requires explanation. Only rarely do the records reveal specific name changes. One case, seemingly typical, was that of Stephen Tancard, a Norfolk, Va., slave who fled his master during the Revolution, was reenslaved in the West Indies, and later jumped ship in Philadelphia, where he assumed the name of Thomas Williams (William Palmer et al., eds., *Calendar of Virginia State Papers*, 11 vols. [Richmond, 1875–93], 4:334–35. I am indebted to Philip J. Schwartz of Virginia Commonwealth University for bringing this case to my attention).

delphia directory, five—Brown, Johnson, Jones, Jackson, and
Miller—account for 15 percent of the entries, and the twelve
most frequently given surnames make up almost one-quarter
of all family names, a far more concentrated naming pattern
than among whites.[37]

This selection of common white surnames seems to indicate that free blacks wished to minimize the chance that they
would be associated, either within the black community or in
the view of whites, with the slave past. To assume the name
Johnson or Jones or Jackson was as neutral as one could get,
and its full meaning can be appreciated only by observing—
to take the Philadelphia case—how studiously blacks avoided
the names of prominent slaveowning families such as Cad-
walader, Wharton, Shippen, and Dickinson.[38] The clustering
of common English surnames among blacks also shows how
far acculturation had proceeded and perhaps indicates a
growing feeling of racial solidarity among freedpeople.[39] The

[37]The other most common surnames were Williams, Morris, Anderson,
Lewis, Butler, Smith, and Davis. The 5 most common surnames among
whites, by contrast, account for only 5 percent of nearly 17,000 family
names in the 1816 directory, and the 12 most common surnames add up
to only 8 percent of the total. A partial analysis of the names of free black
householders in New York and Boston, as given in the 1820 census, indicates the same tendency to assume common English surnames.

[38]Among 105 surnames of blacks in the 1795 Philadelphia directory, 22
are the same as those of slaveowners in 1772. But many of these are such
common surnames—Brown, Miller, Harris, Johnson, Hill, Moore, Williams, and Green—that the link is probably coincidental. Only two distinctive linkages appear: Hester Vandergrief, a free black woman, was probably
the slave of Joseph Vandergrief, and Abraham Ingles was perhaps the
slave of John Inglis. Virtually absent among the surnames of blacks were
the family names of Philadelphia's upper-class slaveowners in the late colonial period.

[39]This evidence of acculturation runs contrary to the undocumented
assertions of J. L. Dillard in *Black Names* (The Hague, 1976), pp. 20–25.
Dillard argues that both northern and southern patterns in naming were
strongly African, but he offers no supporting evidence. His indictment of
Elsdon C. Smith, who believes that freedpeople did not use African names
as surnames because they "tended to remind them of their former bondage," is unwarranted. Among the several thousand surnames I have examined, I have found African names only rarely: James Coffee (Cuffe?),
S. Congo, and Enos Gongo in Philadelphia and Edward Affricane in New

African past had not been forgotten, but in the names by which they established their individual identities northern urban free blacks strove to show that they were both Afro-American and free of slavery's grip.

In leaving thralldom behind, northern free blacks sought to perpetuate or create a family life. They neither easily nor automatically accomplished this. The great disruption of slave family life during the Revolutionary War, the dislocation in the war's aftermath, the postemancipation migration, and the constraints placed on family formation by the poverty that enshrouded freedmen and freedwomen all made the creation of black households a complex, multifaceted process that occurred not instantly but over a period of years, extending through the first generation in freedom. Consequently, emancipated Afro-Americans first extricated themselves from white households; then often combined households, with relatives, friends, and boarders intermingling; and finally, as they were able, established nuclear households. The process proceeded at different rates in the three cities, depending on when slavery ended, but everywhere black family life grew more secure.[40]

Any discussion of the free black family should be prefaced with a few comments on slave family life in the northern cities. First, a majority of slaveowners in Boston and Philadelphia owned only one adult slave, which greatly reduced the possibilities that two-parent slave families could live, work, and raise children together. Of Philadelphia's 905 slaves aged twelve or older in 1767, one-third lived by themselves in the home of their owner, and another third lived with only one other slave.[41] The hundreds of inventories of slaveowner es-

---

York. For Smith's statement see *American Surnames* (Philadelphia, 1969), p. 275.

[40]The following analysis is based on a study of 202 black households in Boston's Ward Six, 243 black households in New York's Ward Six, and 318 black households in Philadelphia's Locust Ward, all listed in the 1820 census. I have used microfilm copies of the manuscript census schedules at the Federal Archives and Records Center, Laguna Niguel, Calif.

[41]Nash, "Slaves and Slaveowners," p. 244, table V.

Table 6: Slave ownership

Number of slaves owned	Number of owners					
	Boston 1685–1775		Philadelphia 1685–1775		New York 1790	
	No.	%	No.	%	No.	%
1	337	58.8	87	42.0	601	55.6
2	145	25.3	51	24.6	208	19.2
3	54	9.4	24	11.6	128	11.8
4	19	3.3	14	6.8	66	6.1
5–8	16	2.8	22	10.6	72	6.7
9+	2	0.3	9	4.3	6	0.6
Total	573	99.9	207	99.9	1,081	100.0

SOURCES: Boston (1685–1775): Inventories of Estate, Office of the Recorder of Wills, Suffolk County Courthouse, Boston; Philadelphia (1685–1775): Office of the Recorder of Wills, City Hall Annex, Philadelphia; New York (1790): *Heads of Families at the First Census of the United States . . . New York* (Washington, D.C., 1907).

tates recorded in Boston between 1685 and 1775 indicate that nearly two-thirds of all slaves lived by themselves or with one other slave. Multiple slaveholding was more common in Philadelphia, with one-third of all slaves living alone or with one other slave, and two-thirds living in groups of three or more (table 6).[42] In New York, where slaveholding was more extensive, the presence of two adult slaves in the same white household was more common in the colonial era. But slave units declined in size over the course of the eighteenth century. In 1790 six of every ten slaveowners held only one slave and another two had only two slaves, meaning that most slave children did not live in two-parent households (tables 6 and 7).[43]

Despite the barriers to living together, slaves commonly married in all the cities, and fertility rates among black women

[42]This conclusion is based on an examination of the inventories of estate of 573 Boston slaveowners in the Office of the Recorder of Wills, Suffolk County Courthouse, Boston, and the inventories of 207 Philadelphia slaveowners in the Office of the Recorder of Wills, City Hall An., Philadelphia. There was no significant change in the pattern of slaveholding over time.

[43]Calculated from *Heads of Families at the First Census of the United States Taken in the Year 1790: New York* (Washington, D.C., 1908), pp. 116–37. I

Table 7: Slave residence in white households of Boston, New York, and Philadelphia

	Boston 1685–1775		Philadelphia 1685–1775		Philadelphia 1767		New York 1790	
	No.	%	No.	%	No.	%	No.	%
Slaves living alone	337	34.5	87	15.8	297	32.8	601	30.7
With 1 other slave	290	29.7	102	18.5	272	30.1	416	21.3
With 2 other slaves	162	16.6	72	13.1	168	18.6	384	19.6
With 3 other slaves	76	7.8	56	10.2	124	13.7	264	13.5
With 4 or more other slaves	112	11.5	234	42.5	44	4.9	290	14.8
Total	977	100.1	551	100.1	905	100.1	1,955	99.9

SOURCES: Boston (1685–1775): Inventories of Estate, Office of the Recorder of Wills, Suffolk County Courthouse, Boston; Philadelphia (1685–1775): Office of the Recorder of Wills, City Hall Annex, Philadelphia; Philadelphia (1767): Tax Assessors Lists for 1767, Van Pelt Library, University of Pennsylvania, Philadelphia; New York (1790): Heads of Families at the First Census of the United States . . . New York (Washington, D.C., 1907).

were similar to those prevailing among white women. In New York, where the best data are available, the child-woman ratio among blacks was the same or higher than among whites in three mid-eighteenth-century censuses and was somewhat lower in 1771.[44] The child-woman ratio in Philadelphia cannot be measured, but the steady procession of slaves who came to Christ Church to be married and who brought their children there for christening provides firm evidence of slave family formation. For example, Richard and Dinah brought their son Salisbury before the church early in 1749. William Allen's slaves, Quaco and Hannah, presented their son Joseph for christening in July 1751, returned with another son, James, in the following year, and brought a daughter, Hannah, to the church in 1755.[45] Between 1742 and 1775 several hundred slave children were christened in a church that included one-third to one-half of the city's slaveowners.

Still, enslaved blacks had to struggle to maintain the sanctity of their family life. Masters not only shattered slave families by sale, but they also bound out slave children, sometimes as young as six years of age. For example, William Masters, one of Philadelphia's largest slaveowners, apprenticed eleven of the seventeen slave children, aged four to sixteen, who had been born to his adult slaves. Both of Bellinda's daughters, aged twelve and seven, were bound out until the age of eighteen, the older daughter to a man in Wilmington, Delaware. Scipio and Chloe had their seven-year-old son and four-year-old daughter at their sides, but three older sons were

---

have excluded Harlem and also the 74 white households which held both slave and free blacks in 1790. Theoretically, a two-parent family could exist only in households with three or more slaves. This was the case in 241 of the 1,050 New York white households where slaves were present in 1790. For a discussion of slave family life in New York City, see Thomas J. Davis, "Slavery in Colonial New York City," Ph.D. diss., Columbia University, 1974, pp. 165–72. For Philadelphia see Merle G. Brouwer, "Marriage and Family Life among Blacks in Colonial Pennsylvania," *Pennsylvania Magazine of History and Biography* 99 (1975):368–72.

[44]Davis, "Slavery in Colonial New York City," pp. 170–71, table 7.1.

[45]Register Books of Christ Church: Marriages, Christenings, and Burials. Also see Brouwer, "Marriage and Family Life among Blacks," pp. 370–72.

bound out.[46] In sum, before the Revolution slaves in northern cities eagerly sought conjugal relationships, frequently parented children in spite of not living together, but had difficulty in keeping their offspring with them because of the common practices of hiring out and sundering family ties through sale.[47]

With freedom, Afro-Americans began to establish separate households and secure an independent family life. But for many extricating themselves from their master's house proved to be a slow and difficult task. In Boston, where slavery had been completely eradicated by 1790, more than one of every three blacks still resided in a white household at the time of the first federal census, most of them without another black in the same residence.[48] Thirty years later, all but 16 percent of the city's blacks were members of autonomous black households. In Philadelphia, where 13 percent of the city's blacks remained enslaved in 1790, half of the free blacks,

[46]William Masters inventory of estate, 1761, Off. of the Rec. of Wills, City Hall An., Philadelphia.

[47]This is somewhat contrary to the view presented in Berlin, "Time, Space, and the Evolution of Afro-American Society," pp. 48–52. Boston fits Berlin's description of northern urban slave society characterized by a "growing disproportion of slave men" and a low fertility rate among slave women. The overall sex ratio in Boston in 1765 was 158, which means that among adult slaves it must have been even higher. But the sex ratio in New York in 1771 among slaves sixteen years of age and older was 116; in Philadelphia the sex ratio among 289 slaves whose sex is indicated in inventories of estate taken between 1740 and 1775 was also 116, although a higher sex ratio is indicated by some other data (see Nash, "Slaves and Slaveowners," p. 238n). Berlin believes that mortality rates were increasing in the northern cities among blacks, but data from Boston show decreasing mortality from 1725 to 1745, a leveling off from 1745 to 1765, and then a small rise in the pre-Revolutionary decade (Lemuel Shattuck, "On the Vital Statistics of Boston," *American Journal of the Medical Sciences*, 2d ser. 1 [1840]:371).

[48]For the rapid manumission of slaves in Boston during the Revolutionary era, see Elaine MacEacheren, "Emancipation of Slavery in Massachusetts: A Reexamination, 1770–1790," *Journal of Negro History* 55 (1970):289–306. The following analysis is based on data in the 1790 and 1820 censuses. For 1790 I have used *Heads of Families at the First Census of the United States . . .* (Washington, D.C., 1907–8). For 1820 I have used the manuscript census schedules.

Table 8: Household residence of free blacks, 1790–1820

	Boston		New York		Philadelphia	
	1790	1820	1790	1820	1790	1820
In black households	63.2%	83.9%	63.9%	62.3%	49.8%	73.3%
In white households	36.8%	16.1%	36.1%	37.7%	50.2%	26.7%

SOURCES: *Heads of Families at the First Census* (Washington, D.C., 1907–8); Population Schedules of the Fourth Census of the United States, 1820 (microfilm at Federal Archives and Records Center, Laguna Niguel, Calif.).

many of them emancipated only in the previous few years, still lived in white households. A generation later, at the time of the 1820 census, only one in four did (table 8).

Economic necessity, which pressed hard on the newly freed, was doubtless the largest factor in keeping emancipated blacks in the households of former masters or obliging them to take live-in domestic jobs in the homes of other whites. The need was probably greatest when a man or woman had no spouse or relatives and was therefore forced to seek the security that service in a white household could provide. A single black, usually a woman, resided in more than half the white households where former slaves remained. The fact that twice as many black women as men continued to live in white households also indicates the demand for live-in domestic servants.[49]

[49]In Boston black females in white households outnumbered males 142 to 108; in a sample of four wards in Philadelphia, by 555 to 300; and in a sample of two wards in New York, by 502 to 246. The following table shows that in most cases it was single free blacks or small partial families who resided with whites.

Free blacks in white households, 1820

Number of free blacks in white households	Number of households					
	Boston		New York		Philadelphia	
	No.	%	No.	%	No.	%
1	120	70.6	1,100	55.2	834	63.4
2	35	20.5	508	25.5	317	24.1
3–4	11	6.5	299	15.0	125	9.5
5+	4	2.4	87	4.4	39	3.0
	170	100.0	1,994	100.1	1,315	100.0

Comparative data for New York confirm the notion that from one-half to two-thirds of northern blacks were able to establish their own households within a few years of gaining freedom, while for the others the process was much slower. In 1790, when New York still had twice as many slaves as free blacks, about 36 percent of the free blacks were living in white households, almost the same proportion as in Boston. Three decades later, when all but 16 percent of Boston's free blacks and all but 27 percent of Philadelphia's had extricated themselves from white households, 38 percent of New York's free blacks still lived among whites, almost the same as thirty years before. Slavery's longer life explains the difference between New York and the other cities. A gradual abolition law was not passed until 1799, and even then it took almost three decades more to end slavery. In 1810, 1,686 blacks remained enslaved in New York City, and many of those who received their freedom in the next decade were probably among the free blacks continuing to reside in white households at the time of the 1820 census.[50] In Boston and Philadelphia, by contrast, the emancipation process began earlier and concluded more rapidly. By the time of the 1820 census, almost all Afro-Americans in the two cities had been free for a generation or more.

Though residence in a white household, often under an indenture lasting seven years or more, was the intermediate step between subservient and autonomous existence for many freed blacks, a large majority of urban blacks lived in black households by 1820 (table 8). The census returns for that year do not indicate exact family relationships within households, so it is impossible to delineate family composition exactly. But this census did for the first time enumerate black residents by age and sex, thus permitting some tentative generalizations about black household and family formation in the early decades of freedom.

In all three cities more than three-quarters of the black

[50]There were still 518 slaves in Manhattan in 1820 according to the census. Probably most of them were born in the 1790s. In 1817 a second emancipation law was passed, declaring that slaves born before July 4, 1799, would be free on July 4, 1827. This legislation ended slavery in New York. See Freeman, "The Free Negro in New York City," pp. 3–6.

Table 9: Black household types, 1820

| | Philadelphia | | Boston | | New York | |
	No.	%	No.	%	No.	%
Nuclear*						
With children	157	48.3	70	33.5	66	26.7
Without children	49	15.1	44	21.1	1	0.4
Total	206	63.4	114	54.6	67	27.1
Augmented†	50	15.4	44	21.1	132	53.4
Single parent						
Female-headed	30	9.2	18	8.6	24	9.7
Female-headed, augmented	9	2.8	14	6.7	22	8.9
Total	39	12.0	32	15.3	46	18.6
Male-headed	2	0.6	1	0.5	1	0.4
Male-headed, augmented	1	0.3	0	—	0	—
Total	3	0.9	1	0.5	1	0.4
Nonfamily‡						
Female-headed	15	4.6	9	4.3	1	0.4
Male-headed	8	2.5	7	3.3	0	—
Total	23	7.1	16	7.6	1	0.4
Grown child plus parent	4	1.2	2	1.0	0	—
Grand total	325	100.0	209	100.1	247	99.9

SOURCE: Population Schedules of the Fourth Census of the United States, 1820 (microfilm at Federal Archives and Records Center, Laguna Niguel, Calif.).

*A nuclear household is a simple two-parent family (with children) or conjugal unit (without children).

†An augmented family is a nuclear type plus kin or non-kin.

‡A nonfamily type contains one adult or two or more adults of same sex only.

households contained at least one adult male and one adult female. This was true of 76 percent of the black households in Boston, 79 percent in Philadelphia, and 81 percent in New York (table 9).[51] Single-parent families were even less frequent in black households containing children under the age

[51]These percentages stand in striking contrast to one city of the upper South, Petersburg, Va., where in 1810 only 43.7 percent of the free black families were double-headed in 1810 and 41.9 percent in 1820 (Suzanne

Table 10: Black household types with children under 14, 1820

| | Boston | | Philadelphia | | New York | |
	No.	%	No.	%	No.	%
Two-parent	86	77.5	205	88.4	181	81.5
Female-headed	24	21.6	25	10.8	39	17.6
Male-headed	1	0.9	2	0.9	2	0.9
Total	111	100.0	232	100.1	222	100.0

SOURCE: Population Schedules of the Fourth Census of the United States, 1820 (microfilm at Federal Archives and Records Center, Laguna Niguel, Calif.).

of fourteen. Such households were overwhelmingly headed by both an adult male and female—in 78 percent of the cases in Boston, 88 percent in Philadelphia, and 82 percent in New York (table 10). In a sample of 1,407 black children under fourteen years of age in 1820, 92 percent lived in households that included at least one adult male and one adult female (table 11).

Still, blacks achieved the goal of a nuclear household slowly. In the immediate aftermath of slavery, unable to establish their own separate households but unwilling to continue to reside with whites, blacks often joined together to form large extended or augmented household units.[52] Black families boarded relatives and friends newly arrived from the countryside and emerging from slavery with no assets or knowledge of urban life. Strong evidence exists for this pattern in New York, where emancipation came later than in Boston or Philadelphia, although the pattern was probably present in the other seaport cities as well in the immediate aftermath of slavery. Thus in 1820 the average black household was far larger in New York than in Philadelphia or Boston: 6.3 persons as compared with 3.9 in Philadelphia and 4.2 in Boston (table 12). This reflected not a larger number of children in

Dee Lebsock, "Women and Economics in Virginia: Petersburg, 1784–1820," Ph.D. diss., University of Virginia, 1977, p. 22). Theodore Hershberg reports that in the censuses conducted by the Pennsylvania Abolition Society in 1847 and 1856, two-parent households "were characteristic of 78 percent of black families" ("Free Blacks in Antebellum Philadelphia," p. 190).

[52]The census returns do not allow for a distinction between extended and augmented families since exact blood or marital relations between household members are not specified.

Table 11: Number of black children under 14 in various types of households, 1820

	Boston		Philadelphia		New York		Total	
	No.	%	No.	%	No.	%	No.	%
Two-parent	209	85.3	575	90.6	505	95.8	1289	91.6
Female-headed	34	13.9	58	9.1	20	3.8	112	8.0
Male-headed	2	0.8	2	0.3	2	0.4	6	0.4
Total	245	100.0	635	100.0	527	100.0	1407	100.0

SOURCE: Population Schedules of the Fourth Census of the United States, 1820 (microfilm at Federal Archives and Records Center, Laguna Niguel, Calif.).

Table 12: Blacks in black households by age and sex, 1820

		Males				Females				Average size of household
		0–13	14–25	26–44	45+	0–13	14–25	26–44	45+	
Boston	Number	112	20	189	31	142	44	271	60	4.2
	Percent of total	12.9	2.3	21.8	3.6	16.3	5.1	31.2	6.9	
	Percent of gender	31.8	5.7	53.7	8.8	27.5	8.5	52.4	11.6	
Philadelphia	Number	211	88	159	80	258	149	210	112	3.9
	Percent of total	16.7	7.0	12.6	6.3	20.4	11.8	16.6	8.8	
	Percent of gender	39.2	16.4	29.6	14.7	35.4	20.4	28.8	15.4	
New York	Number	225	136	205	126	241	203	279	131	6.3
	Percent of total	14.6	8.8	13.3	8.1	15.6	13.1	18.1	8.5	
	Percent of gender	32.5	16.7	29.6	18.2	38.3	22.1	30.4	14.3	

SOURCE: Population schedules of the Fourth Census of the United States, 1820 (microfilm at Federal Archives and Records Center, Laguna Niguel, Calif.).

New York black families[53] but the greater number of "extra" people in the household. While most Boston and Philadelphia black families lived in nuclear units by the second decade of the nineteenth century, the majority of black households in New York remained augmented or extended, and the nonfamily type of household virtually nonexistent. In Philadelphia and Boston 7 to 8 percent of the black households were made up of a single male or female or several adults of the same sex. But in New York only one of 247 households in Ward Six was of the nonfamily type. This circumstance, combined with the large number of blacks living in white households relative to the other cities, suggests that the distance from slavery was often still too short for an individual free black to maintain a household of his or her own (table 9).

Black families generally contained far fewer children than white families. In New York and Boston the number of children per adult woman was more than twice as high for whites as for blacks. In Philadelphia the ratio was 2.7 for whites and 1.6 for blacks.[54] Some of this difference may be accounted for by the extremely high mortality rate among blacks, usually two to three times that of whites.[55] But family limitation

[53]The child-woman ratio (calculated as the number of male and female children under fourteen years of age divided by the number of women between twenty-six and forty-four years) was 1.1 in Boston, 1.4 in New York, and 1.6 in Philadelphia. Table 3 gives the number of persons in each sex and age category.

[54]Calculated from the 1820 census as recapitulated in Everett S. Lee and Michael Lalli, "Population," in David T. Gilchrist, ed., *The Growth of the Seaport Cities, 1790–1825* (Charlottesville, Va., 1967), p. 35. Since the white age categories are infant to nine years of age and ten to fifteen, I have combined the number of children up to nine years old with two-thirds of those aged ten to fifteen in order to gain comparability with black children under fourteen. The number of children has been compared to the number of women of twenty-six to forty-four years of age.

[55]For black mortality in Philadelphia see *The Present State and Condition of the Free People of Color of the City of Philadelphia* (Philadelphia, 1838), pp. 34–35; for New York see John Duffy, *A History of Public Health in New York City, 1625–1866* (New York, 1968), pp. 260, 580, and 587. Brissot de Warville observed in 1788: "Married Negroes certainly have as many children as whites, but it has been observed that in the cities the death rate of Negro

was also a factor. In New York, the one city where we have data from the slave period to compare with the 1820 census figures, it appears that the woman-child ratio actually dropped significantly as slaves passed from bondage to freedom.[56]

These various measurements, although crude, make it clear that the stereotypes about the unstable and matrifocal black family after slavery have little basis in fact, at least so far as concerns the seaport cities of the North. In general, these data support Herbert G. Gutman's contention that "black households and family systems were exceedingly complex in the aftermath of emancipation" but that conjugal and nuclear-family relationships predominated.[57] In all three cities, though the timing differed, freed blacks moved toward the establishment of two-parent nuclear households. Boston, farthest from slavery, had the smallest proportion of blacks living in white households in 1820 (one in six) and a high incidence of nuclear families among black householders (three of five). New York, where 45 percent of the black population remained enslaved in 1800 and 5 percent in 1820, had the largest proportion of free blacks living in white households (nearly two of five) and among black householders a dramatically lower incidence of nuclear families. Philadelphia's free blacks, who were between their counterparts in Boston and New York in terms of distance from slavery, were also between the two extremes in terms of the proportion who lived

---

children is higher" (*New Travels in the United States of America, 1788*, ed. Durand Echeverria [Cambridge, Mass., 1964], p. 232n, quoted in Berlin, "Time, Space, and the Evolution of Afro-American Society," p. 48n).

[56]The ratio of children under sixteen to women sixteen and older in New York City in 1771 was 1.0; in 1820 it was 0.7. For the 1771 data see Greene and Harrington, *American Population*, p. 102. It is impossible to say how much of this decline is accounted for by different mortality rates among slaves and free blacks, but it seems certain that the mortality rate among blacks must have risen as they moved from upper-class homes in less densely settled areas to crowded lower-class sections of the city after emancipation.

[57]"Persistent Myths about the Afro-American Family," in Michael Gordon, ed., *The American Family in Social-Historical Perspective*, 2d ed. (New York, 1978), p. 476.

in white households (one of four) and slightly ahead of Boston in the formation of nuclear families. The effort to create autonomous families was one of the remarkable features of Afro-American life in the early years of freedom.

As they worked themselves free of white households and established households of their own, new patterns of black residence began to emerge. In slave days, of course, Afro-Americans had resided with their masters or with those to whom they had been hired out. Since these masters lived in cities that were only gradually becoming segregated by function and class, slaves lived scattered throughout urban areas. In the first decade of freedom this dispersal continued in some measure, because from one-third to one-half of all manumitted slaves continued to live in white households.

In the 1780s, as blacks began forming their own households, they made independent decisions about where to locate. In Philadelphia, to focus on one case, they began clustering in two areas, one old and one new. The old area, in the northern part of the city, was in North and South Mulberry wards, a relatively poor district of the city with a concentration of Irish and German laboring-class families. Located between Arch and Vine streets west of Fourth, North and South Mulberry wards attracted about 29 of the city's 169 black households by 1790. Another 32 families lived in the Northern Liberties, beyond North Mulberry Ward. The other area was almost entirely new. Located in the southern part of the city, it comprised Cedar and Locust wards and the west part of South Ward. As late as 1785 this had been mostly open land, but within a few years contractors began erecting cheap housing to accommodate the city's growing population.[58] By 1790 some 56 black households had established themselves in the area. They appeared as the advance guard of what would shortly become an enormous movement of black Philadelphians into this southern part of the city. Fifty-

---

[58]The development of the southern part of the city is detailed in Emma Jones Lapsansky, "South Street Philadelphia, 1762–1854: 'A Haven for Those Low in the World,'" Ph.D. diss., University of Pennsylvania, 1975.

two other black families were dispersed throughout the rest of the city.[59]

Because new cheaply constructed tenements rented at a lower rate than older but larger dwellings, black Philadelphians moved steadily into the southern section of the city. But another process, the establishment of African churches and schools, also drew blacks. In 1791, Richard Allen and Absalom Jones were laying plans to build a black church at Sixth and Lombard streets, in some measure because Philadelphia's free blacks had been moving into new housing in this section of Cedar Ward. By 1794 two black churches had opened their doors in the same neighborhood. But if the nascent black neighborhood attracted African churches, the churches, once established, became vital centers of black community life, drawing hundreds of black families as they worked their way out of white households into their own residences. St. Thomas's had a membership of 427 one year after its building was completed; by 1813 it had 560 members, while Bethel Church counted 1,272 communicants.[60]

The lure of the black churches can be seen in the changing residential pattern of blacks in Philadelphia.[61] Black families continued to settle in the northern part of the city, many of

[59]The black residential pattern in 1790 has been plotted from the listings of black households in *Heads of Families at the First Census of the United States: Pennsylvania* (Washington, D.C., 1908).

[60]Lapsansky, "South Street Philadelphia," pp. 180–82. For church membership, Du Bois, *Philadelphia Negro*, p. 199. On the role of the black churches in the creation of neighborhoods where many black families settled, see also Carol V. R. George, *Segregated Sabbaths: Richard Allen and the Rise of Independent Black Churches, 1760–1840* (New York, 1973). In Boston the decision to build the first black church in the west end of town in 1805 hastened the migration of blacks out of the North End (Daniels, *In Freedom's Birthplace*, p. 22).

[61]Between 1790 and 1810 the share of the city's black population living in the northern sector of North and South Mulberry wards and Northern Liberties fell from 25 to 21 percent. During the same period the portion of the black inhabitants living in the southern area of Cedar and Locust wards, Southwark, and Moyamensing (the newest area of black settlement), rose from 29 to 47 percent (calculated from the 1790 and 1810 censuses).

them perhaps because they had jobs in that part of town. But the black population in Cedar and Locust wards grew much faster, from 265 free blacks in 1790 to 4,191 in 1820. This "Cedar Street corridor" of black life, as Emma Lapsansky styles it, was no black ghetto. While free blacks established residences there in great numbers, they were never a majority in this period. Neighborhoods remained mixed, both racially and occupational. Yet the development of racial and class segregation had received a strong impetus as builders constructed primarily cheap housing in new parts of the city and black families sought the security and group consciousness that came through residential consolidation.[62]

To the south of Cedar Ward lay West Southwark and Moyamensing. Still not incorporated into the city at this time, they nonetheless were part of the rapid development of the southern part of Philadelphia. Free blacks moved there by the hundreds after 1790, living in "cabins," "sheds," and "mean low box[es] of wood."[63] Especially in Moyamensing the free black population increased dramatically in thirty years, from 27 in 1790 to 1,174 in 1820. All told, this southern sector of the city, composed of Locust and Cedar wards, West Southwark, and Moyamensing, contained three of every five blacks in Philadelphia by 1820. Moreover, among independent black householders the percentage living in this area was even higher.[64]

[62]Lapsansky, "South Street Philadelphia," pp. 119–40. In Cedar Ward, Locust Ward, and Moyamensing, the areas where black families were most highly concentrated, Afro-Americans represented 27, 24, and 30 percent of the population, respectively, in 1820. For the increasingly class-divided social geography of New York City in this period, see Betsy Blackmar, "Rewalking the 'Walking City': Property Relations in New York City, 1780–1840," *Radical History Review* 21 (1980):131–48.

[63]The descriptions of housing, taken from contemporary newspaper accounts, are quoted in Alexander, *Render Them Submissive*, pp. 21–22.

[64]In many of the more affluent wards of the city, blacks lived primarily in white households. For example, Chestnut, Walnut, and Dock wards contained 514 free blacks in 1820 (5 percent of the city's black population). But only 62 of them, gathered in thirteen families, resided in black households. The large number of free blacks living in white households in wards where there were few independent black households disguises the grow-

Some sense of these emerging neighborhoods, where free black families mixed extensively with laboring-class whites, can be gained from looking at city directories. Gaskill Street, which ran from Third to Fifth between Cedar and Lombard streets, had two black families listed in the 1795 directory and three in the directory of 1811. But five years later, twenty-four black families were spread along Gaskill, all but two of them in the block between Third and Fourth streets. Sometimes families doubled up, as did Richard Bennett, shoemaker, John Bahimy, mariner, and Joseph Reed, laborer, at 62 Gaskill. Charles Brown, porter, and Phillips Exeter, washerwoman, shared 88 Gaskill. By 1816 eighteen black families made their residence on Blackberry Alley, running north and south from the Pennsylvania Hospital. Among the heads of household were a carpenter, painter, carter, porter, plasterer, trader, gardener, waiter, coachman, and laborer. Black families made their homes throughout the Cedar Street corridor, especially in the crowded courts and alleys that builders and landlords were developing in the early nineteenth century.[65]

In the organization of black institutions, closely tied to emerging neighborhoods, free Afro-Americans constructed the social, religious, and emotional ligaments of their communities. The black church, as many historians have noted, stood at the center of this process and marked the strongest tie between the distant African past, the more proximate slave past, and the present and future as free persons. "The Negro church," wrote Du Bois, "is the peculiar and characteristic product of the transplanted African. . . . It has preserved, on the one hand, many functions of tribal organization, and on the other hand, many of the family functions. Its tribal func-

---

ing segregation of black and white residences in the city. The same is true for New York and Boston in this period. For a study of growing residential segregation in Philadelphia between 1811 and 1858, see Norman J. Johnston, "The Caste and Class of the Urban Form of Historic Philadelphia," *Journal of the American Institute of Planners* 32 (1966):334–49.

[65]Lapsansky, "South Street Philadelphia," pp. 141–48, for the rapid deterioration of the recently built lower-class neighborhoods of the "Cedar Street Corridor." For the black families on Gaskill Street in 1811, ibid., pp. 131–32.

tions are shown in its religious activity, its social authority, and general guiding and co-ordinating work; its family functions are shown by the fact that the church is a centre of social life and intercourse."[66]

Two closely related factors led to the organization of the first black churches in northern cities in the 1790s: discriminatory treatment in white churches and "the gradual rise of a community of interest" among the Afro-Americans drawn into the metropolis after emancipation. This separatist church movement drew much inspiration from the indifference of white churches to the social and political injustices that freed blacks confronted at the end of the eighteenth century. It was also grounded in the desire of Afro-Americans for a more evangelical gospel than white churches proffered and in a determination "to arise out of the dust and shake ourselves, and throw off that servile fear, that the habit of oppression and bondage trained us up in."[67] Similarly, in New York and Boston separate black churches emerged not only because of discrimination but also because of "a growing self-reliance and the rise of individual leaders."[68]

To some extent the rise of the independent black church appears to have been triggered as much by concern for the religious care of the dead as by concern for the living. In both Philadelphia and New York free black churches had their origins in the Free African societies established in the late 1780s and early 1790s. In each case one of the society's first acts was to apply for a separate black burial ground.[69] White churches did not permit the mortal remains of black worshippers to be interred in their cemeteries but instead con-

[66]Du Bois, *Philadelphia Negro*, p. 201.

[67]"The Causes and Motives for Establishing St. Thomas's African Church of Philadelphia," in William Douglass, *Annals of the First African Church in the United States of America* . . . (Philadelphia, 1862), pp. 93–95.

[68]Freeman, "Free Negro in New York City," p. 375; Daniels, *In Freedom's Birthplace*, p. 226; George A. Levesque, "Inherent Reformers—Inherited Orthodoxy: Black Baptists in Boston, 1800–1873," *Journal of Negro History* 61 (1975):491–525.

[69]George, *Segregated Sabbaths*, p. 49; Freeman, "Free Negro in New York City," p. 410.

signed blacks to the Potter's Field or "Stranger's Burial Ground," as it was tellingly called in Philadelphia. This extension to the dead of the racial inequalities among the living may have been especially grievous to Afro-Americans, whose African religious heritage stressed ancestor reverence and thus emphasized dignifying the dead.

To signify their group identity and to separate themselves from whites, blacks—from the beginning—named their churches, schools, and mutual aid associations and fraternal societies "African." In 1787 Philadelphia free blacks established their first independent organization and called it the Free African Society. From it derived the African Methodist Episcopal Church and the African Episcopal Church of St. Thomas. The African Baptist and African Presbyterian churches would follow. Among the benevolent societies established in this early period were the Angolian Society and the Angola Beneficial Association in 1808, the Sons of Africa in 1810, the African Female Benevolent Society (founding date unknown), and the Male African Benevolent Society in 1819.[70] The Quaker school for blacks, founded in 1770, became known as the Friends African School in the 1790s. The first black insurance company, in existence by 1809, was called the African Insurance Company of Philadelphia.[71] In New York the term *African* was also used for almost all the early churches, the first black school, and the first mutual aid societies. In Boston the African Society, founded in 1797, established the African School in 1798 and the African Meeting House in 1805.[72] The frequency of the term in the names of

[70]Philadelphia's black organizations and their founding dates are listed in *The Present State and Condition of the Free People of Color of the City of Philadelphia*, pp. 26–27.

[71]Nancy Slocum Hornick, "Anthony Benezet and the Africans' School: Toward a Theory of Full Equality," *Pennsylvania Magazine of History and Biography* 99 (1975):399–421. The insurance company is noted in J. Thomas Scharf and Thompson Westcott, *History of Philadelphia, 1609–1884*, 3 vols. (Philadelphia, 1884), 3:2117.

[72]For free black institutions and their names in New York, see *The Negro in New York: An Informal Social History, 1626–1940*, ed. Roi Ottley and William J. Weatherby (New York, 1967) and Freeman, "Free Negro in New York City," chs. 9–11. For Boston see Donald M. Jacobs, "A History of the

early churches, schools, and benevolent societies, when considered in conjunction with the rapid Anglicization of black personal names in this period, suggests that while free blacks took on common English names as a way of wiping out the slave past, they simultaneously and self-consciously fostered black solidarity by affixing an adjective to their institutions that would unmistakably differentiate them from parallel white institutions.

Establishing independent institutions took time, and the continued enslavement of a sizable portion of the black population delayed the process, partly because the business of obtaining freedom for those still in bondage absorbed the time, money, and energy of those who were free, and partly because it took a generation of freedom for blacks to extricate themselves from white households and establish residences of their own in neighborhoods where black consciousness could thrive. This stifling effect of slavery can be seen in the wide disparity in black institutional development in Philadelphia and New York. The two cities had black populations of roughly the same size in the first quarter of the nineteenth century. But whereas nearly all Philadelphia blacks were free by 1790, it took another generation to extinguish slavery in New York City. Thus by 1813, when Philadelphia blacks had created six black churches with a total membership of 2,366, only two existed in New York, with a membership that cannot have exceeded one-third of Philadelphia's.[73] Similarly, New York's first free black school was founded in 1786 and the second not until 1820. Meanwhile, by 1811 nine black schools were operating in Philadelphia. New York blacks founded their first mutual aid society, the New York African Society for Mutual Relief, in 1810, while Philadelphia blacks

Boston Negro from the Revolution to the Civil War," Ph.D. diss., Boston University, 1968, chs. 2–3, and George A. Levesque, "Before Integration: The Forgotten Years of Jim Crow Education in Boston," *Journal of Negro Education* 48 (1979):113–25.

[73] For the black churches in New York and their difficulties, see Freeman, "Free Negro in New York City," pp. 375–405. Even by 1855 New York's black churches had fewer than 2,000 members (ibid., p. 422). For the Philadelphia church membership figures see Du Bois, *Philadelphia Negro*, p. 199.

had organized eleven benevolent societies by 1813.[74] Where slavery had been expunged soon after the Revolution, black institutional life thrived; where it lingered, it had a deadening effect even on those blacks who did escape its clutches.

At different rates, black institutions took form in all northern cities. Created out of the massing of free blacks in the cities and the rise of an independent black consciousness, these churches, schools, fraternal societies, and mutual aid associations in turn became part of the magnetic pull of urban life. By the 1820s Philadelphia Afro-Americans had created an institutional life that was richer and more stable than that of the lower-income whites with whom they shared neighborhoods. Since Afro-Americans were "blocked from upward mobility out of the neighborhood," writes Lapsansky, "they wanted institutions that would provide them with a reasonable future there." For whites, by contrast, these increasingly class-segregated neighborhoods were seen as a "brief stopping place" on the way to something better. White gangs were the institution better suited to "a transient constituency," for they required no large expenditures for permanent structures, no "long-range planned activity," and no regular commitments of time.[75] Hence, white churches and fraternal organizations fared poorly in comparison to black institutions in the lower-class wards of Philadelphia in this period,

---

[74]On black schools in Philadelphia, see *The Present State and Condition of the Free People of Color*, p. 39. Philadelphia's black schools were private since blacks were excluded from tax-supported public schools until 1822, contrary to the school laws first passed in 1802. See Harry C. Silcox, "Delay and Neglect: Negro Public Education in Ante-bellum Philadelphia, 1800–1860," *Pennsylvania Magazine of History and Biography* 97 (1973):444–64. For black institutions in New York see Daniel Perlman, "Organizations of the Free Negro in New York City, 1800–1861," *Journal of Negro History* 56 (1971):181–97. Perlman concludes that fifty Negro organizations were formed between 1800 and 1850. In 1838 in Philadelphia there were eighty mutual aid societies, with 7,448 members, according to a survey by the Pennsylvania Abolition Society (*Present State and Condition of the Free People of Color*, p. 39).

[75]Lapsansky, "South Street Philadelphia," pp. 205–9. On black consciousness, see George A. Levesque, "Interpreting Early Black Ideology: A Reappraisal of Historical Consensus," *Journal of the Early Republic* 1 (1981):269–87.

and black institutions became the envy of whites in racially mixed neighborhoods. Oppressed both as an economic class and a racial caste, urban freedmen and freedwomen drew upon a collective black consciousness to form their own network of thriving institutions.

"Sir," thundered South Carolina's Robert Y. Hayne in the famous nullification debate of 1830, "there does not exist on the face of the earth, a population so poor, so wretched, so vile, so loathsome, so utterly destitute of all the comforts, conveniences, and decencies of life, as the unfortunate blacks of Philadelphia, New York, and Boston. Liberty has been to them the greatest of calamities, the heaviest of curses."[76] The words were uttered, of course, to shame the North for its treatment of emancipated slaves and to contrast their condition unfavorably with those still held in bondage in the South. Hayne's indictment truthfully acknowledged the wretched effects of northern racism. White urban dwellers in the North, as Leon Litwack has written, "worked free Negroes severely in menial employments, excluded them from the polls, the juries, the churches, and the learned professions, snubbed them in social circles, and finally even barred them from entering some states."[77] Yet this is not the full story, for it focuses on what was done to free blacks rather than on what emancipated Afro-Americans did for themselves. Alongside the history of oppression must be placed the history of people striving to live life as fully, as freely, and as creatively as their inner resources and external circumstances would allow. In the northern capitals of American life after the Revolution, emancipated slaves suffered greatly to be sure, but they also formed communities that would not die and created a viable culture of their own.

[76]Quoted in Litwack, *North of Slavery*, p. 39.

[77]Ibid. It is one of the ironies of this period that southern defenders of slavery, advocates of recolonization, and northern white friends of free blacks, such as the Quakers, tended to describe, each for their own purposes, the plight of urban Afro-Americans in much the same way.

RICHARD S. DUNN

Black Society in
the Chesapeake
1776–1810

FROM THE PERSPECTIVES of black slaves and white slaveholders alike, the Chesapeake during the Revolutionary era was
a region of pivotal importance. In 1776 over half of the blacks
in the United States lived in Virginia or Maryland. Since the
seventeenth century the Chesapeake had been the center of
black life in America, and so it continued to be throughout
the early years of the new Republic. As late as 1810 more
than 40 percent of the blacks in the United States were to be
found there. What Chesapeake blacks accomplished—and
were prevented from accomplishing—during the closing
decades of the eighteenth century had great consequences
for all Afro-Americans. The white slaveholders of Virginia
and Maryland played an equally crucial role. From the 1770s
to the 1820s the Chesapeake's white leadership took an ex-
traordinarily prominent place in national affairs. They led
the rebellion against Britain, took charge of the Continental
army, shaped the new republican government, and nearly
monopolized the American presidency. Although the white
Chesapeake leaders were all slaveholders, most of them protested, publicly or privately, against the institution of slavery.
They were certainly the only men in America who could con-
ceivably have engineered a national emancipation in the 1780s.
The steps they took—and failed to take—greatly affected
the development of the southern slave system down to the
Civil War.

In several important respects the American Revolution
opened new opportunities for blacks in the Chesapeake. A
number of historians have discussed the Revolutionary chal-

lenge to slavery. The war itself had an immediate impact: thousands of Virginia and Maryland slaves served in the British or patriot armies, were carried off as war booty by the British, or deserted their masters to become freemen.[1] Organized religion had a new meaning for blacks: the large-scale evangelical revival that swept through Virginia and Maryland in the 1770s and 1780s brought slaves into the Baptist and Methodist churches, created a number of independent black churches, and persuaded many white slaveholders that enslavement was unchristian.[2] The patriotic agitation against British tyranny also raised ideological doubts about slavery. The Revolutionary call to liberty and natural rights placed slaveholders in an awkward moral predicament.[3] Chesapeake masters manumitted a sizable number of blacks during and after the Revolution; by 1810 the free black population in Maryland and Virginia had multiplied approximately tenfold since 1776 and totaled over 60,000.[4] One-third of the free blacks in the United States lived in the Chesapeake in 1810 and were more numerous there than in any of the northern states.

The American Revolution also precipitated fundamental

[1]Benjamin Quarles, *The Negro in the American Revolution* (Chapel Hill, N.C., 1961); Luther P. Jackson, "Negro Soldiers and Seamen in the American Revolution," *Journal of Negro History* 27 (1942):247–87.

[2]Albert J. Raboteau, *Slave Religion: The "Invisible Institution" in the Antebellum South* (New York, 1978); Lester B. Scherer, *Slavery and the Churches in Early America, 1619–1819* (Grand Rapids, Mich., 1975).

[3]Winthrop D. Jordan, *White over Black: American Attitudes toward the Negro, 1550–1812* (Chapel Hill, N.C., 1968), chs. 8–15; Duncan J. MacLeod, *Slavery, Race and the American Revolution* (Cambridge, England, 1974); and F. Nwabueze Okoye, "Chattel Slavery as the Nightmare of the American Revolutionaries," *William and Mary Quarterly*, 3d ser. 37 (1980):3–28.

[4]The published totals of 33,927 free blacks in Maryland and 30,570 in Virginia in 1810 are incorrectly tabulated, a characteristic problem with early census returns. The Maryland census takers made an error of over 4,000 in adding up the Prince George's free blacks, and the Virginia enumerators made an error of 1,000 in Southampton. Correcting for these errors, the Maryland total becomes 29,656 and the Virginia total 31,570. For general discussion of the Chesapeake free blacks, see Ira Berlin, *Slaves without Masters: The Free Negro in the Antebellum South* (New York, 1974).

changes in the slave-based Chesapeake economy. Throughout the colonial era, tobacco had been the principal export
staple of the region, and tobacco planters had been the principal employers of slave labor. During the Revolutionary War
tobacco exports were largely blocked, and though the tobacco staple revived temporarily in the 1780s, exports col-
lapsed again—this time decisively—with the European wars
of 1792–1815.[5] While many Chesapeake planters had long
been producing wheat, corn, and livestock for export or for
local consumption, the decline in tobacco prices compelled
them to turn from the traditional gang labor system to a style
of mixed agriculture practiced elsewhere in the United States
by small free farmers. Agricultural historians have emphasized the depressed post-Revolutionary farming conditions
in the region: soil exhaustion, declining crop yields, and a
massive outmigration to greener pastures west and south.[6]
One gets the impression that those slaveholders who stayed
in the Chesapeake hardly knew how to keep going, bur-
dened as they were with an obsolete labor force and compelled to find employment for hordes of unwanted and
unneeded black workers.

Yet chattel slavery survived, and indeed expanded, in the
Chesapeake. Despite the military, religious, ideological, and
economic presures upon them, the Virginia and Maryland
statesmen of the Revolutionary era made few legal and insti-

[5]Jacob M. Price, "The Economic Growth of the Chesapeake and the
European Market, 1697–1775," *Journal of Economic History* 24 (1964):496;
idem, *France and the Chesapeake: A History of the French Tobacco Monopoly,
1674–1791, and of Its Relationship to the British and American Tobacco Trades*
(Ann Arbor, Mich., 1973), pp. 682, 729–34, and 841–42. For additional
commentary on the Chesapeake economy in the eighteenth century, see
Carville V. Earle, *The Evolution of a Tidewater Settlement System: All Hallow's
Parish, Maryland, 1650–1783* (Chicago, 1975); Paul G. E. Clemens, *The Atlantic Economy and Colonial Maryland's Eastern Shore: From Tobacco to Grain*
(Ithaca, N.Y., 1980); and Carville Earle and Ronald Hoffman, "Urban Development in the Eighteenth-Century South," *Perspectives in American History* 10 (1976):7–78.

[6]Lewis C. Gray, *History of Agriculture in the Southern United States to 1860*,
2 vols. (Washington, D.C., 1933), chs. 19–28; Avery O. Craven, *Soil Exhaustion as a Factor in the Agricultural History of Virginia and Maryland, 1606–
1860* (Urbana, Ill., 1926).

tutional changes in their slave system. They closed the slave trade, restricted entry of slaves from other states, and permitted individual manumission, but they squelched every move toward general abolition. Thomas Jefferson, the most prominent would-be emancipator, soon retreated into silence and freed few of his own slaves. By the late 1780s Chesapeake abolitionists had lost much of their vigor. In the 1790s they were muzzled. A generation after the Revolution, nearly 90 percent of Chesapeake blacks remained enslaved. By 1810 the slave population in the Chesapeake had nearly doubled since 1776.[7]

How can the Revolutionary challenge to slavery and the large-scale manumission movement in Virginia and Maryland be reconciled with the continuing adherence to slavery by the white leadership and the expansion of Chesapeake slavery in the post-Revolutionary era? One way of doing so is to note the growing divergence between developments in the upper and lower Chesapeake, between black life in Maryland and black life in Virginia. What had been a single region—geographically, economically, and psychologically— began to fragment in the years following the Revolution. Blacks acquired considerably greater independence, mobility, and opportunity—freedom—in the upper Chesapeake than in Tidewater or Piedmont Virginia. But in those Chesapeake districts where most blacks lived, slavery was more deeply rooted when Jefferson stepped down from the presidency than when he composed the Declaration of Independence.

Tax lists and census returns compiled between 1776 and 1810 provide striking evidence of this trend toward black freedom in Maryland and entrenched slavery in Virginia. These enumerations contain much more detailed and comprehensive information about slaveholders, slaves, and free blacks than can be found in any tabulations for the Chesapeake before 1776. They indicate where black people lived, distinguish between slaves and free blacks, and suggest

[7]Robert McColley, *Slavery and Jeffersonian Virginia*, 2d ed. (Urbana, Ill., 1973); Donald L. Robinson, *Slavery in the Structure of American Politics, 1765–1820* (New York, 1971).

something (though not enough) about black occupational structure and the size of black living and working units. Of course such tax lists and census returns reveal nothing whatsoever about black or white *mentalité*. Even from a purely statistical viewpoint these documents are incomplete and inaccurate. Many of the tax lists exclude slave children; most exclude elderly slaves and the poorest whites and thus considerably understate the black and white populations. The census returns, while generally more systematic, were often carelessly compiled. Generally the Maryland enumerations are much better than the Virginia ones for this period, with detailed tabulations from most counties in 1776, 1782–83, 1790, 1800, and 1810.[8] For Virginia similar tabulations exist only for 1782–83 and 1810.[9] Yet despite these shortcomings

[8]The Maryland census of 1776 is incomplete; returns for parts of eight counties are printed in Gaius Marcus Brumbaugh, ed., *Maryland Records: Colonial, Revolutionary, County and Church, from Original Sources*, 1 (Baltimore, 1915); 2 (Lancaster, Pa., 1928). A summary of the Maryland census of 1782 is printed in Stella H. Sutherland, *Population Distribution in Colonial America* (New York, 1936), p. 174. Tax lists of 1783 for six counties are tabulated by Gregory A. Stiverson, *Poverty in a Land of Plenty: Tenancy in Eighteenth-Century Maryland* (Baltimore, 1978), pp. 146–49. The 1790 census is published by the U.S. Bureau of the Census, *Heads of Families at the First Census of the United States Taken in the Year 1790: Maryland* (Washington, D.C., 1907). County totals for 1800 are printed in *Return of the Whole Number of Persons within the Several Districts of the United States . . . for the Second Census* (Washington, D.C., 1801). County totals for 1810 are printed in *Aggregate Amount of Each Description of Persons within the United States . . . in the Year 1810* (Washington, D.C., 1811). The manuscript county schedules for Maryland in 1800 and 1810 have been microfilmed by the National Archives. In addition to surveying all the Maryland county totals for 1776, 1782–83, 1790, 1800, and 1810, I have analyzed the household-by-household county returns for Harford, Prince George's, and Talbot counties in 1776, 1790, and 1810 and also the Maryland Genealogical Society's published *Prince Georges County, Maryland, 1800 Census* (Baltimore, 1969).

[9]A summary of Virginia tax lists, 1782–87, was compiled by Stella Sutherland in *Population Distribution*, pp. 174–76; for major errors in this compilation, see note 12, below. County tax lists for thirty-two Virginia counties in 1782–83 are printed in U.S. Bureau of the Census, *Heads of Families at the First Census. . . . State Enumerations of Virginia; From 1782 to 1785* (Washington, D.C., 1908). An alphabetical file of taxpayers from another thirty-five counties has been compiled by Augusta B. Fothergill and John Mark Naugle, eds., *Virginia Tax Payers, 1782–1787; Other than Those Published by*

the Chesapeake county lists contain important evidence that documents the changes in the structure of black society in the post-Revolutionary years.

Throughout Tidewater and Piedmont Virginia and Maryland the black population grew faster than the white population from the mid-eighteenth century into the early nineteenth century. And as the black population grew, it spread steadily westward toward the Appalachians. As of 1755, twenty years before the Revolution, roughly 165,000 blacks, constituting about 37 percent of the total population, lived in the region. Practically all the blacks were slaves. Comparison of a list of Virginia tithables in 1755 with a summary Maryland census taken in the same year shows that in fourteen of the sixty-three Chesapeake counties, blacks constituted a majority of the population (map 1).[10] Virginia contained all of these

---

the United States Census Bureau (Baltimore, 1966). There are long runs of county tax lists in the Virginia State Library, Richmond, but after the mid-1780s they lose much of their value for present purposes because they generally omit slave children. The Virginia manuscript census schedules for 1790 and 1800 were destroyed during the War of 1812. The county totals for 1790 are printed in *Heads of Families . . . Virginia*, cited above. The county totals for 1800 are printed in *Return of the Whole Number of Persons . . . for the Second Census*. The county totals for 1810 are printed in *Aggregate Amount of . . . Persons . . . in the Year 1810*. The manuscript county schedules for Virginia in 1810 have been microfilmed by the National Archives. In addition to surveying all the Virginia county totals for 1782–83, 1790, 1800, and 1810, I have analyzed the household-by-household county returns for Amelia, Amherst, Fauquier, Frederick, Richmond, and York counties in 1782–83 and 1810.

[10]This and succeeding maps omit the western district of Virginia, which later became the state of West Virginia. The Virginia list of tithables for 1755, on which it is based, is printed in Robert E. and B. Katherine Brown, *Virginia, 1705–1786: Democracy or Aristocracy?* (East Lansing, Mich., 1964), p. 73 and table 1. To arrive at their figures, the Browns multiplied white tithables by four and black tithables by two, a somewhat different procedure from that followed by Stella Sutherland when she computed Virginia tithables for 1782–87 (*Population Distribution*, pp. 174–76). The Maryland census of 1755 is summarized in U.S. Bureau of the Census, *A Century of Population Growth, 1790–1900* (Washington, D.C., 1909), p. 185. See the commentary on this census by Robert V. Wells, *The Population of the British*

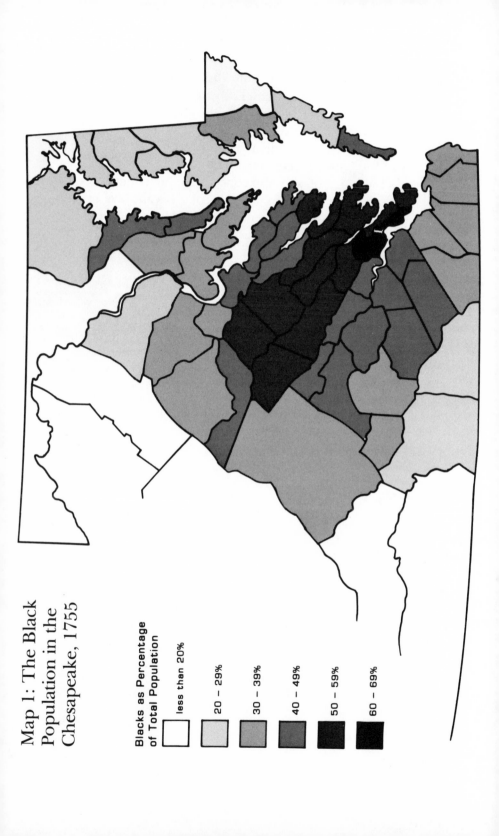

Map 1: The Black
Population in the
Chesapeake, 1755

Blacks as Percentage
of Total Population

less than 20%

20 – 29%

30 – 39%

40 – 49%

50 – 59%

60 – 69%

heavily black counties, reflecting the fact that planters from this colony imported considerably more slaves than their counterparts in Maryland during the first half of the eighteenth century. James City and Warwick counties, where blacks outnumbered whites by nearly two to one, were at the entrance to the James River, convenient to incoming slave ships. The black population was also concentrated in counties served by the York River, the chief avenue for African slave traders in the first half of the eighteenth century. Heavy slaveholding was by no means confined to the Tidewater, however; the black majority extended as far west into the Piedmont as Louisa County.[11]

By 1782, at the conclusion of the Revolutionary War, this pattern had changed considerably (map 2).[12] Blacks had nearly doubled in number since 1755, and they constituted a somewhat larger proportion of the region's population than thirty

---

Colonies in America before 1776: A Survey of Census Data (Princeton, 1975), ch. 5. The Virginia counties with black majorities in 1755 were Caroline, Elizabeth City, Gloucester, Hanover, James City, King and Queen, King William, Lancaster, Louisa, Middlesex, New Kent, Spotsylvania, Warwick, and York.

[11]For discussion of pre-Revolutionary Chesapeake slavery, see three articles by Allan Kulikoff: "A 'Prolifick' People: Black Population Growth in the Chesapeake Colonies, 1700–1790," *Southern Studies* 16 (1977):391–428; "The Origins of Afro-American Society in Tidewater Maryland and Virginia, 1700 to 1790," *William and Mary Quarterly*, 3d ser. 35 (1978):226–59; and "The Beginnings of the Afro-American Family in Maryland," in Aubrey C. Land et al., eds. *Law, Society, and Politics in Early Maryland* (Baltimore, 1977), pp. 171–96. For discussion of the dimensions of the pre-Revolutionary Chesapeake slave trade, see Herbert S. Klein, *The Middle Passage: Comparative Studies in the Atlantic Slave Trade* (Princeton, 1978), ch. 6; and Darold D. Wax, "Black Immigrants: The Slave Trade in Colonial Maryland," *Maryland Historical Magazine* 73 (1978):30–45.

[12]The Maryland county totals for 1782, listed in Sutherland, *Population Distribution*, p. 174, correlate extremely well with earlier and later county enumerations for this colony/state. But the Virginia county totals for 1782, listed in Sutherland, *Population Distribution*, pp. 174–76, are demonstrably in serious error for Caroline, Elizabeth City, Frederick, Rockingham, Stafford, and York. There is, however, no reason to question the general accuracy of the reported black-white ratios in the remaining sixty Virginia counties.

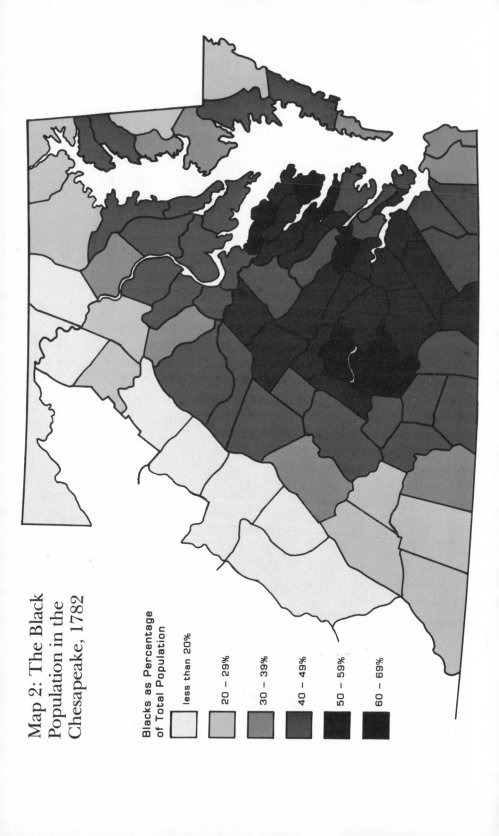

Map 2: The Black Population in the Chesapeake, 1782

Blacks as Percentage of Total Population

less than 20%

20 – 29%

30 – 39%

40 – 49%

50 – 59%

60 – 69%

years earlier. There were now nearly 300,000 blacks in the Chesapeake. More significant, however, the geographic balance of the black population had shifted westward. Cornwallis's invasion of Virginia in 1781 had caused severe dislocations. Eleven Virginia Tidewater counties, most of them in the immediate vicinity of Yorktown, reported a loss in black population. These eleven counties had 12,000 fewer blacks than they had listed in 1755. The decrease turned out to be a temporary wartime loss. In the first federal census of 1790, nine of them reported larger black populations than in 1755, and collectively the eleven pillaged Tidewater counties doubled their slaveholdings between 1782 and 1790.[13] Yet the Virginia Tidewater never recovered its pre-Revolutionary status as the Chesapeake district most heavily committed to slaveholding.

Almost everywhere else in the Chesapeake the number of blacks increased substantially between 1755 and 1782. No Maryland county as yet had a black majority, but sixteen of the state's eighteen counties reported higher percentages of blacks than in 1755. The two exceptions were Frederick and Washington counties in the western interior. In Virginia, blacks outnumbered whites in twenty-four counties, with the most dramatic increase occurring in the southern Piedmont and the Southside, the region of heaviest tobacco production and large-scale slave gang labor in the years between 1750 and 1775.[14] Amelia had the largest black population of any Virginia county in 1782, and one of the highest black ratios in the state. Massive African slave importations to planters on the upper James during the closing years of the colonial era accounted for part of the increase of the black popula-

[13]Caroline, Elizabeth City, Essex, Gloucester, Hanover, James City, King and Queen, King George, King William, Warwick, and York all reported smaller black populations in 1782–83 than in 1755. Of these counties, all but Warwick and York had larger black populations by 1790 than they had in 1755.

[14]The Virginia counties with black majorities in 1782–83 were Amelia, Charles City, Chesterfield, Cumberland, Dinwiddie, Essex, Goochland, Greensville, Hanover, Henrico, King and Queen, Lancaster, Louisa, Middlesex, New Kent, Northumberland, Powhatan, Prince George, Richmond, Spotsylvania, Surry, Sussex, Warwick, and Westmoreland.

tion west of Richmond and south of Petersburg.[15] During the Revolutionary War, Tidewater planters who owned land in the Piedmont appear to have moved a good many of their slaves west, out of reach of the British army. As a result, by 1782 about as many blacks lived in the Virginia Piedmont as in the Tidewater counties, but (as in Maryland) black expansion westward stopped abruptly at the mountains. Scarcely more than 10,000 Virginia and Maryland blacks lived west of the Blue Ridge, and in only one western county, Frederick County in Virginia's Shenandoah Valley, was the black ratio as high as 20 percent.

The federal census of 1810 shows the situation after another thirty years (map 3). In 1810 the Chesapeake black population totaled some 567,000, having once again nearly doubled in a generation.[16] Natural increase accounted for all of this growth, for the importation of blacks from Africa or anywhere else had been banned since 1778. The black ratio for the entire region stood at 42 percent, a 3 percent increase since 1782 and a 5 percent increase since 1755.

The Chesapeake black population continued to grow despite the enormous export of Virginia and Maryland slaves to Kentucky, Tennessee, and other slave-hungry states. Assuming the natural increase of Chesapeake blacks in the 1790s and early 1800s to be 2.5 percent annually, Allan Kulikoff has estimated that some 98,000 bondspeople were moved out of the region between 1790 and 1810.[17] But to Kulikoff's conjectures a corollary should be added: many more whites than blacks migrated out of the Chesapeake during this twenty-year period. Applying to the white population Kulikoff's assumptions about the rate of natural increase suggests that approximately 225,000 Chesapeake whites abandoned

[15]Compare Klein, *Middle Passage*, p. 132, with Kulikoff, "Origins of Afro-American Society," pp. 245–46.

[16]The 1810 census enumerated slaves and free blacks separately, but in order to calculate the size and distribution of the black population, they are here added together.

[17]See the essay in this volume by Allan Kulikoff, "Uprooted Peoples: Black Migrants in the Age of the American Revolution, 1790–1820," table 1.

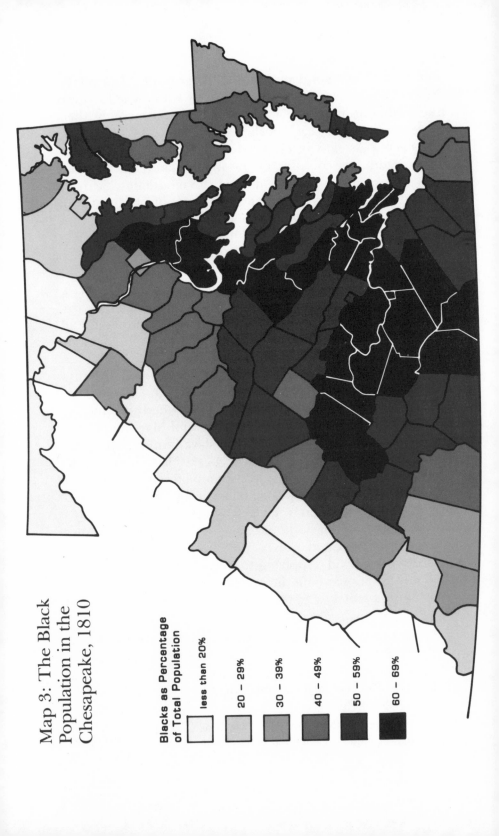

Map 3: The Black
Population in the
Chesapeake, 1810

Blacks as Percentage
of Total Population

less than 20%

20 – 29%

30 – 39%

40 – 49%

50 – 59%

60 – 69%

Virginia and Maryland between 1790 and 1810. These projections for black and white outmigration remain rough estimates, but they fit well with the census figures for Kentucky and Tennessee, which indicate a huge migration into these two states, with white immigrants outnumbering black by nearly four to one.[18] Although new arrivals in Kentucky and Tennessee did not all come from the Chesapeake, a great many of them did. The Chesapeake whites who migrated across the Appalachians during this period appear to have been mainly small planters, with few slaves. In consequence of this massive white exodus, the black proportion of the population remaining in Virginia and Maryland rose appreciably in the generation following the Revolution.

The census returns for 1810 indicate not only long-distance migration out of the Chesapeake but a sizable short-distance migration within the region, whereby both blacks and whites moved west from Tidewater to Piedmont, and from the Piedmont across the Blue Ridge to the Shenandoah Valley and the mountain districts of western Virginia. Once again, comparison of county census figures for 1790 and 1810 demonstrates that more whites than blacks participated in this internal migration process. In the older, settled parts of Maryland and Virginia, fifty-two of the eighty-two counties east of the mountains were more than half black by 1810. Twenty-one Virginia counties and two Maryland counties, Prince George's and Charles on the lower Western Shore, were now more than 60 percent black.[19] However, nowhere in the Chesapeake was the black majority so overwhelming as in lowcountry Carolina and Georgia. The highest black ratios—

[18]The white population of Kentucky and Tennessee rose from 93,146 in 1790 to 540,112 in 1810, indicating a white in-migration of approximately 283,000 if we assume a natural growth rate of 2.5 percent per year. The black population in these two states rose from 15,722 in 1790 to 128,260 in 1810, indicating a black in-migration of approximately 75,000 based on the same assumptions. For Kentucky and Tennessee population figures, see Berlin, *Slaves without Masters*, pp. 46, 396, and 398.

[19]The twenty-one Virginia counties were Amelia, Brunswick, Buckingham, Caroline, Charles City, Chesterfield, Cumberland, Dinwiddie, Essex, Gloucester, Greensville, James City, King George, King William, New Kent, Nottoway, Powhatan, Prince George, Sussex, Warwick, and York.

approaching 70 percent—were to be found in the southern Virginia Piedmont counties of Powhatan, Amelia, Nottoway, and Greensville, and in Prince George's County, Maryland. In 1810, as in 1782 and 1755, black expansion within the Chesapeake stopped at the mountains. The western districts of Virginia and Maryland had grown dramatically since 1782 but remained white man's territory. In 1810, 30 percent of the whites in the two states lived west of the Blue Ridge, but only 7 percent of the blacks. Only three counties west of the Blue Ridge had black ratios above 20 percent: Jefferson, Frederick, and Augusta in the Shenandoah Valley.[20]

Tracing the expansion of black population in the Chesapeake as a whole masks significant differences between Maryland and Virginia. Before the Revolution few free blacks could be found in the Chesapeake. Only 4 percent of Maryland's blacks were categorized as free in 1755, and the Maryland census of 1776 indicated no increase.[21] During and after the Revolution, however, the Maryland free black population grew rapidly. By 1810 over 20 percent of Maryland blacks had gained their liberty. A trend was established that would continue for the next half century: by the eve of the Civil War the Maryland black population was nearly half free. But if Maryland's free black population skyrocketed in the post-Revolutionary era, Virginia's only inched upward. There free blacks constituted only 7 percent of the black population in 1810 and only 10 percent by the time of the Civil War.[22]

With the slave population in the two states, the situation was reversed. In Maryland, the number of bondspeople grew slowly between the Revolution and 1810 and declined thereafter. A small state without a hinterland, Maryland contained

[20]Robert D. Mitchell, *Commercialism and Frontier: Perspectives on the Early Shenandoah Valley* (Charlottesville, Va., 1977), pp. 98–100.

[21]According to the Maryland census of 1755, there were 1,817 free blacks in a total black population of 45,312 (*A Century of Population Growth*, p. 185). In Talbot County, free blacks constituted less than 4 percent of the black population in 1776, but the proportion of freedpeople among the blacks increased to 18 percent by 1790 and to 30 percent by 1810.

[22]Berlin, *Slaves without Masters*, pp. 46–47 and 136–37. Berlin's figures for 1810 should be revised in the light of footnote 4, above.

no room for the westward expansion of slave-based agriculture. Virginia's extensive and underdeveloped hinterland allowed its slave force to nearly double between the Revolution and 1810 and to continue growing, albeit at a lower rate, down to 1860. In consequence, the Maryland free black population outnumbered that of Virginia in 1860, but Maryland's share of the Chesapeake slave population had dropped from 30 to 15 percent between the Revolution and the Civil War.[23] Clearly the Revolutionary era saw the beginning of an important divergence between the two states: a trend toward black freedom in Maryland and toward continued enslavement in Virginia.

The geographical distribution of the Chesapeake slave force suggests some of the sources of this development (map 4).[24] With the major exception of the Tidewater region, Chesapeake slavery more than held its own at the turn of the century. The chief expansion took place in the western Piedmont of Virginia, a region by no means fully developed or fully committed to slavery at the time of the Revolution. In the double tier of sixteen Virginia counties to the east of the Blue

[23]Ibid., pp. 396–401.

[24]Map 4 describes the distribution of the slave population, excluding free blacks. It is based upon Virginia and Maryland county figures for the slave population in the federal censuses of 1790 and 1810. In those counties where slavery is identified as gaining during the twenty-year period, the number of slaves rose by at least 2,000 *and* the slave proportion of the population increased by at least 5 percent. In those counties where slavery is identified as losing or in retreat, either the number of slaves *or* the slave proportion of the population (or both) declined between 1790 and 1810. In the remaining counties there was no loss and little gain: the slave and free populations changed at about the same rate, so that the system stood in equilibrium. By these definitions, slavery expanded in nineteen counties: Albemarle, Amherst, Bedford, Brunswick, Buckingham, Campbell, Charlotte, Culpeper, Fauquier, Frederick, Halifax, Lunenburg, Madison, Mecklenburg, Nelson, Orange, Pittsylvania, and Prince Edward in Virginia, and Charles in Maryland. The *number* of slaves declined in seventeen counties: Calvert, Caroline, Cecil, Dorchester, Kent, Queen Anne's, St. Mary's, and Somerset in Maryland, and Charles City, Elizabeth City, James City, King George, Lancaster, Middlesex, Northumberland, Richmond, and Westmoreland in Virginia. In six additional Chesapeake counties the *percentage* of slaves decreased: Harford, Talbot, and Worcester in Maryland, and Accomack, New Kent, and Northampton in Virginia.

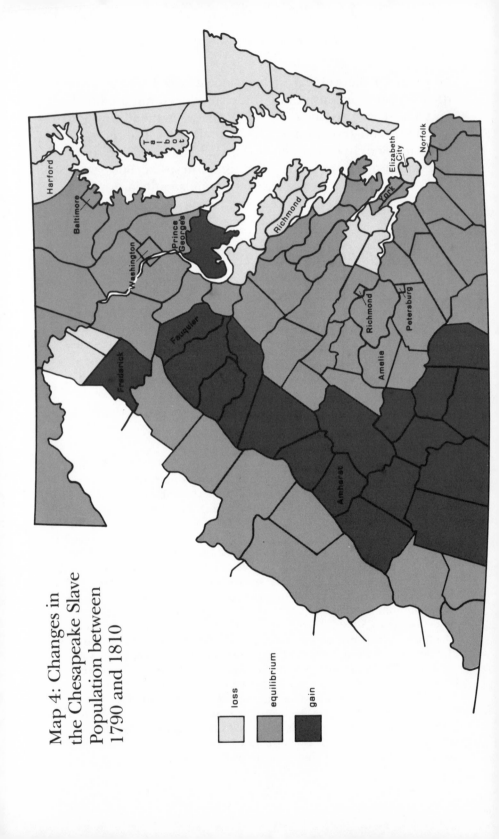

Map 4: Changes in
the Chesapeake Slave
Population between
1790 and 1810

loss

equilibrium

gain

Ridge, the number of slaves rose by 40,000 between 1790 and 1810, and the slave proportion of the population climbed sharply upward from a third to over 40 percent of the whole. Throughout the southeastern Virginia Piedmont, where slaves already outnumbered whites at the time of the Revolution, the slave population continued to expand. In parts of Maryland as well, notably in Charles County on the Potomac, slavery also continued to rise. Yet with no room for westward Piedmont expansion, Maryland slavery had but limited prospects. Most of the Maryland population was concentrated along the shores of the Chesapeake Bay, and the most vigorous development between 1790 and 1810 took place along the upper Western Shore in the vicinity of Baltimore. Slaveholding had always been marginal in this district, and slaves constituted only 20 percent of its population in 1810. The whole Tidewater region, in Virginia as in Maryland, experienced severe agricultural depression in these years. Tidewater slaveholders demonstrated the greatest propensity to transfer or sell or free their slaves. Seventeen Tidewater counties, nine of them in Virginia, suffered outright loss: there were 7,000 fewer slaves in these counties in 1810 than in 1790.[25] This loss was more disruptive of the slave system in Tidewater Maryland than in Tidewater Virginia. On Maryland's Eastern Shore the slave percentage of the population dropped from 36 to 31 percent between 1790 and 1810, so that by the latter date slave labor had become less important in this long-established region than in the more recently settled western Virginia Piedmont. In Tidewater Virginia, despite the slave loss in nine counties, over half the population remained enslaved.

The distribution of slaves within nine geographically dispersed counties—three in Maryland and six in Virginia—offers a closer look at the changing structure of slavery in the post-Revolutionary Chesapeake. In Maryland, Talbot County on the Eastern Shore had a slave ratio that was about average

[25]In Virginia, Charles City, Elizabeth City, James City, King George, Lancaster, Middlesex, Northumberland, Richmond, and Westmoreland counties lost 2,686 slaves between 1790 and 1810; in Maryland, Calvert, Caroline, Cecil, Dorchester, Kent, Queen Anne's, St. Mary's, and Somerset counties lost 4,707.

for the state; Harford County to the north, bordering the Mason-Dixon line, had a notably low and declining percentage of slaves; and Prince George's County on the lower Western Shore had a notably higher one. In Tidewater Virginia, Richmond County on the Rappahannock River had a declining slave population, while York County, in a more commercial neighborhood at the mouth of the York River, was in a state of equilibrium. In Piedmont Virginia, Amelia County to the southeast had one of the highest slave ratios in the Chesapeake, while Amherst County to the west and Fauquier County to the north were more newly settled and had rapidly building slave populations. Across the Blue Ridge in the Shenandoah Valley, Frederick County had a slave count as small as that of Harford County in Maryland, but unlike Harford's, the Frederick slave population was expanding. Collectively these nine selected counties provide a cross section of the Chesapeake slave system which permits developments throughout the region to be compared.[26]

A close analysis of these selected counties demonstrates that an increasing number of Chesapeake whites were becoming slaveholders in the years between 1782 and 1810. In eight of the nine selected counties the number of white families holding slaves increased, with Prince George's County, Maryland, the only exception. Overall, there were about 4,300 slaveholders in these nine counties in 1782, and some 6,200 in 1810. In eight of the nine counties the percentage of white families holding slaves also increased; the only exception was Richmond County, Virginia. Overall, 46 percent of the white families in these nine counties held slaves in 1782; 54 percent held slaves in 1810. The trend can be observed not only in slave-rich Amelia County, where the proportion of slaveholders rose from 78 to 82 percent, but also in slave-poor Har-

[26] For the six Virginia counties, only partial evidence survives since the 1790 and 1800 manuscript census schedules for this state have been destroyed, but county tax lists from 1782–83 can at least be compared with the county census schedules of 1810. For the three Maryland counties, evidence is more abundant, and comparisons can be made of the county enumerations taken in 1776, 1783, 1790, 1800, and 1810. See notes 8 and 9, above.

ford County, where it increased from 29 to 43 percent, and in Frederick County beyond the Blue Ridge, where it rose from 22 to 32 percent.

Slaveholding expanded for a variety of reasons. In western districts such as Amherst, Fauquier, and Frederick, with rapidly enlarging slave populations, slaveholding grew along with slavery. In the eastern and central Chesapeake counties of Talbot, York, and Amelia, where the slave population was static or rising only moderately, the rise in slaveholding had a different source. The outmigration of non-slaveholding whites shrank the white population in these three counties and proportionately increased the number of slaveholders, and it also gave those whites who stayed behind access to a large local slave supply. In the post-Revolutionary era more and more of them became slaveholders. Looking at the Chesapeake as a whole, if these nine counties are representative, a majority of the whites stood outside of the slave system at the time of the Revolution. By 1810 a majority of the whites had a direct personal stake in the system.

The enumerations in these nine counties also provide information on the distribution of Chesapeake slaves among small, middling, and large planters in the generation following the Revolution. Scholars remain woefully ignorant about slave living and working conditions in eighteenth-century America, but it is clear that significant regional differences existed. In the colonies north of Maryland, where the employment of slave labor was always marginal, most blacks worked as domestics, farmhands, craftworkers, or menial laborers appended to white households; they lived singly, in pairs, or in small, family-sized groups. In the Carolina low-country and in the West Indies, where slave labor was employed on a massive scale, planters organized most blacks in rice or sugar gangs; slaves worked and lived in village-sized communities, supervised by white overseers. The colonial Chesapeake displayed a more variegated pattern. A great many slaves, perhaps the majority, worked on tobacco plantations of considerable size, but the large-scale Chesapeake planters generally divided and dispersed their black laborers into "quarters" of thirty people of less. The remaining Ches-

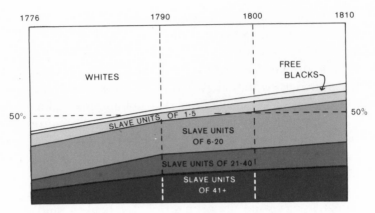

Figure 1: The Distribution of Slaves, Free Blacks, and
Whites in Prince George's County, Maryland, 1776–1810

apeake slaves labored on small family farms or in village or
town households. This dispersion among large and small
masters and among country and town masters meant that
Chesapeake slaves experienced a wide range of living conditions. In the years before the Revolution, the size of the average
Chesapeake slave unit grew larger, providing greater opportunities for autonomous black social life and family development.[27] In the post-Revolutionary era, however, the situation
was more complex.

In Prince George's County, Maryland, one of the four selected counties in which slaves constituted a majority of the
population by 1810, the trend toward larger units of production continued after the Revolution (fig. 1). In this county
there was a large white exodus, the free black population
remained small, and slavery expanded steadily between 1776
and 1810.[28] Increasingly the Prince George's planters pooled
their slaves into living and working units of considerable size;

[27]Kulikoff, "Origins of Afro-American Society," pp. 240–53.

[28]In Prince George's, the white population dropped from approximately 10,000 in 1776 and 9,864 in 1782, to 6,471 in 1810. White householders correspondingly dropped from some 1,800 in 1776 and 1,823 in
1790, to 1,510 in 1810. The slave population rose from about 6,800 in
1776 and about 8,500 in 1782, to 11,539 in 1810. Free blacks constituted
perhaps 2 percent of the black population in 1776 and 5 percent in 1810.

the small planters of 1776 either moved away or enlarged their holdings, and middling and large slaveholders became more numerous. If those owning one to five slaves are categorized as small slaveholders, those with six to twenty slaves as middling slaveholders, and those with more than twenty slaves as large slaveholders, it becomes clear that a significant shift was taking place. In 1776 half of the Prince George's slaves were attached to units of middling size. By 1810 half were in large units.[29]

The same trend can be observed in two other selected counties with slave majorities, Amelia and York. Richmond, the fourth selected county with a slave majority, located in the depressed Northern Neck of Virginia, moved toward somewhat smaller slave units. Nonetheless, the four selected counties with slave majorities collectively displayed a decided overall increase in the number and size of large slave gangs during the post-Revolutionary years. In 1782, 43 percent of the slaves in Prince George's, Amelia, York, and Richmond lived in units of more than twenty bondspeople. By 1810 more than half did so. Only a tiny fraction lived singly or in pairs. In other words, slaveholders placed more and more slaves in groups large enough to permit settled marriage and cohabitation with mates, children, parents, and other kin. Large slave communities also provided some measure of physical— and perhaps psychic—independence from whites.

This pattern was not, however, representative of the Chesapeake as a whole. A different situation existed in another part of Maryland, fast-growing Harford County on the Pennsylvania border (fig. 2). Here, in contrast to Prince

---

[29]Allan Kulikoff has studied the size of slaveholdings in Prince George's County before the Revolution, basing his analysis upon probate inventories dating between 1731 and 1779. He finds in this county, as I do, a definite long-term upward trend in the size of the slaveholding unit, though his inventories show a majority of large units as early as the 1770s. See Kulikoff, "Origins of Afro-American Society," pp. 241 and 248. The discrepancy between his figures and mine for the 1770s is probably partly explained by the incompleteness of the 1776 Prince George's census, from which I worked, and also partly explained by a bias in Kulikoff's sample of inventories toward wealthy planters with large slaveholdings.

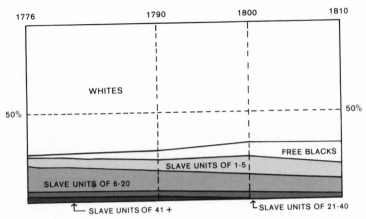

Figure 2: The Distribution of Slaves, Free Blacks, and Whites in Harford County, Maryland, 1776–1810

George's, there was a large influx of whites, so that while the black population doubled between 1776 and 1810, it remained proportionately low. Moreover, an increasing share of these blacks were free, signaling the decline of slavery.[30] Most Harford slaves lived in small or middling units. A rising number of small Harford white householders acquired slaves in the post-Revolutionary years, but the size of the average slave unit dropped to five persons, less than half the size of the average slaveholding in Prince George's. Still, even in Harford County, few slaves lived alone. But the large slave gangs characteristic of Prince George's slowly disappeared in Harford. As late as 1790, six Harford planters held forty or more slaves; by 1810, the largest slaveholder in the county claimed only thirty-two slaves.

In Harford, situated on the Mason-Dixon line, slavery was seriously in doubt. But in four other selected counties in which slaves constituted a minority of the population—Talbot, Amherst, Fauquier, and Frederick—the post-Revolutionary distribution pattern shows a generally stable situation, with

[30]In Harford the white population rose from 9,423 in 1776 to 14,606 in 1810; the black population rose from 3,342 to 6,652. By 1810, 33 percent of the blacks were free. The number of Harford slaves actually rose from 3,411 in 1790 to 4,139 in 1810, but figure 2 shows the slave population as continuing to decline because the proportion of slaves in the total population fell from 23 to 21 percent during these twenty years.

plentiful evidence of continuing adherence to the slave system. Within these counties neither the Prince George's model
nor the Harford model applies, for the relative position of
small, middling, and large slaveholders changed little in the
thirty years following the Revolution. In Talbot, as in Harford, the free black community grew, but within the Talbot
slave population the distribution among large, middling, and
small units was almost exactly the same in 1810 as in 1776.
In the fast-growing western Piedmont counties of Amherst
and Fauquier, slave units of middling size predominated.
Throughout the post-Revolutionary generation half the slaves
in Amherst and Fauquier lived in groups of six to twenty
persons. Across the mountains in Frederick, where slaveholding was more marginal, a few large planters owned a
surprisingly high percentage of the slaves. Here, in sharp
contrast to the situation in Harford, more than 40 percent of
the slaves belonged to large gangs both in 1782 and in 1810.
Thus each neighborhood had its own characteristics. As
Chesapeake slavery expanded after the Revolution, the distribution of slave living and working units became more variegated and more complex.

Before the Revolution the so-called first families of Virginia and Maryland had been the most conspicious practi-
tioners of slavery. Grandees from several dozen Chesapeake
families had built impressive dynastic fortunes on the basis
of slave labor. They had staked out huge tobacco tracts manned
by squadrons of black laborers, and they had parlayed tobacco profits into social aristocracy and political control. These
people occupied the top county and provincial offices, and
their less affluent neighbors commonly deferred to them. They
have been looked up to ever since, both because their political achievements were remarkable and because they left such
tangible legacies: handsome mansions, elegant furnishings,
and valuable collections of family papers for the historian to
study.[31] In the 1780s, according to Jackson Turner Main, sixty-

---

[31]Louis B. Wright, *The First Gentlemen of Virginia: Intellectual Qualities of
the Early Colonial Ruling Class* (San Marino, Calif., 1940); Charles S. Sydnor, *Gentlemen Freeholders: Political Practices in Washington's Virginia* (Chapel

five Virginians held 100 or more slaves apiece.[32] However, this impressive figure needs to be set in perspective. At the close of the Revolution, South Carolina had a slave population only one-third as large as Virginia's but twice as many large slaveholders who owned 100 or more slaves.[33] And Jamaica in the 1780s had a slave population about equal to Virginia's but ten times as many really big slaveholders.[34] Obviously the Chesapeake first families were less dominant than their counterparts farther south. Main argues that the 100 richest Virginians of the 1780s controlled less than 7 percent of the slaves and land in the state. In his view, their economic prominence has been exaggerated: they reached the zenith of their success with the launching of the Revolution, and declined thereafter.[35]

Nonetheless, inspection of the census schedules for 1790 and 1810 finds the Chesapeake grandees still very much in evidence. In the nine selected counties, members of the elite pre-Revolutionary families—bearing such names as Burwell, Calvert, Carter, Digges, Lloyd, Page, Randolph, Tayloe, Tilghman, and Washington—were still the chief slaveholders. In 1782 fifteen planters from these counties held 100 or

---

Hill, N.C., 1952); and Carl Bridenbaugh, *Myths and Realities: Societies of the Colonial South* (Baton Rouge, La., 1952), ch. 1.

[32]Jackson T. Main, "The One Hundred," *William and Mary Quarterly*, 3d ser. 11 (1954):354–84.

[33]The South Carolina census of 1790 lists 141 slaveholders with more than 100 slaves apiece (U.S. Bureau of the Census, *Heads of Families at the First Census of the United States. . . . South Carolina* [Washington, D.C., 1908]).

[34]There were 1,061 sugar estates in Jamaica in 1786, at a time when the average sugar estate was worked by 200 slaves (Richard B. Sheridan, *Sugar and Slavery: An Economic History of the British West Indies, 1623–1775* [Baltimore, 1974], pp. 223 and 230). Of course, some sugar estates had small slave units, some nonsugar estates had large slave units, and some Jamaica planters operated multiple estates. My impression from inspection of slave distribution in western Jamaica is that there were at least 700 Jamaica planters in the 1780s who held 100 or more slaves apiece. By 1832 there were 931 slave units of 100 or more on the island. See B. W. Higman, *Slave Population and Economy in Jamaica, 1807–1834* (Cambridge, England, 1976), pp. 13 and 274–75.

[35]Main, "The One Hundred."

more slaves, as did eighteen in 1810. Slave units of 100 or more were to be found in every one of the sample counties except Harford. The smaller counties had one magnate apiece, the larger ones had several. Six big slaveholders resided in Prince George's in 1790, and four each in Amelia and Frederick in 1810. Edward Lloyd of Talbot operated the largest single slave unit, numbering 420 people in 1810. Collectively, Lloyd and his colleagues controlled only 5 percent of the slaves in these nine selected counties in 1810, but they sustained the hierarchical aura of the system.

Slavemasters did not employ large slave gangs exclusively in agriculture. David Ross staffed his Oxford iron works in Campbell County, Virginia, with slave labor. His was an elaborate industrial enterprise. In 1811 the Oxford slave force of 220 included a full range of technicians to operate the blast furnace, miners to extract iron ore, woodsmen to produce charcoal fuel, smiths to turn the bar iron into tools, and boatmen to transport the finished products to market.[36] Even on a strictly agricultural estate, numerous slave spinners, weavers, shoemakers, smiths, carpenters, masons, gardeners, ostlers and house servants could be found. From a slave's perspective, an establishment of this sort offered advantageous employment as a skilled craftsman or privileged domestic. But even the most skilled bondsmen might be sold away from family and friends. Moreover, most of the slaves worked as field hands, and for them the risk of social dislocation was great, because the big Chesapeake planter usually divided his field hands into a number of relatively small farming crews, moving workers freely from one quarter to another and often separating husbands from wives or parents from children in the process.

For example, during the post-Revolutionary era John Tayloe continually reshuffled the slaves at Mount Airy in Richmond County.[37] The Tayloes were the largest slaveholders in the county from the 1730s to the 1860s. About 200 slaves

---

[36]Charles B. Dew, "David Ross and the Oxford Iron Works," *William and Mary Quarterly*, 3d ser. 31 (1974):189–224.

[37]Richard S. Dunn, "A Tale of Two Plantations: Slave Life at Mesopotamia in Jamaica and Mount Airy in Virginia, 1799 to 1828," *William and Mary Quarterly*, 3d ser. 36 (1977):32–65.

generally lived at Mount Airy, and several hundred more labored on other Tayloe properties scattered from Charles County, Maryland, to Botetourt County, Virginia, beyond the Blue Ridge. The Tayloes regularly removed the majority of blacks born and raised at Mount Airy from their home plantation, sending them to outlying quarters or selling them, customarily when they were in their teens or early twenties. Nor did the Tayloes restrict their operations to the Chesapeake. By the 1830s they had become so discouraged by agricultural prospects in the Northern Neck that they began to open up cotton plantations in Alabama, staffed largely by Mount Airy slaves. In 1860, 169 Tayloe slaves still lived at Mount Airy, but they had numerous relatives and former comrades 800 miles away among the 650 slaves on five Tayloe plantations in Perry and Marengo counties, Alabama.

Most big Chesapeake slaveholders displayed little enthusiasm for manumission. John Tayloe reported one free black living with his 225 slaves at Mount Airy in 1810, and at his death he freed another of his 700 slaves, his faithful body servant Archy. But a few miles from Mount Airy, Robert Carter of Nomini Hall in Westmoreland County concluded that slavery was wicked as well as uneconomic. Since the Carters were the leading slaveholding dynasty in the Chesapeake, Robert Carter's conversion was significant. In 1791 he arranged to manumit all of his 509 slaves over a twenty-two year span. Carter's sons and neighbors worked to frustrate this scheme, and it appears some of Carter's slaves never received their promised freedom.[38] But something was accomplished: the Westmoreland census schedule for 1810 indicates that the Carters no longer operated a slave gang at Nomini Hall, and there were 621 free blacks living in the county, one of the highest county totals in Virginia.

The emergence of a sizable and growing free black community was undoubtedly the most important challenge to Chesapeake slavery in the post-Revolutionary years. When

[38]Louis Morton, *Robert Carter of Nomini Hall: A Virginia Tobacco Planter of the Eighteenth Century* (1941; reprint ed. Charlottesville, Va., 1964), ch. 11.

the Virginia and Maryland manumission laws were liberalized after the Revolution, many whites either freed their slaves or permitted them to earn enough money to buy their own freedom. And when slavemasters promised manumission and failed to deliver, large numbers of blacks barraged the courts with freedom suits. In consequence, the number of free blacks in the Chesapeake rose from a few thousand in 1776 to 60,000 by 1810.

Manumission was not a random process in the Chesapeake. Slaveholders along the coast were more inclined toward manumission than slaveholders who lived inland, and slaveholders in Maryland manumitted more freely than did slaveholders in Virginia. (See map 5 for the distribution of free blacks in 1810.)[39] Freedpeople clustered in the Virginia counties bordering the lower James, in the Maryland Western Shore counties, and throughout the Eastern Shore. Six Maryland counties had 2,000 or more free black residents;[40] no Virginia county had this many, and most reported fewer than 300 freedpeople. But even in Maryland free blacks were still a small minority in 1810. Kent and Queen Anne's counties on the Maryland Eastern Shore had the highest proportion: free blacks composed a sixth of the population. In these counties, as elsewhere on the Eastern Shore, slaves outnumbered free blacks by more than two to one. In the chief Chesapeake towns—Baltimore, Richmond, Norfolk, and Petersburg—free blacks were relatively numerous. Baltimore, the only real city in the region, was the one place in the Chesapeake where free blacks formed a majority of the black population in 1810.

Blacks who lived along the coast and in the towns had the best opportunity to participate in Revolutionary events. Some escaped from slavery by joining Lord Dunmore's Ethiopian Regiment. Some voted with their feet by fleeing north during the fighting. Others earned their freedom by military

[39]This map is based upon the Virginia and Maryland county figures for the free black population in the federal census of 1810.

[40]Anne Arundel, Baltimore, Dorchester, Harford, Queen Anne's, and Talbot.

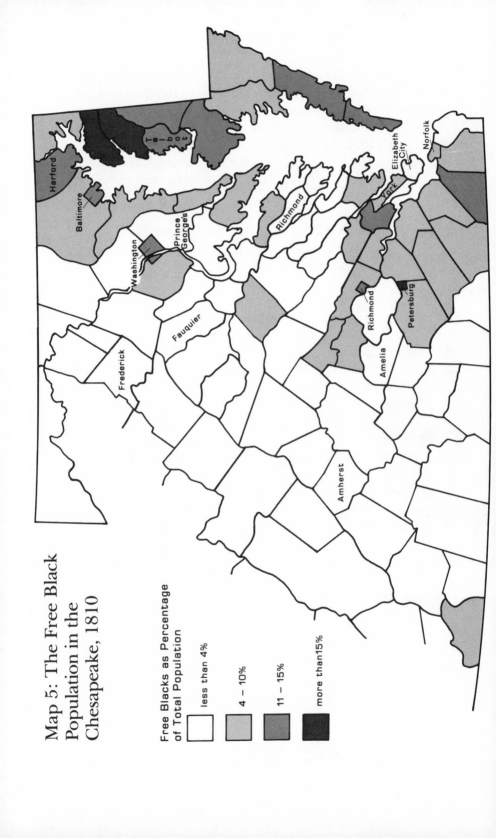

Map 5: The Free Black
Population in the
Chesapeake, 1810

Free Blacks as Percentage
of Total Population

less than 4%

4 – 10%

11 – 15%

more than 15%

service on the patriot side. Blacks who lived in or near the seaport towns or who lived anywhere along the upper Chesapeake could most readily learn about the abolition movement that was gaining momentum north of the Mason-Dixon line and press for their own liberation. In the coastal districts religious developments also helped to erode slavery. Methodists on the Eastern Shore established a number of churches with mixed black and white memberships in the 1780s. Quakers in this area also agitated vigorously against slavery.[41] The coastal towns became magnets for runaway slaves, offering back alley hiding places and casual jobs. Fugitives who could get employment as sailors had perhaps the best chance of passing permanently as free men.[42]

Most Chesapeake free blacks lived in country districts and worked as farm laborers, so the postwar changes in Chesapeake coastal agriculture were clearly important. White farmers in most of the counties bordering Chesapeake Bay had to revise traditional formulas in order to survive. The demands of small grain cultivation and demographic changes forced planters to reconstitute their labor force. They needed to find substitutes for the white tenant farmers who were migrating west and to make more profitable use of their abundant black labor. In some parts of coastal Virginia their solution was to employ slaves as hired hands. In Elizabeth City County, at the mouth of the James River, white propertyholders checked the outmigration of white tenant farmers by supplying them with slave workers, hired on yearly contracts.[43] In this way, the white propertyholders derived rental income from both land and slaves, and the marginal white farmers, who had been excluded from the slave system before the

[41]Ronald Hoffman, *A Spirit of Dissension: Economics, Politics, and the Revolution in Maryland* (Baltimore, 1973), pp. 228–30; Kenneth L. Carroll, "Religion Influences on the Manumission of Slaves in Caroline, Dorchester and Talbot Counties," *Maryland Historical Magazine* 66 (1961):176–97.

[42]For fuller discussion, see Berlin, *Slaves without Masters*, chs. 1–2.

[43]Sarah S. Hughes, "Slaves for Hire: The Allocation of Black Labor in Elizabeth City County, Virginia, 1782 to 1810," *William and Mary Quarterly*, 3d ser. 35 (1978):260–86.

Revolution, became slave users if not owners. The hired slaves received no wages, were separated from family and friends, and probably worked harder than plantation slaves, but they perhaps gained a measure of physical mobility. Planters in neighboring coastal Virginia counties probably repeated the Elizabeth City pattern.

Further north, in Harford and Talbot counties, white propertyholders tried an alternative system that was based on free black labor. They freed large numbers of their slaves and rented their land in small parcels to free black tenants or hired free black laborers on yearly contracts. Why slaveholders in Harford and Talbot freed their slaves, while those in Elizabeth City did not, is not evident. Possibly the scale of religious revivalism on the Eastern Shore and the proximity of free Pennsylvania made slaveholding unattractive. But this does not explain why the number and proportion of slaveholders rose in both Harford and Talbot counties between 1790 and 1810. The situation in Talbot is especially puzzling. In this Eastern Shore county the number of free blacks doubled between 1790 and 1810, rising from 1,076 to 2,103. Meanwhile, the slave population remained steady, rising slightly from 4,777 to 4,878. The number of Talbot slaveholders also rose, from 650 to 685. And though the number of large slaveholders (those with more than twenty slaves) declined from fifty to forty-one during this period, several of the chief Talbot planters built up their slaveholdings appreciably. Thus Richard Goldsborough increased his force from 41 slaves in 1790 to 79 slaves in 1810; Lloyd Tilghman increased his from 66 to 153; Edward Lloyd increased his from 305 to 420. The number of slaves attached to plantations with more than 40 bondspeople rose from 1,052 to 1,848. In this county, slave-based plantation agriculture and free black tenant agriculture developed side by side at the turn of the century.

Some of the free blacks in Harford and Talbot maintained independent households, while others continued to reside in the households of their white employers. Many white farmers in these two Maryland counties commonly employed a mix of free blacks and slaves. William Hickman, one of the largest operators in Talbot, listed twenty-six slaves and fifty free blacks as members of his establishment in 1810. Another Talbot planter, Obadiah Garcy, reported nine slaves and forty-five free blacks. Such large free black units were highly exceptional. Freedpeople were much more likely than slaves to live alone or in very small groups. Most of them must have been very poor. In a population of over 2,100 Talbot free blacks, only 103 are identified on an 1813 tax list as propertyholders.[44] Obviously these people were still oppressed and exploited, but they were better off than their enslaved neighbors and better off than the hired slaves in Elizabeth City. They shared with the Elizabeth City slaves a new impersonal, contractual relationship with whites which broke away from the traditional paternalism.

Inland there is little evidence of a movement toward hired free black labor. In Piedmont Virginia in the post-Revolutionary generation, slave-based plantation agriculture continued in full swing. Unlike the coastal propertyholders, Piedmont planters seem not to have subdivided their land into smaller farms. On the contrary, owners of Piedmont tracts who had rented their land to tenants before the Revolution apparently removed these tenants, replacing them with slave laborers. Comparing the distribution of Chesapeake slaves and free blacks in 1790 and in 1810 (maps 4 and 5) shows, not surprisingly, that slavery was flourishing where free blacks were few in number and vice versa. The nineteen counties with expanding slave populations had insignificant free black populations.[45] In most interior rural districts of Virginia, the ratio of slaves to free blacks in 1810 was at least twenty to one. The Piedmont propertyholders probably sensed that widespread manumission would undermine their slave labor system. The census schedules indicate that everywhere in the

[44]Berlin, *Slaves without Masters*, p. 64.

[45]For identification of these counties, see note 24, above. For discussion of the big Tidewater planters' movement into western Virginia after the Revolution, with removal of nonslaveholding tenants, see Willard F. Bliss, "The Rise of Tenancy in Virginia," *Virginia Magazine of History and Biography* 58 (1950):427–41.

Chesapeake the largest slaveholders permitted few free blacks to live among their slaves. In the nine selected counties 188 planters held more than forty slaves in 1810; 155 of them reported no free blacks attached to their establishments, and the other 33 listed an average of three free black retainers each.

Thus the free black challenge to Chesapeake slavery was limited to the coastal districts, particularly coastal Maryland. In Virginia the General Assembly tightened the slave code in 1792. Shaken by Gabriel's slave conspiracy in 1800, the assembly restricted manumission in 1806.[46] Henceforth Virginia required all manumitted blacks to leave the state. The Virginia legislators who enacted these decrees had a personal stake in the preservation of the slave system: thirty-two of the thirty-three leaders in the House of Delegates during the 1790s were themselves slaveholders, and six held more than 100 slaves each.[47] But they surely voiced as well the wishes of their constituents who were in these years becoming more heavily committed to slave labor than ever before. Although the 1806 manumission law was not always strictly observed, it did have the effect of turning Virginia free blacks into a closed caste and restricting their further increase. Throughout the fifty years before the Civil War, Virginia free blacks remained clustered much where they had been in 1810: in the Southside, in and around the big towns, and in the counties bordering Chesapeake Bay.[48]

North of the Potomac the momentum of the post-Revolutionary years was far more vigorously sustained. By 1860 Maryland was at best only a semislave state. Half of the blacks on the Eastern Shore were free, as were the majority of those in Baltimore. As in 1810, strong pockets of intensive slave-

[46]Gerald W. Mullin, *Flight and Rebellion: Slave Resistance in Eighteenth-Century Virginia* (New York, 1972), ch. 5.

[47]Richard R. Beeman, *The Old Dominion and the New Nation, 1788–1801* (Lexington, Ky., 1972), pp. 249–52.

[48]J. D. B. De Bow, *Statistical View of the United States . . . :Being a Compendium of the Seventh Census . . .* (Washington, D.C., 1854), pp. 320 and 326.

holding remained in the state: on the eve of secession, four lower Western Shore counties—Prince George's, St. Mary's, Calvert, and Charles—had black majorities, and these counties resembled the black belt of Piedmont Virginia, with six slaves to every free black.[49] But when the secession crisis exploded, the slaveholding interest lacked the power to control the entire state. In 1861 the Chesapeake region dramatically split in two. Virginia joined the Confederacy, and Maryland, along with West Virginia, adhered to the Union.

In sum, the years from 1776 to 1810 constituted a crucial transition period in Chesapeake black life. Before the Revolution, Afro-American slavery had taken firm root throughout the region. The white leadership embraced the system, few Marylanders or Virginians who could afford to purchase slaves failed to do so, and few whites questioned the utility of slave labor, evidenced moral scruples, or freed their slaves. While the blacks frequently ran away or shirked or stole, they did not stage many overt rebellions. This pattern was challenged during the years between 1776 and 1810. Chesapeake blacks worked for their freedom far more actively than before. Whites began to doubt the utility or the morality of slaveholding, and some manumitted their slaves. But in most of the Chesapeake, especially in central Virginia, where half of the blacks in the region lived, slaveholding became more widespread and more deeply entrenched than before 1776. Even if Washington, Jefferson, Madison, and Monroe had devoted all their leadership skills to the single cause of black freedom, they would still have failed utterly, for their society was moving inexorably in the opposite direction.

With the cotton boom and the development of the lower South in the fifty years between 1810 and the Civil War crisis, the Chesapeake lost its primacy as the center of black life in America. Virginia still had the largest slave population in the country, but increasingly this was seen as a slave surplus, and Virginia became a great exporter of both white slaveholders and black slaves. Maryland became a border state, with the largest free black population in the country. Thus the choices

[49]Ibid., p. 248.

made by Virginia and Maryland slaveholders during the Revolutionary era proved to have long-range consequences. For some Chesapeake blacks, the Revolution was indeed the first big step toward freedom. For most, however, there was as yet no revolution at all.

PHILIP D. MORGAN

Black Society in the Lowcountry 1760–1810

THE REVOLUTIONARY ERA saw slaves gain formal freedom in the North and "considerably greater independence, mobility and opportunity" in the upper Chesapeake.[1] In lowcountry South Carolina and Georgia, change was much less dramatic; in one sense, the opposite occurred, for slavery became more rather than less entrenched. Indeed, lowcountry planters developed a deeper commitment to slavery than did those in the lower Chesapeake. At the same time, however, black autonomy in the lowcountry assumed dimensions unparalleled elsewhere in mainland North America. The growing entrenchment of slavery and the growing autonomy of the black community constitute the central themes of black life in the lowcountry during the Revolutionary era. This seeming paradox will be explored in two ways: first, through an analysis of the long-term development of black society—a *"longue durée"* stretching from 1760 to 1810—and, second, through an investigation of the disruptions that accompanied the Revolutionary War.

Many of the changes in lowcountry black life during the Revolutionary era had been well underway before the war began and, indeed, had little to do with the conflict. The develop-

---

[1]See the essays in this volume by Gary B. Nash, "Forging Freedom: The Emancipation Experience in the Northern Seaport Cities, 1775–1820," and Richard S. Dunn, "Black Society in the Chesapeake, 1776–1810." The quotation is Dunn's. Although this essay will occasionally introduce information from the Georgia lowcountry, constraints of time and space have required a focus on the South Carolina lowcountry.

ment of the backcountry had been shifting the distribution of South Carolina's slave population for several decades. Less than one-tenth of the colony's slaves resided outside the low-country in 1760; by 1810 almost one-half lived in the back-country (table 1). Although the Revolution did not cause the upcountry migration, the shift in population intensified in the post-Revolutionary years.[2] Similarly, within the lowcoun-try itself the slave population had been growing most rapidly in those districts to the extreme north and south of Charles-ton during the late colonial period, and that trend continued in the late eighteenth and early nineteenth centuries (table 2). Furthermore, planters in post-Revolutionary South Car-olina had as voracious an appetite for slaves as had those in colonial South Carolina. But if the demand for slaves re-mained high, important differences in the pattern of impor-tation emerged. Postwar South Carolina imported slaves from other North American states as well as from Africa, and most slaves were destined for the backcountry rather than the low-country (table 3).[3] In the first decade of the nineteenth cen-

[2]Peter Manigault, for example, reckoned that from at least 1770 on-wards "the great Planters have bought few Negroes. . . . Upwards of two-thirds that have been imported have gone backwards" (Manigault to William Blake, [Dec. 1772], Peter Manigault Letterbook, South Carolina Historical Society, Charleston). Much earlier Henry Laurens had noted the "vast number of people seting down upon our frontier Lands & that with a little management will take off almost insensibly a Cargo by one or two in a Lot, & it has been from such folks that we have always obtain'd the highest prices" (Laurens to Richard Oswald & Co., Feb. 15, 1763, in Philip M. Hamer, George C. Rogers, Jr., and David R. Chesnutt, eds., *The Papers of Henry Laurens*, 8 vols. to date [Columbia, S.C., 1968–], 3:260).

[3]Incidental information attests to the scale of the overland importation of slaves. A committee of the South Carolina House of Representatives was appointed in January 1791 to bring in a bill "to remedy the Evil of Negroes being imported either by land or water into this State for Sale" (Journal of the South Carolina House of Representatives, Jan. 21, 1791. Unless otherwise noted, the South Carolina House and Senate journals cited in this essay are in the microfilm series edited by William S. Jenkins, *Records of the States of the United States of America* [Washington, D.C., 1949]). Over a year later the inhabitants of a parish in Beaufort District petitioned the legislature about the "notorious" practice of northerners who "have for a number of years past been in the habit of shipping to these Southern States, slaves, who are scandalously infamous and incorrigible" (Petition

Table 1: Slaves in lowcountry South Carolina

Year	Number	Percentage of South Carolina slaves
1760	53,257	92.0
1768	71,097	87.0
1790	78,000	72.8
1800	97,170	66.5
1810	110,711	56.4

SOURCES: Office of Public Treasury, General Tax Receipts and Payments, 1760–70 South Carolina Department of Archives and History, Columbia; U.S. Bureau of the Census, Forst, Second, and Third censuses.

NOTE: The lowcountry here includes Beaufort, Colleton, Charleston, and Georgetown districts, and Charleston City (also Marion District in 1800 and 1810, and Williamsburg and Horry districts in 1810).

tury, however, the overland traffic came to a virtual halt as South Carolina reaffirmed its colonial heritage: indeed, in one period of four years (1804–7) South Carolina imported almost twice as many Africans as in any previous five-year period in its history.[4]

Long-term developments in the structure of the slave population matched long-term developments in the movement of slaves into and within the state. For example, the transition from a period of negative to one of positive natural increase occurred among South Carolina's slave population in the early 1750s. The Revolutionary era maintained that pattern, although the massive influx of Africans in the first decade of the nineteenth century temporarily slowed the upward

---

of inhabitants of St. Luke's Parish, Nov. 26, 1792, General Assembly, Petitions, 1792, no. 81, South Carolina Department of Archives and History, Columbia). In the late eighteenth century American slaves born outside South Carolina began to figure prominently in runaway notices; in the 1780s fifty-three were counted (thirteen born in Georgia and nine in New York) and in the 1790s another fifty-three, although now Chesapeake and North Carolina slaves dominated (forty of the fifty-three came from these regions). The complaints and the runaway notices for slaves born outside South Carolina declined in the 1800s.

[4]Compare the number of Africans imported into South Carolina in 1804–7 with that for 1770–74 (table 19).

Table 2: Distribution of slaves in the South Carolina lowcountry

District*	Percentage of slaves in each district, by year					
	1760	1768	1790	1800	1810
Beaufort	12.5	16.6	18.2	16.5	18.9
Colleton	24.4	24.4	21.2	21.1	19.7
Charleston City	8.3	8.8	9.8	10.1	10.5
Charleston	39.7	32.2	33.8	33.1	30.4
Georgetown	15.1	17.9	16.8	19.3	20.4
Total	100.0	99.9	99.8	100.1	99.9

SOURCES: Office of Public Treasury, General Tax Receipts and Payments, 1760–70, South Carolina Department of Archives and History, Columbia; U.S. Bureau of the Census, First, Second, and Third censuses.

*Since the 1800 and 1810 censuses included the parish of St. John's Colleton in Charleston District and the parish of St. George's Dorchester in Colleton District, that arrangement has been adopted for the earlier years. The 1760 and 1768 tax lists described at least one-fifth of the total slaves as "country slaves" owned by city residents; for this analysis, such slaves were distributed among the lowcountry districts and the backcountry.

Table 3: Growth of South Carolina's slave population, 1790–1810

Lowcountry	1790		1800		1810
Population	78,000		97,170		110,711
Actual increase		19,170		13,541	
Hypothetical rate of natural increase		14%		8%	
Projected natural increase		10,920		7,774	
Net in-migration		8,250		5,767	
Backcountry					
Population	29,094		48,981		85,654
Actual increase		19,887		36,673	
Hypothetical rate of natural increase		28%		25%	
Projected natural increase		8,146		12,245	
Net in-migration		11,741		24,428	
Estimated net in-migration for the state		19,991		30,195	

SOURCES: U.S. Bureau of the Census, First, Second and Third censuses.
NOTE: Establishing a plausible figure for the natural rate of increase of the slave population poses the major problem in estimating the components of population growth. In this table it is assumed that the slave population of South Carolina was growing naturally at the rate of about 2 percent a year in the 1790s, not an unrealistic estimate given the average natural rate of increase in the 1770s and 1780s (see table 4). All other estimates (those for the 1800s and for lowcountry and backcountry) were arrived at by making allowances for the influx of Africans in the early 1800s, the more favorable backcountry environment, and general estimates of natural rates of increase of slave populations in other regions of North America. While no great claims can be made for the accuracy of this table, the estimated net migration for the state and the overall rate of increase of the state's slave population which derive from it (table 4) are much more plausible than previous calculations. See Patrick S. Brady, "The Slave Trade and Sectionalism in South Carolina, 1787–1808," *Journal of Southern History* 38 (1972): 618–19.

trend (table 4). This development can be explored in a number of ways. For example, the sex ratio among inventoried adult lowcountry slaves moved in a uniform way from a high point of 133 males for every 100 females in the 1760s to equality by the 1790s. The adult-child ratio followed a similar pattern: in the 1760s there were 120 children for every 100 adult females; by the 1790s that ratio had increased to 150 children for every 100 adult females (table 5).[5] Admittedly fragmentary information further suggests that birth-spacing intervals decreased between the late colonial and early national periods, while the mean age of slave mothers at the birth of their first child rose. Furthermore, the range of ages at which slave mothers gave birth to their first child seems to have increased (table 6).[6] Finally, the proportion of Africans

[5]The term *inventoried slaves* will occur at a number of points in this essay; it refers to those slaves listed in inventories of estates probated between 1760 and 1799 (before 1782 in the whole of lowcountry South Carolina; after 1782 only in Charleston District). The number of slaves listed in inventories during these forty years totals over 80,000; and information is generally available for the name, sex, rudimentary age, value, and, more occasionally, occupation and family tie of each slave. Because only rudimentary ages are available, the construction of adult-child ratios must be imprecise. Generally speaking, however, sixteen years of age can be assumed to distinguish an adult from a child. Other sources generally accord with the resulting ratios. For example, a Georgia planter who wished to purchase a gang of 100 slaves required 24 adult women and 40 children—a ratio of 166 children for every 100 adult females ([Joseph Clay] to [Edward Telfair?], [Dec. 13, 1786], Edward Telfair Papers, Duke University, Durham, N.C.).

[6]Records of the Ravenel family slaves reveal mean birth-spacing intervals of twenty-five months between 1710 and 1750 (81 births, to 14 mothers) and twenty-three months between 1751 and 1790 (79 births to 18 mothers). Records of the Gaillard family slaves reveal a mean birth-spacing interval of twenty-four months between 1786 and 1809 for those mothers who had at least one child before 1800 (190 births to 38 mothers). The Gaillard register is extremely accurate, noting even the births of children who survived only a few days. Of the 193 children born between 1786 and 1809 to mothers who had at least one child before 1800 (three sets of twins account for the difference between 190 births and 193 children), 24 percent died within a year of birth, 6 percent between one and three years, and 6 percent between four and nine years; 58 percent survived at least ten years; and the longevity of 6 percent went unrecorded (Ravenel Papers and Peter Gaillard Account Book, Gaillard Family Papers, both in S.C. Hist. Soc.).

Table 4: Natural increase of South Carolina's slave population

Period	Beginning population	Population increase	Immigrants*	Surviving† immigrants	Natural population increase	Annual rate of natural increase (percentage)
1750–60	49,000	17,000	16,497	11,831	5,169	1.3
1760–70	57,000	25,000	21,840	15,694	9,306	1.6
1770–75	82,000	22,000	18,866	14,261	7,739	1.9
1782–90	79,000	28,094	19,200	14,357	13,737	2.2
1790–1800	107,094	39,057	19,991	15,700	23,357	2.2
1800–1810	146,151	50,214	30,195	21,578	28,636	2.0

SOURCES: Population totals were derived from Evarts B. Greene and Virginia D. Harrington, *American Population before the Federal census of 1790* (New York, 1932), pp. 137–42 and 172–76, and U.S. Bureau of the Census, First, Second, and Third censuses. The 1760 and 1770 figures were modified in the light of Public Treasury General Tax Receipts and Payments, 1760–70, South Carolina Department of Archives and History, Columbia. Colonial immigrant figures were dervied from a re-working of the basic sources: newspaper advertisements for African cargoes: the South Carolina Treasury General Duty Books, S.C. Dept. Arch. and Hist., Columbia; South Carolina Naval Officce Shipping Lists, Public Records Office; and Elizabeth Donnan, ed., *Documents Illustrative of the History of the Slave Trade to America*, 4 vols. (1930–35; reprint ed., New York, 1969), 4: 235–471.

*The post-Revolutionary immigrant totals are problematic. Those for the 1790s and 1800s derive from table 3, and those of the 1780s constitute another estimate based on what is known about African imports (table 19) and what contemporaries said about the scale of overland immigration (see note 3). The number of African immigrants is smaller than the number of Africans imported into South Carolina because re-exports have been taken into account.

†To determine the number of surviving Africans, the survivor schedule outlined by Allan Kulikoff was employed ("A 'Prolifick' People: Black Population Growth in the Chesapeake Colonies, 1700–1790," *Southern Studies* 16 [1971]:421). A less severe survivor schedule was applied to those native-born immigrants who entered the state in the 1780s and 1790s: it was estimated that 77 percent of all such immigrants were alive ten years after arrival.

Table 5: Sex ratios among inventoried adult slaves in the South Carolina lowcountry

	1760–69	1770–79	1783–89	1790–99
Number of males	8,622	8,538	4,761	4,632
Number of females	6,491	6,801	4,523	4,611
Sex ratio: males/females	1.33	1.26	1.05	1.00

Adult–child ratios among inventoried slaves in the South Carolina lowcountry

	1760–69	1770–79	1783–89	1790–99
Number of adults	15,113	15,339	9,284	9,243
Number of females	6,491	6,801	4,523	4,611
Number of children	7,786	8,468	6,427	6,916
Ratio: children/adults	0.52	0.55	0.69	0.75
Ratio: children/adult females	1.20	1.25	1.42	1.50

SOURCES: South Carolina Inventory Books T to CC and Charleston District Inventory Books, vols. A, B and C, South Carolina Department of Archives and History, Columbia.

Table 6: Age of slave mother at the birth of her first child, 1730–1810

Mother's date of birth	Mean age	Range of ages	Number of mothers
Ball family slaves			
1750–74	19.1	16.7–23.2	15
1775–99	20.0	14.3–30.8	63
Ravenel family slaves			
1710–50	19.3	16.7–24.1	5
1751–90	21.0	17.1–29.5	15

SOURCES: Cheryll A. Cody, "A Note on Changing Patterns of Slave Fertility in the South Carolina Rice District, 1735–1865," *Southern Studies* 16 (1977): 457–63: Revenel Papers, South Carolina Historical Society, Charleston.

in the adult slave population declined fairly steadily from about 45 percent in the 1760s to under 20 percent in the 1790s (table 7).

Although ignorant of the details of these demographic developments, contemporaries sensed an improvement in the conditions of slave life. In 1798 one planter pointed out that his tidal swamp plantation was "in a very healthy situation, evinced by the great increase which the present proprietor has had of his Negroes since they have been on it." Another lowcountry planter, when offering his gang of fifty slaves for sale in 1796, singled out the "wenches" as "young and improving." Furthermore, he claimed, these fifty slaves were "not Negroes selected out of a larger gang for the purpose of sale, but are prime[.] Their present Owner, with great trouble and expence selected them out of many for several years past. They were purchased for stock, and breeding Negroes, and to any Planter who particularly wanted them for that purpose, they are a very choice and desirable gang."[7] By

[7]*South Carolina State Gazette*, June 13, 1798, John Dawson; ibid., Mar. 4, 1796, Colcock and Patterson. If the following notice is indicative, there may also have been a new interest in the longevity of Tidewater slaves in the 1790s: "Please to inform your readers that two old men, slaves, died at Mr. Pontoux's, on Ashley River; their ages being traced as well as could be, by old inhabitants, it was found neither could be less than 115 years, but were thought to be from 120 to 125" (*City Gazette* [Charleston, S.C.], Dec. 4, 1798, Charleston News).

Table 7: Africans in South Carolina's adult slave population

Year	Adult* population	Adult† Africans	Percentage African-born	Percentage of Africans among advertised runaways
1760	36,538	16,460	45.0%	68.7%
1770	53,595	23,788	44.4	69.5
1775	67,097	32,942	49.1	67.3
1782	46,471	18,725	40.3	—
1790	62,628	16,759	26.8	54.2
1800	83,995	6,588	7.8	23.4
1810	112,853	22,533	20.0	53.1

SOURCES: Population totals were derived from Evarts B. Greene and Virginia D. Harrington, *American Population before the Federal census of 1790* (New York, 1932), pp. 137–42, and 172–76, and U.S. Bureau of the Census, First, Second, and Third censuses. The 1760 and 1770 figures were modified in the light of Public Treasury General Tax Receipts and Payments, 1760–70, South Carolina Department of Archives and History, Columbia. Colonial immigrant figures were dervied from a reworking of the basic sources: newspaper advertisements for African cargoes; the South Carolina Treasury General Duty Books, S.C. Dept. Arch. and Hist., Columbia; South Carolina Naval Office Shipping Lists, Public Record Office; and Elizabeth Donnan, ed., *Documents Illustrative of the History of the Slave Trade to America*, 4 vols. (1930–35; reprint ed., New York, 1969), 4: 235–471. This information on runaways was drawn from Charleston Library Society, South Carolina Newspapers, 1732–82 (microfilm), The Johns Hopkins University, Baltimore. For the years after 1782: extant issues of the *South Carolina Weekly Gazette* (1783–86), *South Carolina Gazette and General Advertiser* (1783–85), *Gazette of the State of South Carolina* (1783–85), *Columbian Herald* (1784–89), *State Gazette of South Carolina* (1785–89), *Charleston Morning Post* (1786–87), and *City Gazette* (1787–89), Charleston Library Society, Charleston, S.C.; and microfilm copies of *State Gazette of South Carolina* (1790–1802), *City Gazette* (1790–1801), *Columbian Herald* (1790–96), *Columbia Gazette* (1794), *Charleston Courier* (1803–6), and *Times* (1803), University of South Carolina, Columbia.

*Estimated by applying the slave adult–child ratios in table 5.

†For the adult African survivor schedule, see note † to table 4, but with two modifications: the survivor ratio from year 11 to year 20 and from year 21 to year 30 was graduated (all African adults were assumed to have died by year 30). An estimated 25,000 slaves were lost to South Carolina as a result of the Revolutionary War; perhaps one-fifth of these 25,000 were Africans (assuming that native-born slaves found it easier to desert and were more attractive to those who wished to remove slaves). The proportion of Africans in the slave population in 1782 and subsequent periods is therefore reduced by that amount.

1788 the Reverend James Stuart could testify to antislavery forces in Britain that he had been a "Rector of a Parish in Carolina, and was ready to advance that many Estates in that District, though more unhealthy than the West Indies, supported Themselves, by proper Treatment, independently of the Slave-Trade."[8]

Like the structure of the slave population, the environment in which most lowcountry slaves found themselves also changed in the latter half of the eighteenth century. Most lowcountry slaves resided in parishes where they increasingly outnumbered whites. It is not possible to calculate this trend from mid-century, but between 1790 and 1810 the slave population increased more rapidly than that of whites in most lowcountry parishes, so that in 1810 all lowcountry rural parishes were over 80 percent black, and in at least five, blacks numbered over 90 percent of the total (table 8). Furthermore, as time passed, more slaves resided on large plantations than ever before. In the 1760s, 40 percent of inventoried lowcountry slaves resided on plantations of fifty or more slaves; by the 1780s that proportion had risen to 52 percent (table 9). In some regions the late eighteenth and early nineteenth centuries witnessed a staggering degree of concentration. In the rice-growing parishes of All Saints and St. James Santee, for example, about half the slaves in 1790 belonged to planters who owned 100 or more; by 1810 that proportion had risen to 81 and 61 percent, respectively (table 10). Although the degree of concentration was less marked in sea island cotton-producing areas, it remained significant. While in St. Helena the proportion of slaves in units of fifty or more increased by just under 10 percent between 1800 and 1810, in St. John Colleton the proportion almost doubled between 1790 and 1810 (table 10). Lowcountry parishes, then, generally witnessed greater and greater concentration of blacks, both in terms of their distribution in the total population and the size of slaveholding units.

[8]Thomas Clarkson to Lord Liverpool, June 25, 1788, Liverpool Papers, Additional Mss. 38416, British Museum. The Reverend James Stuart was a rector in Prince George's Parish and left with the British in 1777.

Table 8: Slave proportion of the total population of the South Carolina lowcountry, 1790–1810

District	1790	1800	1810
Beaufort District	75.9%	78.5%	80.8%
Colleton District	82.1	82.2	82.8
St. Bartholomew	82.0	76.8	
St. Paul	93.3	89.3	
St. George	70.3	84.4	
Charleston City	47.0	47.9	47.2
Charleston District	85.9	86.8	91.0
St. John Colleton	88.6	90.2	92.5
St. Andrew	86.4	88.6	89.0
St. James Goose Creek	83.7	67.5	84.4
St. John Berkeley	87.3	90.1	93.0
Christ Church	80.5	88.9	85.9
St. Thomas and St. Denis	88.8	91.1	92.7
St. James Santee	88.1	90.6	95.9
St. Stephen	91.7	86.7	88.7
Georgetown District	59.3	72.2	88.4
All Saints	80.7		95.4
Prince George	56.5		86.2

SOURCES: U.S. Bureau of the Census, First, Second, and Third censuses.

Table 9: Proportion of inventoried slaves on plantations of various sizes in the South Carlina lowcountry, 1760–99

Period	Size of slaveholding unit						Number of slaves
	1–9	10–19	20–49	50–79	80–99	100+	
1760–69	12%	13%	35%	21%	7%	12%	23,732
1770–79	11	14	28	18	10	10	24,332
1780–89	10	11	27	15	9	28	16,337
1790–99	11	14	26	18	11	18	16,175

SOURCES: South Carolina Inventory Books T to CC and Charleston District inventory Books, vols. A, B, and C, South Carolina Department of Archives and History, Columbia.

95

Table 10: Proportion of slaves on plantations of various sizes in selected parishes of the South Carolina lowcountry, 1790–1810

Size of slaveholding unit	Predominantly rice-producing				Predominantly cotton-producing			
	All Saints		St. James Santee		St. John Colleton		St. Helena	
	1790	1810	1790	1810	1790	1810	1800*	1810
1–9	6.9%	1.5%	5.2%	1.1%	5.4%	1.6%	1.7%	6.0%
10–19	6.6	2.6	5.9	3.3	8.7	4.0	5.6	9.2
20–49	20.7	4.6	14.4	13.3	46.5	18.0	43.1	28.0
50–79	16.2	3.2	18.1	17.8	20.0	31.6	26.6	20.7
80–99	—	7.3	7.6	3.6	7.4	15.0	10.5	18.0
100+	49.4	80.9	48.7	60.8	12.0	30.0	12.7	18.0
Total	99.8	100.1	99.9	99.9	100.0	100.2	100.0	99.9
Number of slaves	1,795	3,717	3,345	4,687	4,705	7,057	2,657	5,741

SOURCES: U.S. Bureau of the Census, First, Second and Third Censuses.

*Because the 1790 census does not alllow a parish-by-parish analysis of Beaufort District (encompassing st. Helena Parish), the 1800 census was used.

96

The increasing size of plantations reflected other changing economic realities. One of the most significant components of the slaves' economic world was their opportunity to do specialized work. The late colonial period saw a slight but significant upward trend in the skill levels of slaves. By the 1770s about 18 percent of inventoried adult slave men had been exempted from field labor;[9] this upward trend accelerated markedly in the late eighteenth century, when over a quarter held specialized positions (tables 11 and 12).[10] Occupational opportunities for slave women also expanded in the late eighteenth century, but they remained extremely limited: even in the 1790s, nine of every ten adult women worked in the fields. Most of the increase in skills apparently resulted from an expansion in the number of domestic servants (tables 13a through 14b), although the continued expansion in the size of plantation estates also buttressed the trend.[11] A slight decline in the proportion of skilled slaves about the turn of the century probably reflected in part the beginning of the cotton boom, which pulled some skilled slaves out of the lowcountry along with thousands of field hands. And among those skilled blacks who remained in the low-

[9]See Philip D. Morgan, "The Development of Slave Culture in Eighteenth Century Plantation America," Ph.D. diss., University College, London, 1977, esp. pp. 101–7, for a full discussion of the reliability of these figures.

[10]Five advertisements in post-Revolutionary newspapers specified clearly the skill levels required or present in gangs of slaves: the aggregate skill level was 23 percent of 134 adult slaves, and must have been much higher for adult men (*S.C. Weekly Gaz.*, Mar. 6, 1784, Colcock and Gibbons; *State Gazette of South Carolina* [hereafter *State Gaz.*], Aug. 12, 1790, Colcock and Graham; ibid., Oct. 21, 1790, John Parker; ibid., Jan. 20, 1791, Job Colcock; and *Charleston Courier*, Mar. 12, 1805, John Moncrieffe).

[11]Skill levels usually correlate positively with size of estate. See, for example, Richard S. Dunn, *Sugar and Slaves: The Rise of the Planter Class in the English West Indies, 1624–1715* (Chapel Hill, N.C., 1972), pp. 91, 171, and 319.

country, some were pushed into the fields by the resulting shortage of labor. When Charles Ball's slave coffle arrived at a South Carolina inn just after the turn of the century, there was no stableman to tend to the trader's horse, and the landlord explained apologetically "that at this season of the year, the planters were so hurried by their crops . . . that for his part, he had been compelled to put his coachman, and even the waiting-maids of his daughters into the cotton fields, and that at this time, his family were without servants, a circumstance that had never happened before!"[12]

Still, most slaves remained unaffected by expanding or contracting opportunities for skilled work; they continued to labor in the fields as had most adult slaves throughout the eighteenth century. Rice remained South Carolina's premier crop, with the shift to Tidewater cultivation, which had begun as early as mid-century, in full swing. The change in location and methods of rice production generated, on the one hand, a significant improvement in the work routines of the slaves. As John Drayton observed, "River swamp plantations, from the command of water, which at high tides can be introduced over the fields, have an undoubted preference to inland plantations; as the crop is more certain, and the work of the negroes less toilsome."[13] Increasing reliance on tidal culture greatly reduced the heavy hoeing formerly required of slaves in the summer months. The gain to the slaves was evident in one Tidewater planter's boastful description of his estate: "250 acres are cleared, and inclosed with large sub-

---

[12]Charles Ball, *Slavery in the United States: A Narrative of the Life and Adventures of Charles Ball, a Black Man* (1837; reprint ed., New York, 1969), pp. 88–89.

[13]John Drayton, *A View of South Carolina as Respects Her Natural and Civil Concerns* (1802; reprint ed., Spartanburg, S.C., 1972), p. 116. For the evidence that Tidewater cultivation was fully evident by mid-century, see Morgan, "Development of Slave Culture," pp. 77–78.

Table 11: Skilled slaves among inventoried South Carolina adult slaves, 1730–99

Period	Men			Women		
	Total	Skilled	Percent skilled	Total	Skilled	Percent skilled
1730–39	399	62	15.5%	245	3	1.2%
1740–49	828	134	16.2	498	22	4.4
1750–59	1,703	233	13.7	1,249	34	2.7
1760–69	1,618	275	17.0	1,128	60	5.3
1770–79	2,029	371	18.3	1,543	77	5.0
Total	6,577	1,075	16.3	4,663	196	4.2
1780–89	1,250	400	32.0	1,186	88	7.4
1790–99	1,025	293	28.6	1,022	87	8.5
Total	2,275	693	30.5	2,208	175	7.9

SOURCES: Inventories II to CC, Records of the Secretary of the Province, 1730–36, and Charleston District Inventory Books, vols. A, B, and C, South Carolina Department of Archives and History, Columbia.

NOTE: Skill is broadly defined to include not only crafts or trades but also any specialized position. For a breakdown of skills, see tables 13a and 14a.

Table 12: Skilled slaves among advertised runaway South Carolina adult slaves, 1732–1806

Period	Men			Women		
	Total	Skilled	Percent skilled	Total	Skilled	Percent skilled
1732–39	422	37	8.8%	93	7	7.5%
1740–49	492	73	14.8	128	7	5.5
1750–59	675	79	11.7	194	4	2.1
1760–69	1,208	186	15.4	203	16	7.9
1770–79	1,605	281	17.5	310	28	9.0
Total	4,402	656	14.9	928	62	6.7
1780–89	711	150	21.1	239	21	8.8
1790–99	624	173	27.7	184	15	8.2
1800–1806	462	108	23.4	100	8	8.0
Total	1,797	431	24.0	523	44	8.4

SOURCES: Charleston Library Society, South Carolina Newspapers, 1732–82 (microfilm), The Johns Hopkins University, Baltimore. For the years after 1782: extant issues of the *South Carolina Weekly Gazette* (1783–86), *South Carolina Gazette and General Advertiser* (1783–85), *Charleston Morning Gazette of the State of South Carolina* (1783–85), *Columbian Herald* (1784–89), *State Gazette of South Carolina* (1785–89), *Charleston Morning Post* (1786–87), and *City Gazette* (1787–89), Charleston Library Society, Charleston, S.C.; and microfilm copies of *State Gazette of South Carolina* (1790–1802), *City Gazette* (1790–1801), *Columbian Herald* (1790–96), *Columbia Gazette* (1794), *Charleston Courier* (1803–6), and *Times* (1803), University of South Carolina, Columbia.

NOTE: For a breakdown of skills, see tables 13b and 14b.

Table 13a: Skills among inventoried South Carolina adult slaves, 1730–79

Tradesmen	809	(63.6%)	House slaves	249 [196]*	(19.6%)
Woodworkers	634		Waitingman	21	
Cooper	321		Barber	8	
Sawyer	114		Coachman	3	
Carpenter	196		Gardener	5	
Woodman	1		House slave	92 [86]	
Turner	2		Cook	61 [51]	
Wheelwright	13		Seamstress	[20]	
Blacksmith	22		Washerwoman	[28]	
Brazier	2		Ironer	[1]	
Gunsmith	1		Nurse	[4]	
Silversmith	1		Midwife	[1]	
Shipwright	10		Maid	[3]	
Caulker	5		Waitingwoman	[1]	
Bricklayer	34		Spinner	[1]	
Painter	6				
Carter	6		*Town*	10	(0.8%)
Tanner	9				
Currier	2		Porter	3	
Shoemaker	43		Chimney sweep	1	
Tailor	7		Laborer	5	
Butcher	8		Market slave	1	
Baker	2				
Tradesman	2		*Agriculture*	88	(6.9%)
Stockkeeper/ Bookman	2		Driver	70	
			Plowman	1	
Watermen	110	(8.6%)	Hunter	5	
			Indigo maker	3	
Boatman	103		Herdsman	9	
Patroon	1				
Fisherman	6		*Miscellaneous*	5	(0.4%)
			Doctor	5	

Total 1,271 [196]

SOURCES: Inventories II to CC, Records of the Secretary of the Province, 1730–36, South Carolina Department of Archives and History, Columbia.

*Figures in brackets represent female skilled slaves

Table 13b: Skills among advertised runaway South Carolina adult slaves, 1732–79

Tradesmen	384 [10]* (53.5%)	House slaves	100 [46] (13.9%)	
Woodworkers	203	Waitingman	30	
Cooper	69	Barber	9	
Sawyer	38	Coachman	2	
Carpenter	90	Hostler	2	
Cabinetmaker	6	Gardener	3	
Wheelwright	9	Waiter	1	
Blacksmith	12	House servant	17 [12]	
Shipwright	1	Cook	6 [4]	
Caulker	3	Seamstress	[16]	
Sailmaker	2	Washerwoman	[13]	
Brickmaker	1	Nurse	[1]	
Sawmiller worker	1			
Bricklayer	29	*Town*	27 [6] (3.8%)	
Painter	4			
Waggoner	4	Porter	2	
Carter	1	Laborer	1	
Tanner	12	Shoptender	2	
Saddler	2	Market slave	22 [6]	
Shoemaker	27			
Tailor	16	*Agriculture*	8 (1.1%)	
Butcher	10			
Baker	1	Driver	3	
Distiller	3	Plowman	2	
Stocking weaver	1	Hunter	3	
Hired	32 [10]			
Apprentice	10	*Miscellaneous*	12 (1.7%)	
		Doctor	5	
Watermen	187 (26.0%)	Regimental drummer	4	
		Jeweler	2	
Boatman	87	Indian trader	1	
Sailor	87			
Ferryman	1			
Fisherman	12			

      Total 718 [62]

SOURCES: Charleston Library Society, South Carolina Newspapers, 1732–82 (microfilm), The Johns Hopkins University, Baltimore.
  *Figures in brackets represent female skilled slaves

Table 14a: Skills among inventoried South Carolina adult slaves, 1780–99

Tradesmen	407 (46.9%)	House slaves	274 [173]*	(31.6%)
Woodworkers	291	Waitingman	36	
Cooper	73	Barber	3	
Sawyer	55	Coachman	5	
Carpenter	163	Groom	4	
Wheelwright	7	Gardener	20	
Blacksmith	9	Corn grinder	1	
Caulker	11	House servant	79 [59]	
Ropemaker	1	Cook	53 [41]	
Brickmaker	2	Seamstress	[28]	
Bricklayer	26	Washerwoman	[26]	
Painter	1	Ironer	[1]	
Waggoner	4	Nurse	[3]	
Carter	5	Midwife	[5]	
Tanner	5	Spinner	[4]	
Saddler	4	Weaver	[2]	
Shoemaker	30	Dairy	[4]	
Tailor	6			
Butcher	2	*Town*	17 [1]	(2.0%)
Baker	2	Laborer	15	
Tradesman	1	Market slave	2 [1]	
Watermen	74 (8.5%)			
		Agriculture	96 [1]	(11.1%)
Boatman	63	Driver	75	
Patroon	2	Plowman	6	
Pilot	1	Herdsman	13 [1]	
Fisherman	8	Hunter	2	

Total 868 [175]

SOURCES: Inventories AA and Charleston District Inventory Books, vols. A, B, and C, South Carolina Department of Archives and History, Columbia.
  *Figures in brackets represent female skilled slaves.

Table 14b: Skills among advertised runaway South Carolina adult slaves, 1780–99

Tradesmen	205 [1]* (43.2%)	House slaves	120 [31] (25.3%)
Woodworkers	100	Waitingman	39
Cooper	15	Barber	13
Sawyer	10	Coachman	12
Carpenter	73	Gardener	4
Woodman	1	House servant	25 [10]
Cabinetmaker	1	Cook	10 [4]
Wheelwright	1	Seamstress	[9]
Blacksmith	2	Washerwoman	[6]
Shipwright	4	Ironer	[1]
Caulker	2	Attends children	[1]
Sailmaker	6		
Ropemaker	1	*Town*	36 [12] (7.6%)
Bricklayer	16		
Painter	7	Porter	2
Carter	13	Laborer	4
Tanner	2	Works on wharves	7
Saddler	1	Chimney sweep	2
Shoemaker	23	Market slave	16 [11]
Tailor	11	Errand boy/girl	5 [1]
Butcher	3		
Baker	5	*Agriculture*	2 (0.4%)
Hired	4 [1]	Driver	1
Tradesman	4	Plowman	1
Watermen	110 (23.2%)	*Miscellaneous*	2 (0.4%)
Boatman	97	Doctor	1
Sailor	1	Preacher	1
Patroon	6		
Fisherman	6		

    Total 475 [44]

SOURCES: Charleston Library Society, South Carolina Newspapers, 1732–82 (microfilm), The Johns Hopkins University, Baltimore. For the years after 1782: extant issues of the *South Carolina Weekly Gazette* (1783–86), *South Carolina Gazette and General Advertiser* (1783–85), *Gazette of the State of South Carolina* (1783–85), *Columbian Herald* (1784–89), *State Gazette of South Carolina* (1785–89), *Charleston Morning Post* (1786–87), and *City Gazette* (1787–89), Charleston Library Society, Charleston, S.C.; and microfilm copies of *State Gazette of South Carolina* (1790–1802), *City Gazette* (1790–1801), *Columbian Herald* (1790–96), *Columbia Gazette* (1794), *Charleston Courier* (1803–6), and *Times* (1803), University of South Carolina, Columbia.

    *Figures in brackets represent female skilled slaves.

stantial Banks, and subdivided into small squares by other proper Dams, so as to render the Hoeing and Watering each Part distinct, an Advantage few large Plantations have; each Division having fine Flood-Gates and Sluices, which let in the tides from the Front and Back Rivers at the same Time." An advertisement for a river swamp plantation in Georgetown District revealed how the new techniques of production benefited the slaves in still other ways: "The Fields are divided into twelve squares of equal size and separated from each other by good Banks and Ditches, with separate Trunks to each, and three Canals, running through different parts of the Field, and navigable for a Flat up to the Barn-door, for the purposes of Harvesting and Conveying Bbls from the Barn to the River." [14] On the other hand, as these advertisements suggest, "good Ditches and good Trunks are . . . absolutely necessary on a River Swamp plantation," and the construction of these ditches, trunks, canals, and dams increased the labor of slaves in the late winter and early spring months. Thus, late in February the slaves on one Pedee plantation complained "that they had been hard work'd," but the manager argued that "for this there was a kind of necessity, in order to have the Banks secur'd so as to save the crop from being hurted by overflowing Tides." [15]

If the yearly routine of rice culture, while retaining most of its essential character throughout the century, underwent some adaptations, the same may be said of the organization of slave labor. The task system remained the predominant method of labor arrangement in the eighteenth-century lowcountry. However, there had always been elements of the gang system—in clearing new ground, maintaining ditches, working on the roads—and these became more prevalent as a result of the communal work required for Tidewater cultivation. Indeed, in the 1780s one influential planter even recommended that planting could be best achieved through the gang system: "While planting select out of the whole Gang

[14]*S.C. Gaz.*, Feb. 28, 1771, William Williamson; *State Gaz.*, Dec. 28, 1793.

[15]J. Channing to Edward Telfair, Oct. 31, 1787, Telfair Papers; Josiah Smith to George Austin, Feb. 25, 1772, Josiah Smith Letterbook, Southern Historical Collection, University of North Carolina, Chapel Hill.

the ablest Fellows for trenchers, carefullest wenches for sow-
ers & the weakest for Coverers; while employed in this important business . . . they should always be Kept in Gangs or
parcels and not scattered over a field in Tasks as is too generally done, for while in gangs they are more immediately
under the Superintendants Eyes, of course may be much better & more immediately inspected."[16] The task system remained the norm, however, and most slaveowners ignored
this planter's advice. As throughout the eighteenth century,
tasking allowed slaves to appropriate a portion of the day for
themselves by working intensively to complete a task. As one
Georgian put it, after a slave completed his task, "his master
feels no right to call on him."[17]

If significant continuities characterized the work routines
of slaves engaged in rice production, the decline in indigo
cultivation and the emergence of cotton planting marked an
important departure for many field slaves. During the 1750s
planters in the predominantly rice-producing districts had
substituted indigo cultivation for the production of naval stores
during slack periods in the rice-growing cycle. Furthermore,
in the upper parts of lowland parishes and in the estuarine
Tidewater region unsuitable for tidal culture, indigo had become the main crop.[18] The 1790s saw cotton supplant indigo
in both regions, often on the same land that formerly produced indigo. Thus, in predominantly rice-producing regions cotton was grown as a supplement to rice and, while
long-staple cotton became the main crop in estuarine regions, particularly the sea islands, short-staple cotton became
the predominant upland crop.[19] This shift in crop patterns

[16]William Butler, "Observations on the Culture of Rice," 1786, Mss., S.C.
Hist. Soc.

[17]Daniel Turner to his parents, Aug. 13, 1806, Daniel Turner Papers,
Library of Congress, as quoted in Michael Mullin, "British Caribbean and
North American Slaves in an Era of War and Revolution, 1775–1807," in
Jeffrey J. Crow and Larry E. Tise, eds., *The Southern Experience in the Amer-
ican Revolution* (Chapel Hill, N.C., 1978), p. 249.

[18]See Morgan, "Development of Slave Culture," pp. 87–88.

[19]William Abbott to the Right Honourable Henry Dundas, Feb. 27, 1800,
Melville Castle Muniments, Scottish Record Office, Edinburgh. For evi-

not only caused a redistribution of the slave population and a decline in slave skills, as already observed; it also had a powerful influence on the intensity of slave labor and the nature of slave work routines. Cotton was a less demanding crop than either rice or indigo. As one sea island planter noted:

> No culture for our country can be easier than that of the cotton plant. . . . There is, comparatively, *little or no labor* in attending to the crop. . . . The pods, ripening in succession, and continuing for four or five months, make the harvest slow and tedious, but the work is *light and easy*, so much so, that all the pregnant women even, on the plantation, and weak and sickly negroes incapable of other labor, and all the boys and girls above nine and ten years of age, are then in requisition to assist in gathering the wool which hangs from the pods. Children are in fact the most useful hands at the season. From the smallness of their fingers and their low stature, they daily pick in more than many adults.[20]

Making the same point, in a slightly different manner, another planter sought a gang of slaves, but "no cotton Negroes. I want People that can go in the ditch."[21] But if cotton permitted a less arduous regimen, it also required repetitive cultivation that made it ideal for gang labor. Inland planters seem to have adopted the gang system from the beginning. Sea island planters were encouraged to do the same, for one Georgia lowcountry planter was adamant that "there is no possibility of tasking Negroes" in cotton production; never-

---

dence that many plantations combined rice *and* cotton production, see *City Gaz.*, Dec. 12, 1800, John Champneys; ibid., Dec. 17, 1800, Isaac Edwards; *Charleston Courier*, Jan. 18, 1803, Benjamin Stead; ibid., Feb. 2, 1803; ibid., Feb. 7, 1803, William Hasell Gibbs; ibid., Mar. 4, 1803; ibid., Mar. 22, 1803, William Holmes and Co.; ibid., Jan. 7, 1805, Alexander Chisolm; and the plans of plantations in Prince William's Parish belonging to Maj. John Cuthbert and Capt. William Taylor, April 1799, Cuthbert Family Papers, College of Charleston, Charleston, S.C.

[20]Edwin C. Holland, *A Refutation of the Calumnies Circulated against. . . Slavery* (1822; reprint ed., New York, 1969), p. 52.

[21]P. B. to [?], Apr. 6, 1807, Pierce Butler Papers, University of South Carolina, Columbia.

theless, the task system remained standard in this area in the antebellum era.[22]

Compared to the powerful effect of long-term demographic and economic changes, the impact of the Revolution on low-country black life was—in one sense—minimal. Moses Kirkland, a backcountry loyalist, predicted that "the instant that The Kings Troops are put in motion in those colonies, these poor Slaves would be ready to rise upon their Rebel Masters"; unfortunately for his cause, this prediction proved groundless. As one historian has recently put it, "South Carolina blacks apparently did not take advantage of their owners' predicament during the Revolution, nor did lowcountry planters exhibit the anxiety about their slaves' loyalty manifested by Maryland and Virginia slaveholders."[23] Given the intensive preparations of fearful lowcountry slaveholders, it would have been difficult for slaves to do otherwise. According to one newspaper report, militia companies regularly patrolled as early as the summer of 1775; Charleston had to be defended, one patriot general was instructed in the spring of 1776, because "in slave counties so much depends on opinion, and the opinion which the slave will entertain of our superiority or inferiority will naturally keep pace with our maintaining or giving ground." That white South Carolinians would give no ground can be gauged by an admission by one of the state's representatives to the Continental Congress: his state could not defend itself, he claimed, "by reason of the great proportion of citizens necessary to remain at home to prevent insurrection among the Negroes, and to prevent the desertion of them to the enemy."[24] Moreover, even though

[22]*City Gaz.*, Mar. 14, 1796, letter to printers. For evidence that inland cotton planters used the gang system, see Ball, *Slavery in the United States*, pp. 147–48.

[23]Randall M. Miller, "A Backcountry Loyalist Plan to Retake Georgia and the Carolinas, 1778," *South Carolina Historical Magazine* 75 (1974):213; Mullin, "British Caribbean and North American Slaves," p. 236.

[24]*S.C. Gaz. and Country Journal*, June 13, 1775, as quoted in Peter H. Wood, "'Taking Care of Business' in Revolutionary South Carolina: Republicanism and the Slave Society," in Crow and Tise, *The Southern Experi-*

the British army briefly assumed the mantle of an army of liberation through Clinton's 1779 proclamation, once in control of territory that same army worked for the racial status quo. As one British officer ruefully noted, "The Banditts of Negroes who flock to the conquerors . . . do ten thousand times more Mischief than the whole Army put together." Before long, the administrative arm of the British occupation, the Charleston Board of Police, sent parties of soldiers to outlying plantations so that, for example, "the ill behavior and insurrectious conduct of Mr. Isard's Negroes towards their Overseer" could be quelled.[25]

But in another sense the Revolution had a far-reaching impact. Some slaves, of course, stood by their masters. One slave driver demonstrated such fidelity that "during the invasion of the country, [he] never went off with the British, and had the address to prevent any going who were under his care." But many others cared more for their own liberty than for their master's property. For example, driver Andrew "when the British were in possession of Savannah . . . carried off all Mrs. Graeme's negroes that were then in Prince William's Parish; and Mrs. Graeme could not get them back, until she made terms with Andrew."[26] Moreover, the lowcountry's raging civil war and military occupation created unprecedented opportunities for slaves to widen their own freedom within bondage and, occasionally, outside of it. Although planters eventually regained their place in lowcoun-

ence, p. 282; "Instructions to Brigadier General Armstrong," Apr. 10, 1776, Lee Papers, Harvard University, Cambridge, Mass., as quoted in Benjamin Quarles, *The Negro in the American Revolution* (1961; reprint ed., New York, 1973), p. 122; Worthington C. Ford, ed., *Journals of the Continental Congress*, 34 vols. (Washington, D.C., 1904–37), 13:386.

[25]Archibald Campbell to [?], Jan. 9, 1779, Prioleau Papers, S.C. Hist. Soc.; Minutes of the Charleston Board of Police, July 14, 1780, CO5 519, p. 14, Public Record Office.

[26]*S.C. Gaz. and General Advertiser*, June 10, 1783, Colcock and Gibbons; *City Gaz.*, Nov. 30, 1796, J. and W. B. Mitchell. An advertisement offering a gang of forty slaves for sale asserted that "what makes them . . . valuable is that not one ever quitted their owner at a Time when most Negroes had, while this State was in confusion, and invested by the British Army" (*Gaz. of the State of S.C.*, Nov. 27, 1783, Frances-Susanna Pinckney).

try society, wartime anarchy created a power vacuum in the countryside that allowed slaves to expand their liberty. Even those who remained at home became, as one South Carolina mistress observed of her slaves, "insolent and quite their own masters." If few followed Andrew's dramatic example, many slaves could, like those on one Ashepoo plantation, ignore their overseer's orders and be "perfectly free [to] live upon the best produce on the Plantation" or, as on "Watboo" plantation, act "under little or no subjection to the Overseers." As William Bull observed in 1781, since the commencement of the rebellion, the slaves had become "ungovernable."[27]

Lowcountry blacks did not readily surrender their wartime gains. Even after the war many continued to flaunt their increased autonomy. If slavemasters desired to recreate the status quo ante bellum, slaves did not easily return to the old way of life. Many used their wartime experience to win still greater independence. Driver Andrew, as will be noted later, put his wartime experience to good effect some fifteen years after the event. One boatman and pilot presumably treasured the "pass he received from the British during the war," because he used it in 1796 to pass as a free man. Another South Carolina slave, located in St. Augustine in 1784, told his master's envoy that he was prepared to return "willingly . . . but not at present"; the envoy was reduced to hoping that he might "be able to persuade him" to return earlier than the slave intended.[28] These incidental increments in the power of individual slaves suggest a much broader process by which slaves increased governance of their daily affairs in the overwhelmingly black countryside.

The sheer loss of black manpower was the most dramatic

[27]Eliza Pinckney to [?], Sept. 25, 1780, Pinckney Family Papers, Library of Congress; Thomas Pinckney to Eliza Pinckney, May 17, 1779, Pinckney Family Papers, S.C. Hist. Soc.; William Ancrum to James Edward Colleton, July 14, 1780, in J. H. Easterby, ed., *Wadboo Barony, Its Fate as Told in the Colleton Family Papers, 1773–1793* (Columbia, S.C., 1952), p. 4; William Bull to Lord Hillsborough, Mar. 22, 1781, Records in the British Public Record Office Relating to South Carolina, 36:114–17, S.C. Dept. Arch. and Hist.

[28]*City Gaz.*, Jan. 4, 1796, Mr. Snyder; John Douglass to J. Owen and J. L. Gervais, Apr. 14, 1784, J. L. Gervais Papers, Univ. of S.C.

consequence of the Revolutionary War upon lowcountry black life. The best estimate, admittedly far from trustworthy, indicates that South Carolina lost approximately 25,000 slaves during the war, representing about one-quarter of its immediate pre-Revolutionary population.[29] A petition from one lowcountry parish, seeking relief from the usual road duty demands, offers one fairly reliable measure of the local scale of this loss: the basis for the petitioners' claim lay in the fact that the number of adult male slaves in the parish had been nearly halved—from 1,413 in 1774 to 731 in 1784.[30] Many slaves may have died. A British soldier at the siege of Charleston reported that the war had reduced "the poor negroes to a starving condition in many places thereabouts." Both patriot and British soldiers plundered other slaves, and many bondspeople left with the British in 1782.[31] Furthermore, slaves were still found "strolling about the country," as one advertisement put it, some years after the British had evacuated Charleston. In 1784 one African related that he had been "plundered from his master in British times, and taken to Virginia, and now is endeavouring to get back to him." Captured in the Orangeburg District, he remained some hundred miles from his destination. The last capture of a slave uprooted by the war, thus far discovered, was that of an

[29]The South Carolina slave population numbered under 80,000 in 1782 (Evarts B. Greene and Virginia D. Harrington, *American Population before the Federal Census of 1790* [New York, 1932], p. 176) and about 104,000 in 1775. Since the population was growing naturally by the 1770s, South Carolina must have suffered an absolute loss of about 25,000 slaves if the slave population totals are accurate. Some of these 25,000 may have been returned from neighboring states in the early 1780s.

[30]Petition of inhabitants of St. Johns Berkeley Parish, Feb. 15, 1787, General Assembly, Petitions, 1787, no. 32, S.C. Dept. Arch. and Hist. See also Records of the Commissioners of the High Roads of St. John's Parish, Berkeley County, 1760–1853, S.C. Hist. Soc., from which it is possible to discover which individuals lost slaves.

[31]Diary of John Peebles, May 25, 1780, S.R.O. Ralph Izard reckoned that the British, in evacuating Charleston, might "carry with them about Twelve Thousand Negroes, which they have now in Charles Town, & which have been stolen in their various expeditions into the Country" (Izard to his wife, Oct. 7, 1782, Ralph Izard Papers, Univ. of S.C.).

African woman taken up in 1797: "She absented from her owner during the last war, whose name was John Wilkie, and resided between Sunbury and Savannah in Georgia—that her master died soon after she ranaway and his Brother left that state with the British—that she does not know who she at present belongs to, but remembers a Billy and Jacky Groves."[32] Despite his broken and halting English, one fifty-year-old African war refugee related a truly picaresque journey:

> [He] belonged to the estate of George Levington, formerly of Wilmington, North Carolina, and came to Charleston some time before the surrender to the British; that his master bought a plantation on Pedee, of Mr. Huger, from whence (while the British were in Charleston) he was carried thither by two Tories; that he was afterwards taken from thence to the Horse-Shoe by a Mr. Sander's—that he went from that place back to Charleston, and at last, set out on a route to the backcountry; and being taken up at Monck's Corner, was brought up to Santee, where he has been for three years past— He further says, that his master being a Tory, was put in the gaol of George-Town, where he died.[33]

This African was not only uprooted but politically educated, it would seem, by his experience.

This rapid demographic change was not an unmixed blessing for blacks.[34] Much movement was involuntary: masters

---

[32]*State Gaz.*, May 29, 1786, Francis Lann; *Gaz. of the State of S.C.*, Oct. 14, 1784, John Kennerly; *City Gaz.*, June 14, 1797, A. Seixas. For other examples of slaves uprooted by the war, see *S.C. Gaz. and Gen. Adv.*, Nov. 19, 1785, Robert Anderson; *State Gaz.*, Aug. 10, 1786, Workhouse; ibid., Mar. 17, 1788, John Cryer. See ibid., Apr. 7, 1785, George Renerson, for another slave who "seems very desirous to get to his master."

[33]*Columbian Herald*, Aug. 10, 1785, William Murrell.

[34]It is not entirely clear what sort of slaves left the state. One parish return suggests that adult men predominated (see note 30 above); that evidence is confirmed by the fact that the largest reduction in the imbalanced sex ratios occurred between the late 1770s and the early 1780s (table 5). I have begun an analysis of the 3,000 Negroes who left New York for Nova Scotia—many of whom were from the lowcountry—but age, sex, and previous residence are the only systematic evidence that can be tabulated. See Book of Negroes in the Carleton Papers, 30/55/100/10427, P.R.O.

hustled their slaves out of the paths of marauding armies, patriots and loyalists confiscated and sold each other's slaves, both belligerents used blacks as bounties for white volunteers, and unprincipled men with no loyalty except to themselves used the chaos of war to kidnap slaves for their own benefit. Suggesting how events could redound to a slave's detriment, James Brisbane's slave Dick was sold simply because Brisbane had neglected "attending on a General Alarm."[35] Thus, if some blacks used the chaos of war to effect their escape, broaden their horizons, or gain a political education, many others suffered grievously. Indeed, the general loss of black manpower may have stiffened slaveholder commitment to bondage and induced lowcountry masters to press for reopening the slave trade.

The impact of the Revolutionary War on the pattern of lowcountry race relations and white racial ideology was similarly double-edged. In some sense the Revolutionary era produced a new flexibility, an "easing of white racial hostility within a system of continued racial oppression."[36] For example, Charlestonians exhibited a degree of squeamishness

---

For insight into the sort of slaves the enemy might take away, see W. Edwin Hemphill et al., eds., *Journal of the General Assembly and House of Representatives, 1776–1780* (Columbia, S.C., 1970), pp. 93–94.

[35]For an example of a master who moved his slaves to avoid their being taken away by the enemy, see Theodora Thompson and Rosa Lumpkin, eds., *Journals of the House of Representatives, 1783–1784* (Columbia, S.C., 1977), p. 11. I am at present attempting to calculate how many slaves were confiscated (from Commissioners of Forfeited Estates Papers, S.C. Dept. Arch. and Hist.) and how many slaves were used as bounties (from Accounts Audited of Claims Growing out of the Revolution in South Carolina, S.C. Dept. Arch. and Hist.). The case of James Brisbane's slave boy appears in Miscellaneous Record Book RR, p. 588, S.C. Dept. Arch. and Hist. For a good example of uprooted slaves trying to return, see the Journal of the South Carolina House of Representatives, Mar. 22, 1785, which records a case of four slaves, confiscated from a loyalist estate and sold to a resident of North Carolina, who later made their way back to their old South Carolina home.

[36]Ira Berlin, "The Revolution in Black Life," in Alfred F. Young, ed., *The American Revolution: Explorations in the History of American Radicalism* (DeKalb, Ill., 1976), p. 363.

hitherto unsuspected when they recommended that slaves be punished at one central place rather than "in the different streets of the city," for, it was reported, many residents found such a practice "distressing."[37] Masters seemed keen to appear in a good light. One late eighteenth-century sale notice, for example, quickly pointed out that "the cause of [the slave's] being sold is that he does not like to live with his present master."[38] A heightened concern for the integrity of the slave family also became evident. Moreover, in place of the blood-curdling advertisements for runaway slaves that graced the pages of early eighteenth-century newspapers, a more resigned note was struck in many a notice at the end of the century. One master, for example, eschewed a practical in favor of a poetic description: "Charity is gone! Thrice has she departed from my habitation, notwithstanding her abode was comfortable, and her labour with me light. . . . It is supposed she has left the busy city in disgust, and retir'd to rural quiet, on the banks of Stono, to enjoy the company of the sable nymphs and swains, who there cultivate the luxuriant pearly grain."[39] Even a notice that called for the head of a

[37]*City Gaz.*, June 13, 1788, Presentments of the Grand Jury of the District of Charleston.

[38]*City Gaz.*, Jan. 7, 1791, Henry Doggett. For similar advertisements, see ibid., Mar. 23, 1797, Printer; ibid., May 16, 1797; ibid., June 29, 1797; *Charleston Courier*, Dec. 5, 1803, William Stephens. Further evidence of this new self-image is offered in 144 runaway advertisements in the post-Revolutionary era which mentioned that the fugitive would be forgiven if he returned. One master noted in 1797 that "although they [Tom and his wife Rachel] have run-away once before this, from their present owner, they shall be forgiven, if they return to the Subscriber, and have Liberty to choose an Owner" (*City Gaz.*, June 2, 1797, Richard Wall). Only 40 such advertisements were found in the entire colonial period. For the newspapers examined in this analysis, see the sources of table 12.

[39]*State Gaz.*, Dec. 7, 1793, Charles Simmons. Another Revolutionary-era example of the more casual attitude toward running away is an advertisement for Stephen, "well known as a player of the tambourine." He was "requested to come back, when his cruise is out; if he does not, he will get what Paddy gave the drum." To which a later notice replied, "Oho! Massa Conly, mee tink you one paddy; you sa you beet me like one paddy beet him drum, if I no comb homb myself. We poor Nega la, no kitche no

runaway (such advertisements had been frequent in the colonial period) went to great lengths to justify the decision:

> Bristol . . . ran away from John G. Blount esq. some years ago,
> and after weeks of persuasion and many fair promises prevailed
> on the subscriber to purchase him upon an expressly stipulated
> condition that . . . if he ran away after drawing me into a loss by
> inducing me to purchase and then absconding, he would be sat-
> isfied to forfeit his head. . . . He has now left my service without
> the slightest provocation, without having ever been whipped in
> it, without undergoing the most laborious and disagreeable part
> of duty, . . . and under peculiar circumstances of treachery and
> provocation— I do therefore, in consequence of the above men-
> tioned solemn assurance made to him, and with his consent, of-
> fer a reward of FIFTY DOLLARS— . . . [for] his Head.[40]

If a slave lost his head in the Revolutionary era, it would at
least be by his own consent! A more tangible indicator of the
new liberality is the increase in manumissions that occurred
during the Revolutionary years. Masters freed more slaves in
the 1780s than in the previous three decades (table 15), and
occasionally such newfound benevolence can be attributed to
a flexibility in the racial pattern. John Peronneau, like other
emancipators, liberated his slave Romeo in 1781 "in consequence of my aversion to and abhorrence of Slavery which
natural Religion and common sense do equally condemn."[41]

However, even in the arena of manumission the evidence
hardly betokens a substantial easing of white racial hostility.
For one thing, the lowcountry as a whole saw much the lowest rate of manumission in mainland America.[42] For another,
many masters emancipated their slaves on conditions that
signify little change in the slave's status or the master's out-

---

habbee; how paddy beet me den?" (*City Gaz.*, June 25, 1799, John Con-
nolly; and ibid., June 27, 1799, Stephen's answer).

[40]*Times* (Charleston, S.C.), June 1, 1803, Benjamin Smith.

[41]Miscellaneous Record Book TT, p. 36, S.C. Dept. Arch. and Hist.

[42]David W. Cohen and Jack P. Greene, eds., *Neither Slave nor Free: The
Freedmen of African Descent in the Slave Societies of the New World* (Baltimore,
1972), pp. 4 and 10.

Table 15: Manumissions in South Carolina, 1750–90

	Decade			
Location of Master	1750s	1760s	1770s	1780s
Charleston	14	29	61	118
Lowcountry parish	17	6	17	36
Out of state	—	2	8	8
Unknown	22	5	15	36
	53	42	101	198
Sex of manumitted slave				
Adult male	13	12	22	53
Adult female	17	20	44	71
Boy	4	—	11	20
Girl	9	3	11	24
Child, sex not specified	10	7	13	30
	53	42	101	198
Color of manumitted slave				
Negro	25	24	50	68
Mulatto	8	9	28	57
Mustee	4	—	1	—
Mestizo	—	—	1	1
Yellow	—	—	—	3
Moor	—	—	—	6
Unknown	16	9	21	63
	53	42	101	198
Terms of manumission				
Manumission without pay-				
ment	40	33	65	139
Self-purchase	11 (3)*	7 (1)	20 (7)	37 (11)
Purchase by another black	2	2	3	8
Purchase by white attor-				
ney or merchant	—	—	9	11
Purchase by other white	—	—	4	3
	53	42	101	198

SOURCE: Miscellaneous Record Books LL to ZZ, South Carolina Department of Archives and History, Columbia.

*Figures in parentheses indicate cases in which the manumitted slave paid a merely nominal amount.

look. William Glen freed a mulatto slave on provision that both she and her issue "shall serve me . . . during my Natural Life and be worked and employed in such way and manner as I shall think fit."[43] More generally, the Revolutionary era witnessed a heightened racial consciousness rarely found earlier. A few runaway advertisements suggest the degree of increased white racial disdain. One described a slave as "one of those unshapely ill-formed cubs of the creation . . . , bow-legged with the calf fixed on the shin, the length of the foot from heel to toe nearly equal to the leg from ankle to knee; his ankle approaching to the ground, whilst his face bears a very exact resemblance to the picture of a baboon, drawn by a very bad artist." More succinctly, another described a black as having a "monkey face."[44] Furthermore, although slave executions seem to have declined in the late eighteenth century, South Carolina remained a society quick to execute, especially compared to Massachusetts or even Virginia.[45] By the turn of the century, as Winthrop D. Jordan has argued, the interracial mold began to harden into its familiar antebellum shape as tighter restrictions were placed on slaves,

[43]Miscellaneous Record Book XX, pp. 7–8, S.C. Dept. Arch. and Hist. Twelve manumissions were conditional in the 1760s, three in the 1770s, and forty in the 1780s.

[44]*City Gaz.*, Feb. 2, 1788, John Walters Gibbs; *Charleston Courier*, Dec. 5, 1807, Andrew Miller.

[45]The number of slave executions in South Carolina, by year, was: 1746–55, 61; 1756–65, 64; 1766–76, 62;1786–95, 41; 1796–1805, 35; 1806–15, 52. These figures are based on John D. Duncan, "Servitude and Slavery in Colonial South Carolina, 1670–1776," Ph.D. diss., Emory University, 1971, pp. 708–13, and, for the post-Revolutionary era, newspaper reports and the payments for executed slaves found in the annual resolutions of the South Carolina Session Laws, S.C. Dept. Arch. and Hist. The last two sources, when combined, give slightly higher figures than those presented in Michael Hindus, "Black Justice under White Law: Criminal Prosecutions of Blacks in Antebellum South Carolina," *Journal of American History* 63 (1976–77):595, but see that article for comparison with Massachusetts execution rates on pp. 596–97. For slave executions in Virginia (only sixty-six were recorded for the entire period, 1786–1815), see James H. Johnston, *Race Relations in Virginia and Miscegenation in the South, 1776–1860* (Amherst, Mass., 1970), pp. 317–22.

but more particularly upon free Negroes, and as separation of the races at places of social gathering became the norm.[46] If the Revolutionary War loosened the bonds of servitude for some blacks, it tightened them for many others.

In the lowcountry the events of the Revolutionary era and the long-term demographic, economic, and social trends served both to strengthen the slave system and to allow blacks greater autonomy within it. The enlarged role of black drivers illustrates this process. The confluence of long-term changes—the growing creolization of the slave population, the increased size of lowcountry plantations, the continued predominance of rice production, and more widespread white absenteeism—along with the power vacuum created by Revolutionary anarchy, created more opportunities for drivers and thereby allowed blacks to gain greater control of plantation life. In the 1780s and 1790s estate inventories listed drivers much more frequently than did those of the colonial period.[47] Furthermore, if advertisements offering drivers for sale can be trusted, more power reposed with them than ever before. Certainly some late eighteenth-century drivers came with the highest recommendations. One seller described a mulatto driver named Jonathan as "without exception one of the best drivers in this state; and there are few White Men, who have a more general or better knowledge of planting." Another description went further, claiming that "the driver is known to be equal to the management of a rice plantation, without any manager or overseer." Drivers might even have a hand in appointing their fellow drivers: one absentee South Carolina planter advised his partner to "let Sambo point out a Driver for Hampton—He knows better than I do who will answer best."[48] In some instances drivers gained complete control over the plantation routine. Frequent official admo-

---

[46]*White over Black: American Attitudes toward the Negro, 1550–1812* (Chapel Hill, N.C., 1968), pp. 403–26.

[47]Compare the number of drivers in tables 13a and 14a.

[48]*Gaz. of the State of S.C.*, Dec. 20, 1784, Alexander Rose; *Columbian Herald*, Mar. 26, 1789; Pierce Butler to Roger P. Saunders, Sept. 5, 1791, Pierce

nitions to particular individuals for not having a white man on their plantations, as well as recurrent indictments of whole regions for the same offense, suggest that the practice of leaving black drivers to their own devices was widespread. The Grand Jury of Georgetown District, for example, noted as a particular grievance "the number of plantations in this district not having any white person as overseer on them."[49] Even when a white man was present, control might be in other hands. One advertisement, which invited applications from whites for employment on a tide swamp plantation, made the importance of the driver clear: if the white were a shoemaker he could continue to follow his trade, for "the business of the plantation is conducted by a black man."[50] For this reason, no doubt, many a runaway "new Negro" could not recall his master's name but knew that of his driver.[51]

Drivers used their new preeminence to expand their own authority and, by doing so, to enlarge black autonomy within the increasingly black countryside. Most drivers seem to have formed a stable element within the slave community and were conspicuously absent from the numbers of skilled runaways (tables 13a through 14b). Standing his ground and asserting his authority, rather than abandoning his charges, seems to

---

Butler Letterbook, 1790–94, Univ. of S.C. One Georgia planter employed no overseer, preferring to entrust the routine management of his plantation, near Savannah, to his driver, Morris. Even the minimal white supervision that he did employ would have been unnecessary, he noted, had not "the Patrol behaved very ill there last Summer in my absence" (Ebeneezer Jackson to Wells, June 3, 1801, and Jackson to John Lyons, June 3, 1801, in E. Jackson Letterbooks, Duke Univ., as quoted in James H. Stone, "Black Leadership in the Old South: The Slave Drivers of the Rice Kingdom," Ph.D diss., Florida State University, 1976, pp. 149–50).

[49]*State Gaz.*, Dec. 20, 1787, Grand Jury Presentments of Georgetown District. See also, ibid., Nov. 17, 1785, Presentments of Grand Jury of District of Charleston; *S.C. State Gaz.*, Feb. 5, 1794, Grand Jury Presentments of the District of Charleston; ibid., Oct. 12, 1795, Grand Jury Presentments of the District of Charleston; *City Gaz.*, Nov. 12, 1799, Grand Jury Presentments of Beaufort District.

[50]*City Gaz.*, Mar. 12, 1800, Vanderhorst and Miller.

[51]See, for example, *Columbian Herald*, June 15, 1786, John McPherson, and *S.C. State Gaz.*, Mar. 27, 1794, A. Seixas.

have been the driver's overriding concern. A dispute between two drivers on the Pinckney plantations in the late eighteenth century apparently stemmed from the desire of each to maintain or strengthen his own sphere of influence. Much of the contention revolved about the issue of who would make the greater crop. The white manager noted at one point that "as to your Drivers they are often quarreling and jarring with each other which is a disagreeable business to me at times but I believe their jealousy of each other serves to keep them Honest." More to the point, perhaps, it served to keep them on the plantation. The conscientiousness of one of Ralph Izard's drivers was especially notable. Although there had been "considerable embezzlement" on Izard's plantations, the manager reported that on the one "plantation where you make the most to the hand & really a good Crop, there is no overseer but only a Black Driver."[52] Even the exception among drivers—Andrew, whose exploits in the Revolutionary War have already been mentioned—gained his notoriety by being the "most influential fellow in the gang" of slaves from "Ca Ira" plantation, belonging to J. and W. Mitchell. In March 1796 he led away the entire gang, some seventy slaves; eight months later only one slave had been apprehended, although evidence of their camps had been found only a quarter of a mile from a plantation mansion in Prince William's Parish, and Andrew himself had been sighted fishing in full view of that plantation. (Prince William's Parish had been Andrew's home during the Revolutionary War.) By the end of the year the Mitchells had become so exasperated at the influence of this adroit pied piper of men that they offered a $1,000 reward for the return of the gang.[53]

The growing independence of lowcountry blacks—to be seen in their numerical dominance of lowcountry parishes, in widespread black management, and augmented in the tra-

[52]William Frazer to Mrs. Harriott Horry, Oct. 8, 1792, and to Thomas Pinckney, Feb. 5, 1793, Pinckney Family Papers, Library of Congress; Charles Cotesworth Pinckney to Ralph Izard, Dec. 26, 1794, Manigault Papers, S.C. Hist. Soc.

[53]*City Gaz.*, Nov. 10 and 30, 1796, J. & W. B. Mitchell.

ditional task system—was also reflected in their ability to accumulate small amounts of property and engage in local trade. This property often originated in the produce that lowcountry slaves managed to grow by planting in their own time after completing the daily task. One late eighteenth-century planter's diary records that slaves took entire weekdays off in the height of the planting season "to finish planting their own crop." A land dispute that reached the Privy Council in 1784 revealed that one litigant's slaves "had all along [for 10 years] planted for themselves a little field on the same land." A planter in St. Paul's Parish instructed her overseer in 1783 that since the "field will be more than I shall want, what you think is to spare, let it be divided among the Negroes." One late eighteenth-century journal for a Georgetown plantation simply listed the amount of rough rice belonging to various slaves that was stored in the barn.[54]

Slaves dearly valued the property they acquired in this painstaking way. Thus, in 1779, when Eliza Pinckney wanted her slaves to move out of range of the marauding British army, the slaves refused because they were so "attached to their homes and the little they have there." On other occasions the slaves' attachment to their property could benefit their masters. In a fascinating description of a hunt for seven runaways in 1800, their owner made the telling remark that he was "convinced these runaways would not go far, being connected at home and having too much property to leave."[55] In 1772 the Charleston District Grand Jury gave an indication of the property slaves might acquire when it objected to "Negroes being allowed to keep horses . . . contrary to Law." A declaration in a dispute between a slave and his master is revealing of what one particular slave did with his horses:

[54]Allard Belin Plantation Diary, May 31, 1798, and June 1–2, 1797, S.C. Hist. Soc.; Adele Stanton Edwards, ed., *Journals of the Privy Council, 1783–1789* (Columbia, S.C., 1971), p. 132; Miscellaneous Record Book VV, pp. 213–14, S.C. Dept. Arch. and Hist.; Fairfield Plantation Book for 1773–97, undated entry, S.C. Hist. Soc.

[55]Eliza Pinckney to Thomas Pinckney, May 17, 1779, Pinckney Family Papers, S.C. Hist. Soc.; William Read to Jacob Read, Mar. 22, 1800, Read Family Papers, S.C. Hist. Soc.

This is to certify that in the year 1781 or 1782 I heard Mr. Lewis Dutarque say to his old fellow Will that he had been a faithful servant to him and if he had a mind to purchase his freedom he should obtain the same by paying him three hundred pounds old currency and [,] says he[,"] Will[,] you have two Horses which will nearly pay me. I will allow you two hundred pounds old currency for a Roan Gelding and forty five currency for your Gray[,"] for which the fellow Will readily consented to the proposals and Mr. Dutarque took possession of the Horses and the fellow Will was to pay the Balance as soon as he could make it up. Mr. Dutarque also borrowed of the fellow Will a small Black mare which he lost and he said she was worth six Guineas and would allow him that price for her.[56]

Trading horses for one's freedom was no doubt unusual, but the ability of lowcountry slaves to barter their produce (and some of their master's produce, perhaps) with the patroons of schooners, passing peddlers, and hawkers was a constant aggravation for lowcountry planters.[57] Perhaps the most striking indication of the autonomy of this black trading network is provided by a notice placed in a South Carolina newspaper: "On Sunday last was apprehended by the patrol in St. George's parish, a certain negro man who calls himself *Titus* and his son about 10 years who is called *Tom*; he was trading with the negroes in that neighborhood, and he had in possession 2 horses . . . , one poultry cart, and several articles of merchandise, consisting of stripes, linens, and handerkerchiefs."[58]

The character of city life intensified many of the changes that took place in the countryside. The Revolution no more threatened urban bondage than it did rural thralldom, but,

[56]*S.C. Gaz.*, Jan. 25, 1772, Charlestown District Grand Jury Presentments; Miscellaneous Record Book VV, p. 473. One runaway was said to be "possessed of a canoe" which he used for fishing (*City Gaz.*, Apr. 7, 1794, Henry Osborne).

[57]Lark E. Adams and Rosa Lumpkin, eds., *Journals of the House of Representatives, 1785–1786* (Columbia, S.C., 1979), p. 343; Journal of the South Carolina House of Representatives, Feb. 11, 1788; ibid., Dec. 7, 1791; *S.C. State Gaz.*, Feb. 10, 1797.

[58]*State Gaz.*, Oct. 26, 1793.

as in the countryside, urban slaves gained greater independence even as slavery became more entrenched. The number of slaves in Charleston doubled between 1760 and 1800, although the proportion of lowcountry slaves resident in the city increased only slightly during those years (table 2). By the late eighteenth century a sizable number of slaves had grown up in an urban environment. If the skill level among lowcountry slaves rose in general in the late eighteenth century, it did so most intensively for urban slaves. In the late eighteenth century a whole host of white mechanics—house carpenters, bricklayers, shoemakers, master tailors, and master coopers—bombarded the South Carolina legislature with petitions complaining of the threat posed to their respective livelihoods by the "Number of Jobbing Negro Tradesmen in the city."[59] Similarly, if trading was a possibility for rural slaves, urban opportunities were that much greater. Slave women hawked cakes, tarts, and bread about the streets; others sold milk, garden produce, and fruit; and one even sold sand.[60] Slave men dominated the fishing trade, the fish market, and the butchering business.[61] Whites commonly associated black urban trading with criminality: one owner learned that his two runaways subsisted "by picking chickapins, which they sell in town, and what poultry, hogs or plunder of any kind they can lay their hands on"; two runaways from the parish of St. James Goosecreek were frequently "seen going backwards and forwards to town, by land and water; and since they have got a canoe, they have been seen three or four times in the lower market, selling what they have plundered

[59]Senate Journal, Feb. 22, 1783, Petition of House Carpenters and Bricklayers of Charleston; *State Gaz.*, Nov. 9, 1793, Cordwainers and others; ibid., Dec. 7, 1793, Master Taylors; *S.C. State Gaz.*, Oct. 12, 1795, Grand Jury Presentments of the District of Charleston.

[60]See, for example, *State Gaz.*, Feb. 13, 1786, Ichabod Atwell; *City Gaz.*, July 18, 1788, Mrs. Meyers; ibid., July 8, 1789, Richard Wayne; *Charleston Courier*, Sept. 30, 1806, S. Benoit; *S.C. State Gaz.*, Feb. 10, 1796, Caspar C. Schutt; ibid., Dec. 22, 1796, John Love; ibid., Sept. 14, 1798, Mathew D'Harriot; *Charleston Courier*, Feb. 10, 1803, John Gensel.

[61]See, for example, *City Gaz.*, Apr. 4, 1788, Francis Breen; *Charleston Courier*, Nov. 18, 1807, Joseph Seabrook; *S.C. State Gaz.*, Oct. 15, 1796, Bryan Connor; *City Gaz.*, July 11, 1799, John Strobel.

from neighbouring plantations"; another runaway was known to be in "company with a fellow of Mr. George Rise on Daniels Island, and some of Mr. Isaac Barkers negroes. They have a boat and go a fishing, and are frequently on South Bay selling fish."[62] Slave control of lowcountry marketing often amounted to a near monopoly, and white authorities accused them of withholding goods to raise prices and increase their profits. By 1799 Charleston's Grand Jury recommended that "the laws against forestalling may be put in execution, as this grievance is grown to a very great magnitude; and that the clerk of the market may be empowered to remove the number of negro hucksters from about the markets." In 1803 the City Council imposed new regulations, but it is doubtful whether they eradicated the central role of slave marketeers.[63]

The same combination of long-term forces and short-run events that allowed slaves to enlarge their independence also allowed them to secure their family life. The growing proportion of creoles in the slave population; the consolidation of Tidewater rice production and the rise of sea island cotton cultivation, both of which tied lowcountry slaves ever more closely to the coast; and the direct importation of slaves to meet backcountry demand—all facilitated the amplification of slave family ties in the lowcountry. As a result, late eighteenth-century masters seemed more respectful of those ties than their predecessors. For example, gangs would often be sold "in families" rather than individually, and many a prospective purchaser stated a preference for family units.[64] One

[62]*S.C. State Gaz.*, Oct. 15, 1796, Timothy and Mason; *City Gaz.*, Aug. 21, 1798, James W. Gadsden; *S.C. State Gaz.*, Apr. 21, 1798, John Marshall. See also *Charleston Courier*, July 11, 1804, Jacine Laval.

[63]*S.C. State Gaz.*, Feb. 7, 1799, Presentments of the Charleston Grand Jury. See also *State Gaz.*, Feb. 23, 1786, Presentments of the Charleston Grand Jury; ibid., June 20, 1791, Presentments of the Grand Jury for the District of Charleston; *Times*, June 23, 1803.

[64]For examples of gangs that would only be sold "in families," see *State Gaz.*, Nov. 6, 1786, John Walker Gibbs; *Charleston Courier*, Jan. 18, 1803, Benjamin Stead.

planter advertised for twenty or thirty native-born field hands "in large families, the more so the more agreeable," and another would not purchase "any gang where any of the slaves have been separated from their families."[65] The sale of loyalist slave gangs demonstrates the point. The majority of slaves in those gangs were bought by a single purchaser who generally kept whole families together (table 16). Masters who respected the integrity of slave family life were probably acceding to slave demands rather than acting on their own initiative. Occasionally this new concern can be seen emerging: when one master's patroon became "dissatisfied, and desirous of being sold," his wife had also to be sold, "for a principle of humanity *alone*," the master assured prospective buyers, "as they were very unwilling to be separated."[66] A humorous notice in a late eighteenth-century South Carolina newspaper reflected black assertiveness in domestic affairs:

A minister being possessed of a wench to whom a certain Negro man made his addresses: The parson having some objections which he made to the poor black, who, not liking this opposition to his courtship took the liberty to ask him a question, viz. *Massar no wat de elebenth commandment be?* The parson could not tell. "Well," says the negro, "me tell wat it be: *De elebenth commandment is* BES WAY EVERY ONE MINE HE OWN BISNESS."[67]

Even when they broke slave family ties, masters recognized their importance. Thus when Thomas Wright decided on his deathbed to give a slave boy to his friend Stephen Tamplet, the boy's mother was directed to bring him into the dying man's room so that the gift could be sealed, but "Mr. Wright observing that it might occasion some uneasiness amongst his Negroes, ordered the wench to carry out the child, and rising

[65]*State Gaz.*, June 23, 1788, Robert Norris & Co.; *S.C. State Gaz.*, Sept. 28, 1797, Francis Levett.

[66]*City Gaz.*, Dec. 15, 1800, John Webb & Co.

[67]*State Gaz.*, Nov. 26, 1793. Less humorous but no less assertive was the response of a gang of thirteen slaves, comprising three families, who ran away when "ordered to remove" from their Jack Savannah plantation (ibid., Apr. 3, 1786, Abraham Ladson).

Table 16: Sales of various loyalist estates

Slave gangs belonging to various loyalists	Two-parent families		Single-parent families		Extended families		Solitaries	Total persons	Percent of slave gang bought by named purchaser
	No.	Children	No.	Children	No.	Persons			
George Saxby's slaves Purchased by J. Allston	9	17			3	14		49	89%
Dr. Gibb's slaves Purchased by J. Stanly	6	16					3	31	74
Dr. Crokatt's slaves Purchased by J. Allston	1	0	2	6			9	19	73
Thomas Boone's slaves Purchased by N. Greene	4	7	7	21			8	51	65
Richard Pendarvis's slaves Purchased by W. H. Wigg	5	3					1	14	38
Purchased by A. Gibbon	4	2					4	14	38

SOURCE: Commissioners of Forfeited Estates: Sales of Lands and Negroes, South Carolina Department of Archives and History, Columbia.

up in his Bed, delivered a penknife to Stephen Tamplet as earnest of [the] Gift."[68]

If black desires as much as white solicitude *and* heartlessness shaped slave family life, the institution itself continued to grow in strength and complexity. From the 1770s to the 1790s, just under a third of all inventoried slaves were listed in families (table 17). These statistics, however, are heavily reliant upon the whim of estate appraisors (some noted family ties, others did not). Focusing only on those inventoried plantations whose slaves were ordered in families, some two-thirds of the slaves on such estates were listed in families in the 1760s, whereas by the end of the eighteenth century that proportion had risen to four-fifths.[69] Similarly, in the 1760s only 2 percent of such slaves were ordered in extended families; by the 1790s that proportion had risen to 11 percent. Indeed, by the late eighteenth century extended families began to make an appearance in notices for runaway slaves. One group, for example, spanned four generations, with a great-grandmother, a thirty-five-year-old grandmother, a mother, and her child running away together.[70] So commonplace had the legitimacy and stability of slave marriages become that planters could specially note illegitimate births. One lowcountry planter registered 160 slave births between 1730 and 1805; of these, 9, to four different slave mothers, were listed as illegitimate.[71] By the 1780s family units constituted 12 percent of all runaways; in the 1760s the proportion had been only 4 percent.[72] Furthermore, of those advertised run-

[68]Miscellaneous Record Book RR, p. 349, Oct. 28, 1775.

[69]For a discussion of the methodology involved in calculating which inventories can be incorporated into this analysis, see Morgan, "Development of Slave Culture," pp. 313–14.

[70]*State Gaz.*, Aug. 8, 1785, Charles H. Simmons. For less dramatic examples, see *S.C. State Gaz.*, Nov. 17, 1796, Colcock and Paterson; *City Gaz.*, June 20, 1797, Leo Harth; *Charleston Courier*, Jan. 3, 1806; *State Gaz.*, Sept. 18, 1788, A. Waight; *Charleston Courier*, Nov. 18, 1807, Joseph Seabrook.

[71]Notebook, Ravenel Papers.

[72]Fifty-two slaves ran away in family units in the 1760s; 118 in the 1780s. A runaway slave woman with a young child was not counted as a family unit in this tabulation. For the newspapers examined, see table 12.

Table 17: South Carolina slave families as revealed in inventories, 1760–99

Period	Two-parent families			Single-parent families		Extended families		Solitaries	Total slaves on plantation	Percentage of slaves in families
	No.	Childless	No. of children	No.	No. of children	No.	Persons			
1760–69	895	330	1,175	270	534	16	77	1,952	5,798	66.3%
1770–79	1,504	516	2,247	445	941	29	97	3,027	9,765	69.0
1783–89	822	266	1,363	344	660	75	398	1,318	5,727	77.0
1790–99	764	252	1,369	427	936	98	556	1,289	6,105	78.9

SOURCES: South Carolina Inventory Books T to CC and Charleston District Inventory Books, vols. A, B, and C, South Carolina Department of Archives and History, Columbia.

*NOTE: The figures in this table derive only from those inventories that reveal unequivocally the existence of family ties. Such inventories represent 17 percent of all inventoried slaves in the early 1760s and 30 percent in the late 1790s.

aways for whom a motive was given, more than two-thirds in every decade of the Revolutionary era were thought to be "visiting" either friends, acquaintances, or relatives (table 18). By the late eighteenth century, the network of acquaintances and relatives by whom a runaway might be sheltered grew so large as to render virtually meaningless the advertised predictions of a fugitive slave's whereabouts. One forty-five-year-old woman, for example, "had a husband at the plantation of Hugh Willson, esq., James Island, has relatives at the plantation of the Rev. Dr. Frost, Goosecreek and has a son at the plantation of Doctor Jones, in the same parish; she is well known in the city, probably she may make for Georgetown, being well acquainted there."[73]

The character of post-Revolutionary Afro-American culture reveals growing black independence within an increasingly powerful slave system. The need to compensate for wartime manpower losses and a resilient and, later, booming economy led Georgia and South Carolina to reopen the African slave trade. Thus, although the proportion of Africans in South Carolina's adult slave population declined from 45 percent in 1760 to about 9 percent in 1800—and then rose slightly to about 20 percent in 1810 as African imports reached the state—that proportion of Africans was still higher than was to be found in any other region of mainland North America (table 7). Moreover, the pattern of the post-Revolutionary slave trade allowed newly arrived Africans a greater degree of cultural coherence than their declining proportion in the slave population suggests. Analysis of the regional origins of slaves imported from Africa indicates that while African cargoes had become increasingly more heterogeneous in the late colonial period, one or two regions dominated the trade during the two periods in the post-Revolutionary era when Africans were imported (table 19). Indeed, in the first decade of the nineteenth century, South Carolina imported almost half its Africans from Angola. Only in the 1730s had any regional group dominated the trade to anything like the same extent. Traders sent a majority of these Africans to the

[73]*Times*, Jan. 6, 1803, John Cape.

Table 18: South Carolina runaway slaves as advertised in newspapers, 1760–1806

Runaways	Decade				
	1760–69	1770–79	1780–89	1790–99	1800–1806
Fugitive slaves advertised	901	1,209	640	648	391
Captured slaves advertised	526	719	343	187	179
Total	1,427	1,928	983	835	570
Percentage of slaves running away in groups	39%	32%	37%	24%	25%
Percentage of slaves with attributed motives who were said to be visiting	70%	72%	73%	70%	73%

SOURCES: Charleston Library Society, South Carolina Newspapers, 1732–82 (microfilm), The Johns Hopkins University, Baltimore. For the years after 1782: extant issues of the *South Carolina Weekly Gazette* (1783–86), *South Carolina Gazette and General Advertiser* (1783–85), *Gazette of the State of South Carolina* (1783–85), *Columbian Herald* (1784–89), *State Gazette of South Carolina* (1785–89), *Charleston Morning Post* (1786–87), and *City Gazette* (1787–89), Charleston Library Society, Charleston, S.C.; and microfilm copies of *State Gazette of South Carolina* (1790–1802), *City Gazette* (1790–1801), *Columbian Herald* (1794), *Columbia Gazette* (1790–96), *Charleston Courier* (1803–6), and *Times* (1803), University of South Carolina, Columbia.

NOTE: This analysis has not yet been extended to 1809, and all newspapers published in the post-Revolutionary years have not yet been searched. These figures are therefore provisional.

backcountry (table 3), but the sea islands also received a disproportionate share. For example, a listing of Col. John Stapleton's slaves on St. Helena Island in 1810 reveals that almost
half the adults were recently purchased Africans.[74]

The pattern of the slave trade thus allowed some Africans
to maintain ethnic ties in the early national lowcountry. In
1785, for instance, two recently imported Africans left an
Edisto Island plantation, and their master "supposed they
went off with two new negroes (countrymen of theirs) belonging to Mr. John Jenkins, in his four-oared boat"; an "Ebo"
slave who ran away the same year was seen with "a tall, ill-
looking fellow of the same country"; a "Mandingo" slave who
absconded in 1807 was "supposed to be secreted by some of
his country people."[75] Other newly arrived blacks maintained
shipmate relationships. The master of one African reckoned
that his slave had absconded to a shipyard near Charleston
where there were "some negroes [who had been] purchased
out of the same ship."[76] For yet others, commandeering a
canoe, as ten new Negroes did in 1785, in order "to return
to their own country," was another, albeit foolhardy, course
of action.[77] However successful various ethnic African groups
were in maintaining a loose association, it is indisputable that
the African slave was still very visible in the late eighteenth-
century lowcountry. Occasionally a glimpse of African culture in the new land is captured: a "Mandingo NEGRO MAN"
arrived at a Santee plantation in 1805 and spoke "the Guinea
language to one of [the] Negroes" on the plantation.[78] Much

---

[74]List of Negroes belonging to Colonel Stapleton on his Plantation at St.
Helena, Mar. 15, 1810, John Stapleton Papers, Univ. of S.C. I estimate, as
table 3 indicates, that four times as many Africans went to the backcountry
as to the lowcountry between 1800 and 1810 (or, more precisely, between
1804 and 1807).

[75]*Columbian Herald*, May 23, 1785, Charles Daily; *S.C. Weekly Gaz.*, July
26, 1785, James and Edward Penman; *Charleston Courier*, Aug. 14, 1807.

[76]*S.C. Weekly Gaz.*, Oct. 18, 1785, Charles Morgan.

[77]Ibid., Oct. 27, 1785, Charleston News. Interesting in this regard is the
case in 1807 of twelve slaves from Angola who accompanied a native-born
slave "who was persuading them that he was taking them back to their own
country" (*Charleston Courier*, Dec. 28, 1807, William Boyd).

Table 19: Origins of South Carolina's African slaves

Coastal region of origin	Percentage of slaves of identifiable origin				
	1760–64	1765–69	1770–74	1783–87	1804–7
Senegambia	22%	23%	30%	15%	6%
Sierra Leone	11	6	18	3	2
Windward Coast	25	29	14	13	23
Gold Coast	11	16	18	46	13
Bight of Benin	3	2	4	—	1
Bight of Biafra	—	—	2	4	3
Angola	27	23	14	19	49
East Africa	—	—	—	—	2
Total	99	99	100	100	99
Number for whom origins known	8,810	9,981	16,882	5,777	35,321
Total number of imported Africans	10,308	13,055	21,735	c. 10,000	39,519

SOURCES: Colonial sources: South Carolina Treasury General Duty Books; South Carolina Naval Office Shipping Lists; South Carolina newspapers; and Elizabeth Donnan, ed., *Documents Illustrative of the History of the Slave Trade to America*, 4 vols. (1930–35; reprint ed., New York, 1969), 4:235–471. Early national sources: Donnan, ed., *Documents Illustrative of the Slave Trade*; post-Revolutionary newspapers; and South Carolina Archives Microcopy no. 6, *Duties on Trade at Charleston, 1784–89*.

more commonplace must have been the sight of filed teeth, African jewelry (one woman from the "Gola contry" wore "5 strings of red and blue beads round her neck; also a link with 2 red and 1 green ditto in her right ear, and a small iron ring in her left ear") and the inevitable cicatrizations (he has "two scars on each side of his face, as we suppose he had from his country, as most of them have").[79]

Black independence was not predicated, however, on the maintenance of African culture. Slaves knowledgeable of white ways also maximized their independence. By the late eighteenth century, slaves born and reared in North America had assimilated Anglo-American culture to an extent that included its distinct regional dialects. A slave imported from Baltimore had a "remarkable speech like persons from the back parts of Virginia"; many others were simply said to "speak the back country dialect"; another was "Virginian by birth and has that accent."[80] Runaway advertisements offer further indications of slaves' increasing familiarity with Anglo-American culture. Fugitives included slaves who could play European musical instruments;[81] more runaways could read and write than had been the case earlier in the century;[82] other individual fugitives understood "French cookery," wore "goggles" to compensate for weak eyes, dressed in finery that "excel[led] that of his master," or "[wore] false hair under a

[78]*Charleston Courier*, Mar. 23, 1805, Elias Horry; see also *State Gaz.*, Nov. 6, 1786, Charles Ferguson.

[79]Post-Revolutionary newspaper advertisements described 47 runaway slaves with filed teeth and 140 with ethnic markings. For the slave with jewelry, see *State Gaz.*, July 21, 1785, Workhouse. For the newspapers examined, see table 12.

[80]*City Gaz.*, Apr. 24, 1788, Snowden, Lothrop & Forrest; *Charleston Courier*, July 20, 1803, Margretta D. Schutt; ibid., Aug. 7, 1805, Roger Moore Smith.

[81]Post-Revolutionary newspapers mentioned twenty-two such slaves, compared to eighteen cited in the colonial press. For the newspapers examined, see table 12.

[82]Post-Revolutionary newspapers mentioned fourteen such slaves, compared to nine cited in the colonial press. For the newspapers examined, see table 12.

handkerchief or hat."[83] As many blacks gained a knowledge of the countryside, control over work routines, and even a degree of literacy, the perpetual testing of wills between master and slave assumed new dimensions. Toward the close of the century, for example, one master wrote to his overseer that a runaway named Philip should be confined to the "sugar house" when captured; Philip intercepted the message and was far from dismayed by its contents; rather, he was "so sattisfi'd" at not having to return to his master that he immediately surrendered himself and claimed his punishment. The overseer felt constrained to countermand the order so as to retain some semblance of authority.[84]

The slaves most knowledgeable of Anglo-American culture had been brought up in Charleston. For this reason, when an errand-boy and cook were required by one master, he specified that "country Negroes not well acquainted with Town, would be preferred"; similarly, when offering a thirteen-year-old girl for sale, her master was quick to point out that she was "free from all town tricks."[85] Many masters equated "town tricks" with drunkenness. Thus one Charleston resident reckoned his domestic slave might "make a valuable servant to a person residing in the country, where he cannot get at liquor." Another urban master described his cooper as "too much inclined to drink" but thought he could "answer any Planter in the country, and will not be sold to reside in town."[86] Even the Negro boys in Charleston were vexing. A lady who exercised daily on the road leading from Charleston informed the residents that "repeatedly Boys and *even very small ones*, accompanied by *Negro Boys* are imprudently intrusted

[83]*City Gaz.*, Aug. 26, 1800, Joseph Jahan; ibid., June 21, 1797, Thomas Frost; ibid., July 19, 1797, Patrick Byrne; ibid., Apr. 20, 1798, William Roper.

[84]Michael Boineau to J. E. Colhoun, June 11, 1798, John Ewing Colhoun Papers, Univ. of S.C.

[85]*Gaz. of the State of S.C.*, May 6, 1784; *City Gaz.*, June 22, 1797, William Marshall.

[86]*City Gaz.*, Jan. 3, 1788, Sims White and Company; *S.C. State Gaz.*, Mar. 2, 1798, Francis Robertson.

by their parents with Guns, and often shoot across the road, by which means danger will often happen by accident, either by their shot or frightening the horses." Taken to task by the harassed lady, one of the black boys responded that "he *belonged to himself* and *did not care*."[87] Presumably it was boys like these who led "A Magistrate" to suggest in 1794 that a building on the outskirts of the city be converted for the ginning and cleaning of cotton. This enterprise would then recruit, according to this gentleman, the "2,000 idle profligate little negroes and mulatoes, whose employ is to parade through our streets, fighting, swearing, stealing, and, in fact, training up to the gallows and destruction, corrupting the morals of our infants just peeping into life."[88] The insouciance of the urban runaway is captured in one master's claim that his fugitive could be "very easily caught, as he is very lazy [and] sleeps pretty late." Insolence more aptly characterizes another urban slave who was sold "for no other fault than being too much her own mistress. If locked out at ten o'clock, she jumps the fence and forces a window open to get into the house." But the ultimate in self-possession must be reserved for the "negro man [who] stole into the house No 2 St. Michael's alley, and, while the family were at supper in the adjoining room began to pack up every thing that was portable; but perceiving himself seen by a young girl, he told her that he was come for his master's great coat, and gave her a hat to carry into the next room, while he leisurely walked down stairs and escaped."[89] Such was the stuff of which the late eigh-

---

[87]*Charleston Courier*, Nov. 7, 1806.

[88]*S.C. State Gaz.*, Apr. 21, 1794, A Magistrate.

[89]*State Gaz.*, Aug. 2, 1793, Laval; *City Gaz.*, July 24, 1800, M. Russell; ibid., Apr. 3, 1788. Not all the activities of urban blacks proved objectionable. The Charleston Guard forced its way into a house late one November night where a "Negro dance" was being held, only to encounter a white magistrate who claimed "that there was none in the House but friends . . . who were amusing themselves." At least two other whites were present. As one of the Negro women was taken into custody, she handed the magistrate "her Head Dress and Bonnet and desired him to take Care of it for her" (Depositions of Peter S. Ryan, William Johnson and James Allison, James McBride, and Henry Moses, Nov. 7, 1795, General Assembly, Governor's Messages, no. 650, Nov. 24, 1795, pp. 9–30, S.C. Dept. Arch. and

teenth-century urban slave was made—the most sophisticated segment of an increasingly sophisticated slave group.

And yet most lowcountry slaves in the late eighteenth century were neither Africans nor urban Afro-Saxons. Instead,
they had begun to create their own culture, incorporat-
ing many of the characteristics of both the newly arrived
Africans and the alien world of their masters. The new
Afro-American culture could be observed most readily in the
language of lowcountry slaves. While a small minority spoke
African languages and another minority could be described
as speaking "correct English," perhaps even with a pronounced regional accent, the majority carved out something
just as distinctive. Runaway advertisements offer the best insight here: he "speaks a little more properly than Negroes do
in general," and he speaks "plain and tolerably free from the
common negro dialect" are just two ordinary descriptions that
suggest how whites viewed the speech of the common run of
lowcountry slaves.[90] One lowcountry mistress was even more
illuminating. She acknowledged that one of her slaves, Ralph,
"speaks [English] very badly; I cant understand him," although another of her slaves assured her that Ralph himself
"understands English very well." Another master described
one of his slaves who had been a longtime resident in South
Carolina as having "generally much to say tho' he is not easily
understood, unless by those who have been used to him."[91]
Even one or two American-born slaves were described as
speaking "broken English."[92] But perhaps the most revealing

---

Hist. Sexual liaisons between whites and blacks in Charleston are implied
in an account of "Gentlemen" visiting "some Mulatto Girls" (Diary of Catherine De Rosset, July 8, 1798, De Rosset Family Papers, S. Hist. Coll., Univ.
of N.C., Chapel Hill).

[90]*Gaz. of the State of S.C.*, Nov. 1, 1784, Paul Hamilton; *State Gaz.*, Feb.
18, 1790, James Kennedy. See also ibid., Aug. 14, 1786, Henry Bell; *City
Gaz.*, July 26, 1799, Mary Eddings.

[91]Eliza Pinckney to Harriott Horry, c. Mar. 1775, in Elise Pinckney, ed.,
"Letters of Eliza Lucas Pinckney, 1768–1782," *South Carolina Historical
Magazine* 76 (1975):151; *City Gaz.*, Jan. 17, 1798, John Glen.

[92]See *State Gaz.*, June 30, 1785, John Gerley; ibid., Sept. 1, 1785, John
Gerley.

comment came from a Baptist minister who was "puzzled respecting the language [an instructional text designed for the
use of Negroes] should be written in." He seems to have decided on a standard English style rather than "the Negro stile,"
for he reckoned "the language will suit the whole state at
large better than strictly the lowcountry Lingo." From his
"acquaintance with the Negroes," he noted that "there is a
great diversity in their manner of expressing themselves. Many
words they will pronounce their own way, let them be spelt
as they may. Those of them who can read, learn to read by
our common spelling, & would be at a loss to read their own
lingo as we would spell it."[93]

Just as native-born lowcountry slaves grew up speaking a
language that was neither African nor necessarily standard
English, so slave life for the majority became in many ways
(not just linguistically) disengaged from the white world. This
detachment might go no further than a name. One "Gullah"
slave was "named Castania," according to his master, but "the
name he gave himself last was *Bram*." A slave named Abner
was "commonly called Plenty by the negroes of his acquaintance."[94] Or the social distance might be signified by personal
decoration. One runaway was described as having "very bushy
hair which he usually ornaments into several small plaits."
Plaiting rather than queuing, wearing a handkerchief rather
than a hat, were small but probably significant means of self-
assertion.[95] More substantive was the nighttime dancing that
occasionally came to the attention of whites. One visitor to
Beale's Wharf in Charleston witnessed the return of about
forty black men and women from Sullivan's Island at 6:00 in

[93]Edmund Botsford to Dr. Richard Furman, Oct. 15, 1808, Botsford
Papers, Baptist Historical Collection, Furman University, Greenville, S.C.

[94]*City Gaz.*, Oct. 29, 1790, Jacob Sass; *S.C. State Gaz.*, Jan. 5, 1796, Ben-
nois & Co. One slave reported that his "name is Marcelah but for shortness
is called General Moses"; since the latter is hardly an abbreviation of the
former, it seems likely that the name had a more personal significance (*City
Gaz.*, July 28, 1797, A. Seixas).

[95]*City Gaz.*, Oct. 26, 1799, John Ward. See also *S.C. State Gaz.*, Oct. 5,
1798, T. W. Price; *City Gaz.*, July 25, 1800, William Kingsborough; ibid.,
Dec. 25, 1800; *Times*, Mar. 7, 1803, B. D. Roper.

the morning. "Curiosity," he reported, "led me to enquire what such a number had been amusing themselves with during the night, and I found they had been dancing and carousing from Saturday night, until near sunrise . . . to the number, I was informed, of about one hundred."[96] There were also rare glimpses of a distinctive set of magical beliefs. Thus various slave testimonies against a slave named John, executed on suspicion of poisoning a white, revealed that John had boasted of going "to a free school to learn To Conjure sixteen years"; the slave Nat testified that John had "told him that he could give poison that [Nat's] father Could not Cure (viz. this s[ai]d Nats father is allowd to be one of the most skilful doctors in these pa[r]ts of a negro—also in Conjuration)"; others told of being rubbed by John and falling ill, of resorting to an "old Negro Conjurer" to ward off John's powers, of hearing John wish for a "Rattle snakes head [so that] he Could do well Enough."[97]

Patterns of resistance, and white perceptions of them, changed as the new Afro-American culture emerged. For one thing (as table 18 suggests), the overall number of runaways seems to have decreased as the African component in the population declined. (South Carolina's runaway population had always been dominated by Africans, as table 7 indicates). Secondly, group running away also declined (table 18). As the population as a whole creolized, individual escapes became the norm.[98] Equally important, however, given the presence of a still sizable group of Africans and a partially assimilated majority, collective action persisted. The most spectacular examples of maroon groups in South Carolina history occurred during the middle years of the 1780s and from the southernmost extremities of South Carolina and northernmost Georgia; some of these groups could trace a direct link to the period of wartime anarchy. More surprising perhaps was the continued presence of runaway camps even

[96]*Charleston Courier*, Aug. 14, 1804, A Bye Stander.

[97]Petition of Leroy Beauford, General Assembly, Petitions, 1800, no. 174.

[98]For parallels, see Gerald W. Mullin, *Flight and Rebellion: Slave Resistance in Eighteenth-Century Virginia* (New York, 1972).

in the vicinity of Charleston.[99] Finally, although the last decade of the eighteenth and first few years of the nineteenth centuries were notable for producing a number of slave-insurrection scares, lowcountry masters appear to have come to terms with a black majority that had staked out its territory. Significantly, most of the scares were perceived to stem

[99]For accounts of the most spectacular maroon groups, see William B. Stevens, *A History of Georgia* . . . , 2 vols. (1859; reprint ed., Savannah, 1972), 2:376–78; Edwards, *Journals of the Privy Council*, pp. 186 and 203–4; *State Gaz.*, Jan. 8, 1787; Journal of the South Carolina House of Representatives, Mar. 19, 1787; J. L. Bourquin Jr. to J. Hartshone, Mar. 14, 1787, General Assembly, Governor's Messages, no. 423, Mar. 19, 1787, pp. 11–12; Account of Expenditures . . . , General Assembly, Governor's Messages, no. 459, Feb. 26, 1788, pp. 5–8. Perhaps the best account of one such expedition not previously referred to by historians comes from the *Charleston Morning Post*, Oct. 26, 1786, and deserves quotation in full: "A number of runaway Negroes (supposed to be upwards of 100) having sheltered themselves on Belleisle Island, about 17 or 18 miles up Savannah River, and for some time past committed robberies on the neighboring Planters, it was found necessary to attempt to dislodge them. On Wednesday the 11th inst. a small party of Militia landed and attacked them, and killed three or four, but were at last obliged to retire for want of ammunition, having four of their number wounded. The same evening, near to sunset, fifteen of the Savannah Light Infantry and three or four others drove in one of their out guards, but the Negroes came down in such numbers that it was judged advisable to return to their boats, from which the Negroes attempted to cut them off, but were prevented by Lieutenant Elfe of the artillery, who commanded a boat with 11 of the company, and had a field piece on board, which he discharged three times with a grape shot, and it is thought either killed or wounded some of them, as a good deal of blood was afterwards seen about the place to which the shot was directed. On Friday morning General Jackson with a party proceeded to their camp, which they had quitted precipitately on his approach. He remained 'till Saturday afternoon, when he left the island, having destroyed as much rough rice as would have made 25 barrels or more if beat out, and brought off about 60 bushels of corn, and 14 or 15 boats and canoes from the landing. He also burnt a number of their houses and huts, and destroyed about four acres of green rice. The loss of their provisions it is expected will occasion them to disperse about the country, and it is hoped will be the means of most of them being soon taken up."

For examples of runaway camps near Charleston, see *Columbian Herald*, May 18, 1786, Charleston News; *City Gaz.*, June 13, 1788, William Cunnington; ibid., Aug. 21, 1797, John Freaser; *Gaz. of the State of S.C.*, Nov. 18, 1784, James Thomson; Executive Journal of Governor John Drayton, 1800, p. 114, S.C. Dept. Arch. and Hist.

from outsiders: whites feared either slaves imported from the Chesapeake, free blacks from Saint-Domingue, or even blacks supposedly landed by a French fleet.[100] South Carolinians began to boast, in the words of James Allison, that "not a single negro of our own country was in any way concerted" in these threatening events.[101] Furthermore, these persistent scares produced only two slave executions; and from about 1802 to the Denmark Vesey plot in 1822, lowcountry whites seem to have been little disturbed by the threat of insurrection. The good fortune attending lowcountry whites can be explained by the convergence of many of the trends and features of lowcountry society already outlined—from the ability of whites to mobilize forces of repression to the ability of the slaves to carve out a meaningful, if necessarily constrained, social world.

Throughout the latter half of the eighteenth century, long-term demographic and economic trends that had been fully evident at midcentury increasingly made themselves felt. Slaves

[100]For fears about imported Chesapeake slaves, see *City Gaz.*, June 4 and 11, Aug. 6 and 17, and Sept. 5, 1792, and Pierce Butler to John Bee Holmes, Nov. 5, 1793, Pierce Butler Letterbook, 1790–94. For the fear of repercussions from Saint-Domingue, see *State Gaz.*, Sept. 15, 1791; ibid., July 29, Aug. 12, and Nov. 2, 1793; letters from "Rusticus" (attributed to Alexander Garden) addressed to "Gentlemen," June 20 and Aug. 7, 1794, Misc. Mss., S.C. Hist. Soc.; Mary Pinckney to Mrs. Manigault, Feb. 5, 1798, Manigault Family Papers, Univ. of S.C.; Jacob Read to Charles Pinckney, Nov. 28, 1798, General Assembly, Governor's Messages, no. 722, Nov. 28, 1798, pp. 91–94; petition of John Desbeaux, Dec. 4, 1798, General Assembly Petitions. For one insurrection scare in 1800, concerning a ship with black troops under French command in British employ which arrived in Charleston from Jamaica, see Executive Journal of Governor John Drayton, 1800–1801, pp. 33, 34, 35, 41, and 42–43. For another scare in 1800, this one concerning the repercussions of Gabriel's insurrection in Virginia, see ibid., pp. 170–72, and Col. A. Vanderhorst to Maj. J. Pucey, Sept. 27, 1800, Vanderhorst Regiment Records, S.C. Hist. Soc. For fears about a landing of French Negroes, see Howard A. Ohline, "Georgetown, South Carolina: Racial Anxieties and Militant Behavior, 1802," *South Carolina Historical Magazine* 73 (1972):130–40. For the best insight into the anxieties plaguing planters in 1802, see A. Vanderhorst to Thomas Cooper Vanderhorst, Nov. 1, 1802, Vanderhorst and Duncombe Collection, Bristol Record Office, Bristol, England.

[101]J. Allison to Jacob Read, Dec. 5, 1797, Read Papers, Duke Univ.

were distributed more evenly throughout the lowcountry, they increasingly outnumbered whites, they resided on larger and larger units, their families became ever more important to them, drivers became progressively more prominent in the slave community, and property accumulation and trading proceeded apace. There were subtle changes: if importation was still a mechanism that the lowcountry could not disavow, seasoned as well as African slaves were now brought in; if work routines did not change markedly in the late eighteenth century, the rise of cotton production and expansion of Tidewater rice cultivation maintained the stability of the lowcountry population. If the thrust of these trends was toward the greater entrenchment of slavery and the increased autonomy of blacks, the Revolutionary War appears to have intensified the process. It was the convergence of these long-term trends, subtle changes, and wartime experiences that produced a distinctive lowcountry social world—one in which planters were more deeply committed to slavery and slaves enjoyed a larger degree of autonomy than anywhere else on mainland North America.

ALLAN KULIKOFF

Uprooted Peoples
Black Migrants in the
Age of the American Revolution
1790–1820

THE ERA OF the American Revolution witnessed major changes in the lives of Afro-American slaves in the Chesapeake, the Carolinas, and Georgia. During the middle two-thirds of the eighteenth century, many creole blacks had secured a stable family life, and few had been forced to move more than twenty miles from their birthplaces. Black bondsmen and women had established flourishing communities on the increasingly large quarters of the Chesapeake region and on the vast plantations of coastal South Carolina and Georgia. The Revolutionary settlement, however, freed white farmers and planters to evict Indian tribes from lands west of the Allegheny Mountains, and thousands of whites poured into Kentucky, Tennessee, Georgia, Mississippi, and Alabama during the generation following the adoption of the Constitution. The white man's new opportunities disrupted whatever security slaves had enjoyed before the Revolution. Between 1790 and 1820, white slaveowners took nearly a quarter million of them hundreds of miles from their families and friends to cultivate tobacco or cotton on frontier plantations, thereby smashing the fragile security of the slave community. Even

The author completed this essay while a Fellow at the Charles Warren Center for Studies in American History, Harvard University. He would like to thank Herbert G. Gutman, Michael Mullin, Darrett Rutman, the editors of this volume, and especially Stanley L. Engerman for their comments.

143

this huge migration failed to meet the frontier demand for labor, and at least 100,000 Africans destined for the back-country landed at Savannah and Charleston between 1783 and 1807.[1]

The disruption of colonial black life began during the 1770s when both the patriots and the British and their loyalist allies vied for the allegiance of slaves. Wherever British soldiers or sailors fought, blacks ran away in large numbers to join them and escape slavery. About 5,000 Virginia and Maryland slaves from the Eastern Shore and the lower James River reached British lines, and as many as 13,000 South Carolina slaves escaped to the British, the chaotic Carolina backcountry, Florida, or elsewhere. These fugitives, along with others from North Carolina and Georgia, constituted around 5 percent of all blacks in the southern colonies.[2] While many of the fleeing slaves died from hunger or disease or met death on

[1]Most of the work on slave migration focuses on the antebellum period, but useful materials can be found in Philip D. Morgan's essay in this volume, "Black Society in the Lowcountry, 1760–1810"; Patrick S. Brady, "The Slave Trade and Sectionalism in South Carolina, 1787–1808," *Journal of Southern History* 38 (1972):601–20; Paul F. LaChance, "The Politics of Fear: French Louisianians and the Slave Trade, 1786–1809," *Plantation Societies* 1 (1979):162–97; Frederick Bancroft, *Slave Trading in the Old South* (Baltimore, 1931), ch. 2; Elizabeth Donnan, ed., *Documents Illustrative of the History of the Slave Trade to America*, 4 vols. (Washington, D.C., 1930–35), 4:474–635; Michael Tadman, "Slave Trading in the Ante-Bellum South: An Estimate of the Extent of the Inter-regional Slave Trade," *Journal of American Studies* 13 (1979):195–220; and Robert W. Fogel and Stanley L. Engerman, *Time on the Cross: The Economics of American Negro Slavery*, 2 vols. (New York, 1974), 1:44–52. The estimates cited here are from tables 1 and 2.

[2]Most estimates of black runaways have been highly inflated. The Virginia figure is based upon known runaways and the number of slaves who left New York in 1783 with the British; it is documented in Allan Kulikoff, *Tobacco and Slaves: The Development of Southern Cultures in the Chesapeake Colonies, 1680–1780* (Chapel Hill, N.C., forthcoming), ch. 10, n. 83. The South Carolina estimate is based upon the 1770 and 1790 censuses, the level of slave imports, 1771–75 and 1782–90, and several assumptions about the deaths of immigrant slaves and the natural increase of the remainder. For the data sources, see Evarts B. Greene and Virginia D. Harrington, *American Population before the Federal Census of 1790* (New York, 1932), pp. 175–79; U.S. Bureau of the Census, *Historical Statistics of the United States: Colonial Times to 1970*, 2 vols. (Washington, D.C., 1975), 2:1168 and 1172–73; and Morgan, "Black Society in the Lowcountry," tables 4, 7, and 19.

the Revolution's battlefields, over 3,000 left with the British at war's end and ultimately reached Nova Scotia.[3] Threatened by such large-scale slave desertions whenever British troops approached an area, masters attempted to protect their investment in slave property by forcibly removing untold numbers of chattels from the battle regions to safer upcountry districts. After the war ended, planters brought their slaves back to the Tidewater and resumed farming.[4]

If the war disrupted black life in some respects, it stabilized it in others. The large majority of slaves lived far from the fighting and had few opportunities to escape, but, at the same time, war conditions forestalled their relocation and prevented familial separation by limiting their masters' mobility. Many young white men, who usually predominated among the westward-moving pioneers, spent the war years in the patriot or loyalist armies. Until the fighting concluded, the movement of planters and their slaves from Tidewater to Piedmont in the Chesapeake and from lowcountry to upcountry in South Carolina and Georgia temporarily ceased. So too did the importation of slaves. Since the British dominated the slave trade to North America and patriots refused to trade with them, no Africans entered the united colonies until 1783, when peace returned to the country.

When the war ended, whites resumed the settlement of backcountry Carolina and Georgia, migrated to Spanish Louisiana, and crossed the Allegheny Mountains into the new states of Kentucky and Tennessee. Nearly all of Virginia and Maryland was already thickly seated with farms and plantations, and young men seeking their fortunes had to leave that region. Groups of Chesapeake migrants, including slaves, traveled to Kentucky, Tennessee, and the backcountry of the Carolinas and Georgia during the 1780s and 1790s. Other

[3]James W. Walker, *The Black Loyalists: The Search for a Promised Land in Nova Scotia and Sierra Leone, 1783–1870* (London, 1976), chs. 1–2.

[4]Benjamin Quarles, *The Negro in the American Revolution* (Chapel Hill, N.C., 1961), ch. 9 and pp. 126–27; Mary Beth Norton, "'What an Alarming Crisis Is This': Southern Women and the American Revolution," in Jeffrey J. Crow and Larry E. Tise, eds., *The Southern Experience in the American Revolution* (Chapel Hill, N.C., 1978), pp. 223 and 233; Richard S. Dunn, "Black Society in the Chesapeake, 1776–1810," in this volume.

whites living along the Carolina and Georgia coast migrated further inland to the fertile piedmont areas. Some settlers even reached Spanish Louisiana, where, after 1785, white Protestants were welcomed for the first time.[5]

Planters demanded black slaves to provide the labor necessary to break the ground and plant marketable crops on their new farms. While Kentucky pioneers could procure enough slaves from Virginia and Maryland, Chesapeake blacks were too few to meet the demands of frontier Georgia, South Carolina, and Louisiana planters. Only resumption and continuation of the African slave trade could satisfy their needs, and they renewed importations soon after the peace treaty was signed. The foreign slave trade added nearly 20,000 blacks to South Carolina's population between 1782 and 1790, and slavers also docked at Spanish New Orleans and Natchez after the mid-1780s.[6]

These planters and their political representatives wanted to protect their access to African slaves. At the Constitutional Convention in Philadelphia, only the South Carolina and Georgia delegates supported continuation of the foreign slave trade, but in a crucial compromise the new Constitution permitted importations until 1808. Since planters feared Congress would end the trade as soon as it could, slave traders stepped up the pace of importation. The two decades following adoption of the Constitution witnessed the most massive infusion of African slaves that ever reached the North American mainland. When it became constitutionally possible, Congress ended the trade, and after January 1, 1808, no for-

[5]See Paula Martinac, "'An Unsettled Disposition': Social Structure and Geographic Mobility in Amelia County, Virginia, 1768–1794," Master's thesis, College of William and Mary, 1979, ch. 3; George R. Gilmer, *Sketches of Some of the First Settlers of Upper Georgia* (1835; reprint ed., Baltimore, 1980); Gilbert C. Dinn, "The Immigration Policy of Governor Esteban Miro in Spanish Louisiana," *Southwest Historical Quarterly* 73 (1969):156–75; and idem, "Spain's Immigration Policy in Louisiana and the American Penetration, 1792–1803," ibid. 76 (1973):255–76.

[6]Morgan, "Black Society in the Lowcountry," table 4; May Wilson McBee, ed., *The Natchez Court Records, 1767–1805: Abstracts of Early Records* (Ann Arbor, Mich., 1953), pp. 40–53.

eign slaves could legally be imported into the country. Some smuggling continued until the Civil War, but the Constitutional ban effectively limited these imports.[7]

The comparatively small numbers of Africans spirited into the country could not meet the large demand for slave labor in the new Southwest.[8] The only alternative supply of slaves was to be found in the Chesapeake states and North Carolina, but relatively few whites from these areas moved southwest and brought slaves to sell. As a result, domestic slave traders began to purchase slaves from Chesapeake planters, transport these chattels over land or by sea, and sell them to families in the new Southwest.[9]

The forced migration of black Americans between 1790 and 1820 can be divided by both time and region. During the 1790s and 1800s hundreds of Chesapeake planters took their slaves to Kentucky and Tennessee, but relatively few blacks born in Virginia or Maryland reached states farther to the southwest. At the same time, Georgia and South Carolina planters and farmers purchased thousands of enslaved Africans. After the legal slave trade ended in 1808 and imports of human labor nearly ceased, these two streams of migration merged. During the second decade of the nineteenth century nearly all interregional black migrants came from

[7]Brady, "Slave Trade and Sectionalism," pp. 601–20; W. E. B. Du Bois, *The Suppression of the African Slave Trade to the United States* (New York, 1904), chs. 5–7.

[8]Joe G. Taylor, "The Foreign Slave Trade in Louisiana after 1808," *Louisiana History* 1 (1960):36–43; Fogel and Engerman, *Time on the Cross*, 1:25. Du Bois, *Suppression of the African Slave Trade*, pp. 109–30, suggests higher numbers but presents no numerical estimates. See table 2 for my estimate of the number of Africans smuggled in the 1810s.

[9]Bancroft, *Slave Trading*, ch. 2; Ulrich B. Phillips, ed., *Plantation and Frontier*, 2 vols. (Cleveland, 1910) 2:55–56; William Calderhead, "The Role of the Professional Slave Trader in a Slave Economy: Austin Woolfolk, a Case Study," *Civil War History* 23 (1977):197–99. Far more work is needed on the origins of the internal slave trade system in the 1810s, for most works begin in the late 1820s, when the system was already well established.

the Chesapeake states, but they were scattered throughout the South, especially concentrating in the newest territories and states.

Residents of Virginia and Maryland—both white and black—rapidly peopled the new states of Kentucky and Tennessee between 1780 and 1810. At first, poor whites who settled on lands earned by war service or purchased cheap acreage comprised most of these pioneers, but wealthier planters soon moved west and, between 1790 and 1810, forced some 75,000 Chesapeake slaves to relocate with them (table 1). While most migrating whites owned only a slave or two, a few gentlemen—usually the younger sons of the best Virginia families—moved with a large entourage of blacks. Robert Carter Harrison, for instance, migrated from Virginia to Fayette County, Kentucky, in 1805 with around a hundred slaves, thus bringing nearly as many black chattels as fifty of his poorer neighbors.[10]

An organized slave trade between Virginia and Kentucky apparently failed to develop during the 1790s and 1800s. Nearly all slave migrants crossed the Blue Ridge and the Alleghenies with their masters, to settle on new farms in the West. The absence of an organized trade slowed the transfer of slaves but did not mitigate the condition of those who moved. Though few professional slave traders purchased Virginia slaves for the Kentucky or Tennessee market, slaves sold in Chesapeake markets or inherited by Virginia planters might well wind up in the new regions, far from friends and family.[11]

Farmers and planters living in upcountry South Carolina, Georgia, and states farther southwest had limited access to distant Chesapeake markets. Chesapeake planters who wished to sell or transport slaves turned first to neighboring Ken-

[10]Joan W. Coward, *Kentucky in the New Republic: The Process of Constitution Making* (Lexington, Ky., 1979), pp. 37 and 63; Anita S. Goodstein, "Black History on the Nashville Frontier, 1780–1810," *Tennessee Historical Quarterly* 38 (1979):401–20; J. Winston Coleman, Jr., *Slavery Times in Kentucky* (Chapel Hill, N.C., 1940), pp. 19–21.

[11]Goodstein, "Black History on the Nashville Frontier," pp. 403–6; Coleman, *Slavery Times in Kentucky*, pp. 144–47.

Table 1: Conjectural estimates of net slave migration to and within the United States, 1790–1810

States receiving slaves	Number of slaves exported from			Number of in-migrants
	Chesapeake states	Africa	West Indies	
Kentucky	54,000	0	0	54,000
North Carolina	6,000	0	0	6,000
South Carolina	4,000	15,000	0	19,000
Georgia	4,000	48,000	0	52,000
Tennessee	25,000	12,000	0	37,000
Mississippi & Louisiana	5,000	18,000	3,000	26,000
Total	98,000	93,000	3,000	194,000

SOURCES: J. D. B. De Bow, *Statistical View of the United States . . . : Being a Compendium of the Seventh Census . . .* (Washington, D.C. 1854), pp. 63 and 82; Paul F. LaChance, "The Politics of Fear: French Louisianians and the Slave Trade, 1786–1809," *Plantation Societies* 1 (1979): 196–97; David C. Rankin, "The Tannenbaum Thesis Reconsidered: Slavery and Race Relations in Antebellum Louisiana," *Southern Studies* 18 (1979): 21.
NOTE: For an explanation of method used in compiling this table, see appendix, pp. 168–71.

tucky, where planters and their slaves readily found a home and where slaves were easily sold. Not only did the great distances between the Chesapeake and backcountry South Carolina and Georgia inhibit slave relocation and trade, but political leaders in South Carolina further discouraged the influx of Chesapeake slaves by prohibiting the domestic slave trade and restricting the free sale of slaves by migrants, actions taken in response to Gabriel's conspiracy in Virginia in 1800. As a result of the lure of the Kentucky market and the inhospitality of the Carolina one, Chesapeake slaveholders sent fewer than 15,000 slaves to South Carolina, Georgia, Mississippi, and Louisiana between 1790 and 1810, and most of these probably accompanied their masters (table 1).

Since the revolt in Saint-Domingue tainted West Indian slaves with the "Cancer of Revolution," only a continuation of the African slave trade would satisfy backcountry planters in the lower South. While lowcountry legislators in South Carolina succeeded in suppressing the African slave trade in 1788, ships freely plied their human cargoes at Savannah, Georgia, until 1798, and after intensive pressure from upcountry legislators, South Carolina reopened the African trade in 1804. Meanwhile, American settlers in Louisiana could purchase Africans only fitfully: the slave trade was open (to Spanish ships only) from 1790 to 1795, closed from 1795 to 1800, open to Spanish and British ships from late 1800 to 1803, and closed to direct trade after the passage of the Louisiana Ordinance in 1804 by the United States.[12]

Despite these various restrictions, roughly 30,000 slaves reached the United States from Africa in the 1790s, and 63,000 more came in the 1800s. During the 1790s African slavers landed the majority of them in Savannah and sold them to local traders or upcountry planters, who shipped them northwestward along the Savannah River to backcountry Georgia. Smaller groups reached backcountry South Carolina, Tennessee, and Louisiana. Almost no African slaves were sold to Chesapeake or Kentucky planters during this period. After the South Carolina legislature reopened the trade in 1804, slavers shifted their business from Savannah to Charleston. Before the trade closed, they landed over 39,000 Africans in Charleston, most of whom were purchased by backcountry traders and planters from the expanding frontier region of the South some hundreds of miles inland. South Carolina planters, in contrast, probably purchased fewer than a third of them. Another 24,000 Africans either landed along the Gulf coast or were smuggled into Georgia or South Carolina during those few years when the trade there was illegal.[13]

During the 1790s and 1800s, few West Indian slaves reached

[12]LaChance, "Politics of Fear," p. 195.

[13]Brady, "Slave Trade and Sectionalism," pp. 611–13. Morgan, "Black Society in the Lowcountry," tables 3 and 4, assumes a low rate of natural increase for South Carolina's black population and calculates that 50,000 blacks migrated to the state, all of them from overseas. The estimate of smuggled slaves is derived from table 1 and textual estimates of the African trade. About 93,000 slaves came from Africa between 1790 and 1810 (table 1); of these, 39,000 entered Charleston between 1804 and the close of the trade, and another 30,000 arrived during the 1790s. The 24,000 African imports who remain unaccounted for are assumed to have been landed along the Gulf coast or smuggled into Georgia or South Carolina.

the United States in spite of the demand for slave labor. The largest group of them, numbering around 3,200 came to New Orleans with their refugee masters in 1809. These slaves and their owners had earlier migrated from Saint-Domingue to Cuba after the defeat of the French in 1803, and had then been expelled in 1809. While French-speaking citizens of Louisiana welcomed the refugees, English-speaking residents feared both the French culture brought by the whites and the possible rebelliousness of the slaves. The United States government reluctantly permitted them to remain after ascertaining the loyalty of the masters and examining the cost of deporting the slaves.[14]

The close of the international slave trade to the United States on January 1, 1808, accelerated the domestic slave trade and shifted its terminus. Between 1810 and 1820 roughly 137,000 slaves from the Chesapeake states and North Carolina spread over the frontier South. Kentucky was no longer the destination of most Chesapeake blacks. Nearly six of every ten migrants left Virginia and Maryland for Mississippi, Alabama, and the territories and states west of the Mississippi River; the rest of the Chesapeake migrants went to Kentucky, Tennessee, and Georgia. Most slaves from North Carolina were probably moved to Tennessee (table 2).

Chesapeake slaves reached the West in three ways during the 1810s. A substantial but probably declining proportion of them came with their masters. These included most slaves who went to Kentucky and other nearby areas. But only the wealthiest planters who wished to take advantage of the cotton boom could afford to move the great distance from the Chesapeake to the lower South. One such man was Leonard Covington, a former Maryland congressman and descendant of an old gentry family. In 1808 he moved from Prince George's County, Maryland, to the Mississippi frontier, taking thirty-one of his fifty-seven slaves with him.[15] Since few Chesapeake planters followed Covington's lead, Chesapeake

[14]LaChance, "Politics of Fear," pp. 187–93.

[15]Phillips, *Plantation and Frontier*, 2:201–18; Charles S. Sydnor, *Slavery in Mississippi* (New York, 1933), pp. 146–50.

Table 2: Conjectural estimates of net slave migration to and within the United States, 1810–20

States receiving slaves	Number of slaves exported from			Number of in-migrants
	Chesapeake states	North Carolina	Africa	
Kentucky	24,000	0	0	24,000
Tennessee	10,000	13,000	0	23,000
Georgia	13,000	0	2,000	15,000
Mississippi & Alabama	51,000	0	2,000	53,000
Louisiana, Arkansas, & Missouri	26,000	0	3,000	29,000
Total	124,000	13,000	7,000	144,000

SOURCE: J. D. B. De Bow, *Statistical View of the United States . . . : Being a Compendium of the Seventh Census . . .* (Washington, D.C., 1854), pp. 63 and 82.

NOTE: For an explanation of method used in compiling this table, see appendix, pp. 168–71.

slaves often moved "down the river" with professional slave traders.

Between 1810 and 1819 such professionals carried at least a third of all the forced black migrants.[16] While a few operated in the Chesapeake states before 1808, professional slave traders became active in large numbers during the second decade of the nineteenth century. An anonymous traveler in Virginia immediately after the end of the foreign slave trade contended that "the Carolina slave dealers get frequent supplies from this state, particularly from the eastern shore" and lamented the cruelty of the trade. Before 1820 slave traders established offices in most important Virginia cities, including Fredericksburg and Alexandria. A regular trade from Kentucky to the lower South also began to emerge as slave traders transported slaves from the Bluegrass State down the Ohio and Mississippi rivers for sale at Natchez and New Orleans. Not everyone depended on professional traders.

[16]If none of the slave migrants to Kentucky and Tennessee found in table 1 were sold and only half of those who migrated elsewhere from the Chesapeake were carried by slave traders, then 36 percent of the slave migrants were sold to traders.

Some planters traveled to the Chesapeake to purchase their own slaves. Men of wealth and substance already established in the Gulf states sometimes increased their labor forces through direct purchases in Virginia or Maryland. For example, Farish Carter of Baldwin County, Georgia, in the cotton-producing backcountry, owned but four slaves in 1816; the next year he possessed fifty, apparently purchased on local markets. In 1821 Carter journeyed to Virginia, where he bought sixty slaves of all ages to augment his already large work force.[17]

The forced migration of blacks into and across the South had enormous human consequences: migrants left loved ones at home, departed familiar surroundings, often changed masters, lost some of the privileges they had previously enjoyed, and were forced to live among strangers—both free and enslaved—when they reached their destinations. But while migration disrupted the lives of all black participants, its effects differed depending on the origins of the migrants, their destination, and their mode of transit. African migrants, slaves transported by their masters, and blacks sold in the domestic slave trade experienced the move south or west in diverse ways, and these in turn influenced the rapidity with which blacks could reconstruct their lives and create new slave communities.

The African survivors of the Middle Passage lost their social identity. Captured in African wars, driven to the coast, sold to European slave traders, and herded into crowded and unsanitary ships, they left their families behind and found themselves surrounded by strangers, both African and European. Though most of their enslaved shipmates came from a small region, few spoke their language or belonged to their own community. They sometimes developed friendships with their shipmates, but these were usually limited to members of their own sex. Their prospects, once they reached South

[17]Phillips, *Plantation and Frontier*, 2:55–56; Sydnor, *Slavery in Mississippi*, pp. 146–50; Bancroft, *Slave Trading*, pp. 21–27; Coleman, *Slavery Times in Kentucky*, pp. 144–45; Ralph B. Flanders, *Plantation Slavery in Georgia* (Chapel Hill, N.C., 1933), pp. 119–21.

Carolina or Georgia, were bleak. They might be sold several times, first to a seaport merchant, then to a backcountry trader, and finally marched to the interior and sold to a planter hungry only for their labor. In such circumstances slave communities developed slowly. Not only were newly arrived Africans separated from their shipmates, but with few African women included among their numbers, transplanted Africans had difficulty establishing families. Slave traders remained as selective as they had been earlier in the century, preferring men and boys over women, girls, and small children of either sex. On two African slave ships reaching Charleston in 1786 and Savannah in 1797, there were nearly two men for every woman, and three boys for every girl; and almost two-thirds of the Africans on these ships were adults.[18]

The enslavement in 1788 of Ibrahima, a Muslim prince of the Fulbe, illustrates the adjustments a new African slave had to make even before he reached the United States. Since he was a military leader captured by a neighboring tribe during a war, no sum of money would buy Ibrahima's repatriation. His captors sold him to slave traders, who carried him down the Gambia River and onto a crowded slave ship. Ibrahima's new masters chained him to a fellow passenger, where he remained for about a month and a half until the ship landed at Dominica, a new British colony. There fifty-six Africans, including Ibrahima, were sold to a Philadelphia merchant and transshipped to New Orleans, then a Spanish possession. Although four months had passed by the time Ibrahima landed in New Orleans, his travels had not ended, for after a month his new owner placed him in a third ship and took him up the Mississippi River to Natchez, where an American settler purchased him. On a frontier Mississippi plantation he began the difficult transformation from African to Afro-American.[19]

The social dislocations faced by slaves sold in the interstate

[18]Brady, "Slave Trade and Sectionalism," pp. 614–17; Donnan, *Documents Illustrative of the Slave Trade*, 4:491–92 (*Gambia*, to Charleston in 1786, 86 slaves); ibid., p. 633 (*Eagle*, to Savannah in 1797, 237 slaves); Sydnor, *Slavery in Mississippi*, pp. 141–42.

[19]Terry Alford, *Prince among Slaves* (New York, 1977), chs. 2–3.

slave trade or carried by masters to the Southwest differed from those of Africans. Creole slaves understood their master's expectations, spoke the same language as other slaves and whites, and some of them even migrated with their families. Yet their lives were disrupted as well. No matter how humane a master might be, migration inevitably separated families. Even the largest planter did not own *all* the significant relations of his slaves, and many husbands and wives lived on the plantations of different owners. A youth sold in the slave trade, even if unmarried, left behind parents, siblings, and other relatives and friends who had lived and worked nearby. The proportion of slaves who migrated southwest from Maryland and Virginia, and therefore the number of families torn asunder, grew rapidly after the end of the international slave trade. About one in twelve slaves in the Chesapeake moved to Kentucky or further south in the 1790s, and one in ten migrated during the 1800s, but the proportion forced to move doubled during the 1810s, reaching one in five.[20]

Slaves who migrated with their masters often retained some family ties, especially if they were owned by a wealthy planter. Before moving to Mississippi, Leonard Covington wrote to his brother Alexander, who was already living there, to inquire about slave life on the frontier. He wanted to know, among other things, if "the negroes in the country generally looked as happy and contented as with us, and do they as universally take husbands and wives and as easily rear their young as in Maryland?" Despite his concern, Covington divided his slaves, taking some families with him and leaving

[20]For the development and significance of kin ties in the Chesapeake, see Allan Kulikoff, "The Beginnings of the Afro-American Family in Maryland," in Aubrey C. Land et al., eds., *Law, Society, and Politics in Early Maryland* (Baltimore, 1977), pp. 171–96; and the essay in this volume by Mary Beth Norton, Herbert G. Gutman, and Ira Berlin, "The Afro-American Family in the Age of Revolution." The proportion of slaves who moved was computed by adding the slave census population of Maryland and Virginia in 1800, 1810, and 1820, respectively, to the estimated number of slave outmigrants from these states (see tables 1 and 2), and then dividing the numbers of migrants by the slave population in the census year plus the number of migrants.

others on his Maryland farm. Among the slave migrants were five men, four women, and twenty-two children under the age of sixteen. They included at least one family containing a father, mother, and two children, as well as another two mothers with four children each; but a number of the older children probably left parents on the Maryland plantation, and several of the adults may have been married to slaves Covington did not own. Covington apparently wanted youths on his new plantation, for he left behind in Maryland seven of his nine slaves older than thirty. He consigned the thirty-one migrant slaves, along with about twenty others, to a D. Rawlings, who transported them down the Ohio and Mississippi rivers. Rawlings must have kept them under close control, perhaps even chaining them to each other, for they passed through Pennsylvania, a state committed to black emancipation.[21]

Few slaves willingly consented to leaving their families behind. Alexander Covington's slave Sam refused to travel with a group of slaves his master's brother Leonard was shipping to Mississippi. Leonard reported that Sam maintained "a sullen silence on the subject and neither yields consent to accompany my people, or to be sold or exchanged." Sam's wife and family probably lived in the neighborhood, and he did not want to leave them. Leonard Covington finally sold Sam locally, purchased another slave in return, and sent that one to his brother.[22]

The insecurity of creole slaves increased greatly when the international slave trade ended and the domestic trade accelerated. A black man or woman sold to a slave trader had to endure not only disruption of daily work and communal activities but also separation from family members, forced relocation to an unknown and possibly dangerous place, and the probability of working far harder for a new master on the cotton frontier. Planters knew that slaves preferred to

[21]Phillips, *Plantation and Frontier*, 2:210–18 (the passage from Leonard Covington's letter is on p. 202). Family relationships among Covington's slaves were inferred from a list of slave migrants and nonmigrants on p. 208 and random comments in the Covington letters reprinted by Phillips.

[22]Ibid., pp. 206–7 and 211.

remain in familiar surroundings near friends and kin, and they used the threat of sale to control their chattels' behavior. "In Maryland," Charles Ball reported, "it has always been the practice of masters and mistresses, who wished to terrify their slaves to threaten to sell them to South Carolina where it was represented, that their condition would be a hundred fold worse." Ball considered "such a sale of myself as the greatest of evils that could befall me, and had striven to demean my-self in such manner to my owners, as to preclude them from all excuse of transporting me to so horrid a place."[23]

All too often, however, planters sold their slaves to traders, vividly reminding both those who were sold and their kin who stayed behind of the precarious circumstances of slave families and communities. Stephen Penbroke, born in Mary-land in 1804, understood the fear of being sold, for his "father was sold five times. The last time he was knocked down and seized by three men" before being forcibly carried away. The scene of his father's removal deeply affected the younger Penbroke, and his master, sensing this, played upon the young slave's desire to remain near his family by threatening to send him "further South" if he requested a lighter work load.[24]

The life of Charles Ball encapsulates the common experi-ences of men and women sold from the Chesapeake to the cotton South. Ball, born about 1780 in Calvert County, Mary-land, learned early in life that masters did not respect slave family bonds. During the first years of his life, Ball's mother, father, and grandfather lived apart on plantations operated by different masters. When Ball was about five years old, his mother's master died, and that portion of his family living

[23]Charles Ball, *Fifty Years in Chains*, Philip S. Foner, ed. (New York, 1970). Ball's narrative, originally published in 1837, was challenged by contem-poraries as a fabrication, and it was probably ghost-written, as were many slave narratives. Nonetheless, I have relied on it here because it is the ear-liest slave narrative, the only one that covers the period under considera-tion, and it has generally been accepted by present-day scholars, including Foner (see his introduction, pp. v-vi) and John Blassingame, who checked every possible fact mentioned in the narrative with original records (see Blassingame, ed., *Slave Testimony: Two Centuries of Letters, Speeches, Interviews and Autobiographies* [Baton Rouge, La., 1977], pp. xxiii-xxvi).

[24]Blassingame, *Slave Testimony*, pp. 108–9, 167–69, and 211–13.

with his mother was sold, each member to a different master. The new arrangement not only further splintered the family, but also prevented his father and mother from seeing one another. Unable to visit his wife, Ball's father became distraught and behaved sullenly toward his owner, who feared he would run away. The master therefore resolved to sell him to a Georgia slave trader. But before the sale was completed, the elder Ball fled to the North, leaving Charles with only his African grandfather for companionship in the old neighborhood.[25]

Before reaching adolescence Ball saw his family disintegrate several times. When he was twelve his master died, and the estate was administered by his father's former owner, a harsh taskmaster who hired Ball out to a shipowner as a cook at a Washington shipyard. During his early twenties, Ball worked at the Washington Navy Yard and then returned to live in Calvert County under two different masters. After returning to Calvert, he married and started a family, but, like his father, he was destined to be separated from them: his last Maryland master sold him to a Georgia slave trader. Ball asked his new master, the trader, if he "could be allowed to go to see my wife and children, or if this could not be permitted, if they might not have leave to come to see me; but was told that I would be able to get another wife in Georgia."[26]

The Georgia trader took no chances and treated Ball and his other temporary charges harshly. Though the nineteen women in the group "were merely tied together with a rope, about the size of a bed cord, which was tied like a halter around the neck of each," the thirty-two men, including Ball, suffered more severe restraint. "A strong iron collar was closely fitted by means of a padlock round each of our necks. A chain of iron, about a hundred feet in length, was passed through the hasp of each padlock, except at the two ends, where the hasps of the padlocks passed through a link of the chain. In addition to this, we were handcuffed in pairs, with iron staples and bolts, with a short chain, a foot long, uniting the hand-

[25]Ball, *Fifty Years in Chains*, pp. 15–24.

[26] Ibid., pp. 25–37.

cuffs and their wearers in pairs." A routine was established of marching rapidly during the day (ignoring, by the way, the cries of the pregnant women in the group) and sleeping "promiscuously, men and women, on the floors of such houses as we chanced to stop at."[27]

Ball's sale to a slave trader and separation from his family traumatized him. At first, he "longed to die, and escape from the hands of my tormenters; but the wretched privilege of destroying myself was denied; for I could not shake off my chains, nor move a yard without the consent of my master." He dreamed about his grandfather, wife, and children and longed to see them, but "in a few days the horrible sensation attendant upon my cruel separation from my wife and children, in some measure subsided."[28]

During the early years of the Republic the majority of creole slaves neither suffered the indignities of the internal slave trade nor were forced to migrate with their masters hundreds of miles to new plantations, yet stories such as Ball's were repeated with sufficient regularity that most slaves might reasonably expect to be separated from their families, and those left behind feared that they might be next. An adult slave born in Maryland or Virginia early in the nineteenth century could expect many family separations and had a good chance of being sold during his adult lifetime. If each forced migrant during the 1810s left behind only two close kindred in the Chesapeake, then almost two-thirds of Virginia and Maryland blacks were affected by interstate migration in that decade alone.[29]

Forced migration of Africans and creoles to the New South broke many of the fragile ties of kinship and friendship that held together black communities in Africa and slave communities in the United States. Eventually slaves redeveloped

---

[27]Ibid., pp. 36–37 and 41.

[28]Ibid., pp. 39 and 68–69.

[29]Table 2; Herbert G. Gutman and Richard Sutch, "The Slave Family: Protected Agent of Capitalist Masters or Victim of the Slave Trade?" in Paul A. David et al., *Reckoning with Slavery: A Critical Study in the Quantitative History of American Negro Slavery* (New York, 1976), pp. 110–11.

the family networks and familial ideology that bound them together, but broader processes of accommodation have not been extensively studied.[30] It seems clear, however, that the demographic environment—in particular, the age, sexual, and ethnic composition of the migrant population—determined the limits of the possibilities that slaves had for a secure social life in new areas. Furthermore, slave communities and extended kin networks could not emerge unless a substantial number of slaves lived on relatively large units of twenty or more slaves, where neighborhood blacks could gather, visit kindred, find spouses, and harbor fugitives. Since the demographic makeup of frontier slave populations and the typical number of slaves who lived on each plantation varied by region and time during the generation after the adoption of the Constitution, the ability of slaves to develop a strong social life differed from place to place as well.

Although the internal slave trade and massive migration disrupted family life on plantations in the Chesapeake states, those slaves who remained behind regrouped and reconstructed their extensive networks of kinship and friendship. They forged new ties of marriage with neighborhood slaves, reared their children, and memorialized the departed family members by naming children after them. Within a generation, or even less if the master lived, maintained his credit, and did not sell any of his slaves, large plantations of interconnected kindred reemerged.[31]

The 113,000 Chesapeake slaves who migrated to Kentucky and Tennessee, mostly with their masters, struggled to re-

[30]For the best discussions of this issue, see Herbert G. Gutman, *The Black Family in Slavery and Freedom, 1750–1925* (New York, 1976), ch. 4; and Cheryll Ann Cody, "Naming, Kinship, and Estate Dispersal: Notes on Slave Family Life on a South Carolina Plantation, 1786 to 1833," *William and Mary Quarterly*, 3d ser. 39 (1982):192–211. Cody's work on one South Carolina plantation between 1782 and 1833 and Gutman's more extended work on two lower South plantations later in the nineteenth century are the only studies of this sort thus far completed.

[31]Gutman, *Black Family*, pp. 137–39, provides a valuable model of the destruction and re-creation of kinship networks after the breakup of plantations.

create the same kind of communities they had left behind. Planters apparently brought a cross section of slaves with them: close to half the adults were women, and on average two children under fifteen accompanied each woman between fifteen and forty. Since most white migrants owned few slaves, many husbands and wives had lived on different plantations and must have been separated by the move west. Once they reached Kentucky or Tennessee and recovered from the shock of involuntary divorce, many of these slaves probably remarried, started new families, and attempted to redevelop extensive kinship networks. This task was difficult, despite their relative cultural homogeneity and rough sexual balance. Most of them lived on small units of only a few slaves: the typical slaveholder in Kentucky in the 1790s owned only four slaves, and only a quarter of all whites possessed any at all. Youthful slaves faced further disruptions once they arrived, for non-slaveholders frequently purchased slaves from planters. In Davidson County, Tennessee, some 700 slaves were sold in the years between 1784 and 1802. Nearly two-thirds of them were sold singly and most of the rest in small groups of mothers and their young children. Nearly all of those sold were under thirty years old; perhaps half were less than sixteen.[32]

African, Chesapeake, and Carolina migrants to the lower South faced even greater difficulties in creating new communities during the years between 1790 and 1820. These black settlers formed culturally distinct groups. Africans and Chesapeake slaves, in particular, spoke different languages, practiced different customs, and related to their slavery in distinctive ways. While Africans fought the system of slavery itself, Virginia and Maryland slaves—the grandchildren and great-grandchildren of African immigrants—knew from long experience how to disrupt slavery or gain privileges from within the system. In addition, the Chesapeake slave men

[32]Coward, *Kentucky in the Early Republic*, pp. 37 and 63; Goodstein, "Black History on the Nashville Frontier," pp. 403–5; Tadman, "Slave Trading in the Ante-Bellum South," pp. 198 and 201, gives suggestive data on the age and sex composition of slaves taken south by their masters between 1820 and 1860.

probably found wives more easily than did the African men. Cultural differences and conflicts over scarce women may well have created tensions between the groups.[33]

The pattern of the international and interstate slave trade shaped the development of Afro-American culture in the lower South. The first black residents of the frontier Southwest were probably creole slaves brought by their masters. But after the first plantations were established, whites began to import blacks from Africa, and despite the continuing influx of creoles in the 1790s and 1800s, Africans soon far outnumbered the black creoles. The geographical origins of slaves sold in Louisiana's Natchez district in the 1780s illustrate these patterns. Between 1781 and 1785, when the first American pioneers arrived, only 22 slaves were sold in Natchez—16 from the United States, 2 from the West Indies, and 4 from Africa. When planter demand increased, merchants began bringing shiploads of Africans to Natchez. As a result, nearly three-quarters of the 157 slaves sold in Natchez between 1786 and 1788 were Africans; only a sixth came from the United States and a tenth from the West Indies.[34] Nearly half the Africans were bought singly, and another third were sold in pairs. Men and boys dominated the immigrant group, making marriage and the formation of slave families difficult for African men. Nearly twice as many males as females were sold, and almost two-thirds of the males were between the ages of twenty and thirty, prime candidates for marriage.[35]

African slaves shared a number of cultural characteristics.

[33]This paragraph relies heavily on three works on colonial slavery: Peter H. Wood, *Black Majority: Negroes in Colonial South Carolina from 1670 through the Stono Rebellion* (New York, 1974); Allan Kulikoff, "The Origins of Afro-American Society in Tidewater Maryland and Virginia, 1700 to 1790," *William and Mary Quarterly*, 3d ser. 35 (1978):226–59; and Ira Berlin, "Time, Space, and the Evolution of Afro-American Society in British Mainland North America," *American Historical Review* 85 (1980):44–78.

[34]McBee, *Natchez Court Records*, pp. 1–60.

[35]Ibid. The sex ratio (196 men per 100 women) is based upon the 136 cases where the African's sex was known. There were 103 cases in which age (often "heaped" at 20 or 30) was given; in this group there were 13 males under age sixteen (13 percent of the group; 19 percent of the men),

Almost half the slaves imported into Charleston between 1804 and 1807 came from the Congo and Angola regions of Africa, and nearly three-quarters of them probably belonged to a handful of ethnic groups clustered around the Congo River. These Africans may have spoken relatively similar languages and been familiar with each other's customs. Nearly a quarter of the African immigrants came from the Windward Coast; no more than an eighth of them came from any other region. Given the wide dispersion of Africans throughout the Southwest, however, probably few of them found countrymen living near their homes.[36]

The small size of most plantations during the pioneer period also made it unlikely that countrymen or shipmates would reside together. For example, over half the slaves in four upland Georgia cotton counties in the 1790s and 1800s lived on plantations with fewer than ten slaves; at most, a sixth of them worked with twenty or more other blacks. Equally small units could be found in two Mississippi counties in 1816 (table 3). These plantations became polyglot communities of slaves from various African communities and, as women married and bore children, creole slaves as well. To cite one instance, John Fitzpatrick, a merchant who lived near New Orleans, bought six African slaves, from different African nations, in the 1770s and 1780s; when he died in 1791 he owned these and five creole slaves as well, all children of two African women.[37]

African immigrant slaves living in the Southwest—like Africans who came to the Americas earlier in the century—refused at first to cooperate with the slave system. Many slaves probably emulated the behavior of Ibrahima, the African

---

6 females under fifteen (6 percent of the group; 18 percent of the women), 2 men between sixteen and nineteen, and 48 men between twenty and thirty (47 percent of the group; 69 percent of the men). There were 25 women between sixteen and twenty-eight (24 percent of the group; 76 percent of the women), 8 men over thirty and 2 women over twenty-eight.

[36]Morgan, "Black Society in the Lowcountry," table 19; Donnan, *Documents Illustrative of the Slave Trade*, 4:474–635.

[37]Margaret F. Dayrymple, ed., *The Merchant of Manchac: The Letterbooks of John Fitzpatrick, 1768–1790* (Baton Rouge, La., 1978), pp. 425–32.

Table 3: Distribution of slaves on plantations in upper Georgia counties, 1784–1820, and in two Mississippi counties, 1816

Year	Percentage of slaves living on units of				Number of slaves
	1–3 slaves	4–9 slaves	10–19 slaves	20+ slaves	
Georgia*					
1794	22%	29%	38%	11%	1,980
1800/1802	20	35	32	13	2,788
1805/1807	16	38	30	17	15,218
1810/1811	12	30	34	24	20,429
1820/1821	9	24	30	37	24,835
Mississippi†					
1816	17	39	30	14	1,151

SOURCES: Calculated from data in Ralph B. Flanders, *Plantation Slavery in Georgia* (Chapel Hill, N.C., 1933), p. 70; E. Russ Williams, *Records of Marion County, Mississippi* 3 (1965):7–8; and E. Russ Williams, ed., *Resource Records of Pike/Walthall Counties, 1798–1910* (Easley, S.C., 1978).

*For 1794, Oglethorpe County; 1800, Oglethorpe; 1802, Wilkes and Hancock; 1805, Oglethorpe and Clark; 1807, Hancock; 1810, Oglethorpe and Clark; 1811, Wilkes and Hancock; 1820, Oglethorpe, Clark, and Wilkes; 1821, Hancock. The data from the source for Georgia included number of slaves and a distribution by slaveowners; the proportion of slaves on plantations was estimated from that data, after a spot-check of the original lists.

†Marion and Pike counties. The sources are nominal lists.

prince who was forced into slavery in Mississippi. Thomas Foster, a local planter and himself a recent arrival, purchased Ibrahima and another African from a slave trader in 1788. Trouble began soon after they reached Foster's plantation when Foster attempted to clothe Ibrahima in breeches and cut his hair in an acceptable fashion. Ibrahima's hair style symbolized his position in his former society, and he fought vigorously but unsuccessfully to retain it. That humiliation completed, Foster set him to work in the fields, a role beneath his former status. When the slave resisted, Foster whipped him, and after several days' punishment, Ibrahima ran away. Weeks later he returned to Foster's plantation, having learned that escape was impossible. He became a "model" field hand.[38]

[38]Alford, *Prince among Slaves*, ch. 3.

The numerical dominance of Africans on the frontier disappeared in the decade following the closing of the African slave trade. While thousands of Africans died before they were fully immune to the disease environment of the South, 100,000 slaves born in the Chesapeake states replaced them on frontier plantations in Georgia, Alabama, Mississippi, Louisiana, Arkansas, and Missouri. A majority of these Chesapeake bondspeople were probably sold to slave traders and carried south overland, by sea, or down the Ohio and Mississippi rivers. Most were young, and nearly equal numbers of men and women came south with slave traders. In 1820 the sex ratio (number of men per 100 women) of slaves between fourteen and twenty-six—the age group that accounted for nearly half the overland domestic slave trade—ranged from 96 to 107 in the frontier states of Arkansas, Missouri, Alabama, and Mississippi. However frequently these forced migrants had been separated from parents, siblings, and spouses, they soon remarried and began families. While the migrant black population had included only 1.4 children under the age of fourteen for each adult woman, by 1820 there were nearly 2 children for every black woman aged fourteen to forty-five in Missouri and Alabama—a ratio that suggests substantial natural increase—and about 1.5 children under fourteen for each black woman in Arkansas and Mississippi.[39]

Even though African and Chesapeake slaves formed two separate subgroups in the black population of the frontier South in the second decade of the nineteenth century and probably competed for wives among the available black women, tensions and conflicts among them soon diminished and a cohesive Afro-American community began to develop

[39]Tadman, "Slave Trading in the Ante-Bellum South," p. 201; the data on 1820 sex ratios and child-woman ratios come from the 1820 federal census. Louisiana was excluded from consideration because a portion of that territory had long been settled by Spanish and French planters who had already successfully established a plantation system, and because of the resulting ethnic complexity of the slave population. The census does not allow for the disaggregation of the frontier and older settled regions of Louisiana or the disaggregation of the slave population along ethnic lines.

along the cotton frontier. In the first place, the enormous influx of Chesapeake-born slaves soon overwhelmed the surviving Africans, who became a small minority of the adult slave population even in areas where they had previously dominated. In time Africans found accommodation to Afro-American norms and values somewhat easier, for they now spoke English and could participate in black family life and community activities. The development of an Afro-Christian faith further unified blacks from the Chesapeake, lowcountry Carolina, and Africa living in the cotton South, because that faith encompassed values and ideals they all shared.

African and creole slaves joined together to make a new black community, based upon both kinship and activities in the slave quarters. As the proportion of Africans in the adult population diminished, adult sex ratios among slaves declined as well, and African men who survived to 1820 probably did find wives and begin families. By 1820, after many Africans had died and some creole women had come to the frontier, there were five men for every four women under age 45—which probably included most of the Africans—in Arkansas, Missouri, Alabama, and Mississippi. Not only could nearly all slaves start families, but more family members also lived together. Most mothers and their small children resided in the same hut, and by 1820 a few larger kin groups may have begun to appear on established frontier plantations. At that date over a third of the slaves in middle Georgia lived on quarters with twenty or more other slaves, and these plantations probably housed complete families of parents and children, and perhaps a few other kin. Families and work groups on these quarters were of sufficient size to cook, eat, and celebrate with each other and with slaves from nearby farms after the day's work was complete.[40]

The great migration of African and Afro-American slaves to the Southwest coincided with a remarkable resurgence of evangelical Protestantism throughout the United States. Slaves—no matter where they were born—shared in this re-

---

[40]Table 3 and 1820 federal census. See also Kulikoff, "Beginnings of Afro-American Family in Maryland," in Land, *Law, Society, and Politics*, pp. 178–84.

ligious fervor. By 1820 at least 70,000 slaves belonged to Baptist or Methodist churches, and thousands of others probably participated in revivals. African and creole slaves together created an Afro-Christian faith from the West African ethos they shared. Visionary experiences, the call-and-shout, and particular views of God and eternity could be found in African religions, in the culture of the most assimilated Chesapeake slaves, and (to a degree) among white evangelicals.[41]

The great migration of slaves—both African and creoles—that began after the Revolution was one of the most significant events in the history of black society in the United States. Nearly a third of a million African and Chesapeake slaves had moved southwestward by 1820, and another three-quarters of a million blacks were forced to migrate between 1820 and 1860. As slaves were taken from Africa to the cotton South and from seaboard states to the interior, different combinations of ethnic backgrounds appeared in the Chesapeake and Kentucky, in coastal Carolina and Georgia, and in the Southwest. The migration of slaves varied over time as well and was heavier during booms in cotton prices than during years of depression. Any understanding of Afro-American societies and cultures in the nineteenth-century South should begin with an appreciation of these differential patterns of movement in time and space and assess their impact on the lives of slaves.

[41]The best accounts of Afro-Baptist religion can be found in Mechal Sobel, *Trabelin' On: The Slave Journey to an Afro-Baptist Faith* (New York, 1979); Albert J. Raboteau, *Slave Religion: The "Invisible Institution" in the Antebellum South* (New York, 1978); Donald G. Mathews, *Religion in the Old South* (Chicago, 1977), ch. 5; and Eugene D. Genovese, *Roll, Jordan, Roll: The World the Slaves Made* (New York, 1974), pp. 159–324. The data on black church membership are summarized in Sobel, *Trabelin' On*, pp. 182–83.

Appendix
Migration Estimates

The migration estimates in tables 1 and 2 were generated from the numbers of slaves and free Negroes counted in the fed-federal population censuses between 1790 and 1820 and from several Spanish censuses of Louisiana, utilizing a forward projection method.[1] First, I assumed that the rate of natural increase of the black population equaled 2.5 percent each year throughout the South (except for 1810–20 in the exporting states, where a rate of 2.6 percent was used), a number derived from study of colonial black populations of Maryland and Virginia.[2] Then I multiplied the 1790, 1800, or 1810 slave populations of each state by the 2.5 percent growth rate over ten years and subtracted that sum from the succeeding census figure, which included the slave population of that year and blacks manumitted within that decade (defined as the growth of free black population above 2.5 percent a year). Since the total decennial growth within the region in each decade (but particularly before 1810) was greater than the estimated natural rate of growth, the remainder had to be blacks imported in the foreign slave trade. The resulting data, reported in tables 1 and 2, were separated into two periods, 1790–1810 and 1810–20.

Three assumptions must be granted before these conjectures can be given credence. First, I have assumed that the rate of under- or over-recording of the censuses was constant. If census A was underrecorded by 25 percent, while census B missed only 10 percent, then part of the population "growth" between the two censuses resulted from better coverage on the second document rather than from migration or natural increase. A spot check of Maryland and Virginia

[1] J. D. B. De Bow, *Statistical View of the United States . . . : Being a Compendium of the Seventh Census . . .* (Washington, D.C., 1854), pp. 63 and 82; Paul F. LaChance, "The Politics of Fear: French Louisianians and the Slave Trade, 1786–1809," *Plantation Societies* 1 (1979): 196–97; David C. Rankin, "The Tannenbaum Thesis Reconsidered: Slavery and Race Relations in Antebellum Louisiana," *Southern Studies* 18 (1979):21.

[2] Allan Kulikoff, "A 'Prolifick' People: Black Population Growth in the Chesapeake Colonies, 1700–1790," *Southern Studies* 16 (1977):409–14.

county-level census data and a comparison of these data with state tax censuses suggest that this problem is probably minor.[3]

Second, I assumed a uniform rate of natural increase across the South. This proposition is clearly untenable, for the number of creole slaves grew far more slowly in the South Carolina and Georgia lowcountry than in the Chesapeake states where they were concentrated. The rate of in-migration, then, was probably higher in South Carolina, Georgia, and other places of lower natural increase than is indicated in tables 1 and 2. Philip D. Morgan estimates that 50,000 slaves were imported into South Carolina between 1790 and 1810, nearly triple my figure. If one reduces the South Carolina rate of natural increase to 1.5 percent a year, then 49,000 slaves (including 45,000 Africans) were forced to relocate in South Carolina between 1790 and 1810. Such a procedure would raise the total African *survivors* to 123,000, an estimate one-third higher than Philip D. Curtin's suggestion that 92,000 entered North America between 1782 and 1810. If one assumes that only one-fifth of the Africans died before the 1790 census (a low estimate), then 116,000 Africans landed between 1790 and the close of the slave trade, by the conjectures of table 1, or 150,000 by the revised conjecture. This last number seems very high, given the rapid rate of natural increase in the Chesapeake region. The rate of natural increase in the upper South between 1810 and 1820 was raised from 2.5 percent to 2.6 percent a year because the 2.5 percent rate suggested an unrealistically high number of smuggled slaves.[4]

Third, the estimates assume that children under ten mi-

---

[3]De Bow, *Statistical View*, pp. 63 and 82; Evarts B. Greene and Virginia D. Harrington, *American Population before the Federal Census of 1790* (New York, 1932), pp. 132–33 and 150–55; Allan Kulikoff, "Tobacco and Slaves: Population, Economy, and Society in Eighteenth Century Prince George's County, Maryland," Ph.D. diss., Brandeis University, 1976, pp. 428–33; "A State of the Inspector's Accounts from Oct 1786 to Oct 1787," Auditor's Item no. 49, Virginia State Library, Richmond.

[4]Philip D. Morgan, "Black Society in the Lowcountry, 1760–1810," in this volume, tables 3 and 4; Philip D. Curtin, *The Atlantic Slave Trade: A Census* (Madison, Wis., 1969), p. 140.

grated as frequently as did adults and youths. Since frontier planters primarily wanted laborers, perhaps a lower proportion of children migrated and my estimate of interstate forced migration is too high. Nonetheless, I have adhered to this possibly biased procedure because planters rarely separated young children from their mothers and because the child-woman ratios among frontier slaves remained high despite the negative influence of migration.[5]

Two caveats ought to be kept in mind while using these estimates of the flow of slave migrants. First, they probably reflect a reasonable ranking of the sending and receiving areas, but not the exact magnitude of movement. A lower estimate constructed by Claudia Goldin using a survivor technique shows roughly similar directions of movement and similar orders of magnitude for 1790–1810, when differences in estimated rates of natural increase and survival rates are considered, and for 1810–20, when Goldin's exclusion of children is considered.[6] Second, the numbers represent minimal estimates of long-distance migrants because they are net figures that include only surviving resident populations. The high rate of slave mortality suggests that the true number of Africans who landed may have been much higher: if a quarter of the Africans died between migration and census, then the number of African immigrants rises to 124,000 (using my estimate) or 164,000 (adding 30,000 to South Carolina). Fewer creole slaves died after moving, but neither slaves who moved twice nor those who moved long distances within states are counted in the statistic. Even more important, reciprocal exchanges of slaves between states (say, Kentucky and Tennessee, or Virginia and Maryland) are not included.

The numbers and destinations of foreign and interstate migrants are educated guesses based upon the assertions of

[5]In probate inventories, small children are nearly always listed with mothers, but older children are listed separately. For the relationship between migration and fertility, see Richard H. Steckel, "The Economics of United States Slave and Southern White Fertility," Ph.D. diss., University of Chicago, 1977, pp. 224–26.

[6]Robert W. Fogel and Stanley L. Engerman, *Time on the Cross: The Economics of American Negro Slavery*, 2 vols. (New York, 1974), 1:44–52; 2:43–48.

various authorities.[7] I began with the African trade and assumed that no Africans reached the Chesapeake states, Kentucky, or North Carolina, because no slave ships came to Chesapeake ports after the Revolution. Then I distributed the Africans among the remaining areas: Georgia, 75 percent of the trade in the 1790s, 40 percent in 1800–1810, and 29 percent of those smuggled into the United States in the 1810s; South Carolina, 20 percent in the 1790s and 15 percent in the 1800s; Louisiana and Mississippi, 30 percent in the 1800s; Mississippi and Alabama, 29 percent in the 1810s; Louisiana and further west, 43 percent in the 1810s; and Tennessee, 5 percent in the 1790s, and 15 percent in the 1800s (a remainder which is much too high). These distributions were suggested by the dominance of Charleston and Savannah in the trade before 1808 and the probability that smuggled slaves came from Spanish Florida or landed along the Mississippi River thereafter, as well as by the expansion of food and cotton production in the new Southwest.

The interstate movements of slaves were calculated by subtracting the African imports from total net in-migration and then distributing the remainder among the various sending regions. Between 1790 and 1810, the Chesapeake provided all the rest of the migrants, except for some 3,000 slaves who came from Cuba in 1809 with their masters, exiles from Saint-Domingue.[8] During the 1810s both the Chesapeake states and North Carolina sent slaves across state boundaries, and here I assumed that all the North Carolina slaves migrated to Tennessee.

These conjectures could be improved through a detailed study of slave sales in newspapers and local deeds, and examination of planter's records of slave movements. The distributions these records suggest could then be used to reconstruct both the demography of migration and the destinations of particular groups of slaves.

[7]All the works listed in notes 1, 10, 15, and 17 were consulted, along with other state studies of slavery.

[8]LaChance, "Politics of Fear," pp. 187–93.

II

The Transformation of Afro-American Institutions in the Age of Revolution

MARY BETH NORTON
HERBERT G. GUTMAN
IRA BERLIN

The Afro-American
Family in the
Age of Revolution

DURING THE EIGHTEENTH century Africans became Afro-Americans in mainland British North America. The chronology of this transformation differed from place to place, depending upon, among other circumstances, the labor requirements of particular crops; the timing, volume, and source of the slave trade; the sexual balance among blacks; the geographical concentration or dispersion of the slave population; and the ratio of blacks to whites. But despite profound regional differences, the emergence of Afro-American society and culture was everywhere made possible by the development of generational linkages within the slave population. A close look at black families in the last quarter of the eighteenth century in two distinct regions, the Chesapeake and the Carolinas, reveals a good deal about the nature of that transformation, the workings of black society, and—since the Afro-American family matured in the midst of a larger struggle for political independence and self-definition—the role of the black family in defining the extent of black autonomy during the age of revolution.

Afro-American domestic life at the end of the eighteenth century can be seen most clearly in the records of the great planters who periodically inventoried their holdings, kept birth lists of their bondsmen and women, or indicated slave family connections in ration rolls and estate censuses. In 1773 Charles

Carroll of Annapolis listed his several hundred bondspeople and noted their relationship, age, residence, and occupation. The heirs of his only son, Charles Carroll of Carrollton, compiled a similar though less detailed list after the latter's death nearly a half century later. These documents, combined with earlier inventories dating back into the seventeenth century, offer an unparalleled view of the evolution of black domestic life over nearly a century and a half.[1] Similarly, Thomas Jefferson enumerated the slaves on his Piedmont Virginia plantations at least once each decade from the 1770s until his death fifty years later.[2]

Examined within the context of these extensive records, the fragmentary accounts of other planters—like Robert Carter, who regularly tallied his Northern Neck (Virginia) bondsmen and women and listed all five hundred in his 1793 manumission deed, and Edward Lloyd, the largest planter on Maryland's Eastern Shore, who recorded his holdings monthly and noted births and deaths—supplement knowledge of the development of Afro-American family life.[3] In addition, some nineteenth-century slavemasters recorded their

[1]"A List of Negroes on Doohoregan Manor taken in Familys with their Ages Decr 1 1773" and related lists of slaves at Poplar Island, Annapolis, and Annapolis Quarter, Feb. and July 1774, and Charles Carroll (Settler) Inventory, 1721, Charles Carroll Account Book (microfilm), Maryland Hall of Records, Annapolis; Charles Carroll (Carrollton) Real Estate Inventory, 1831–33, Maryland Historical Society, Baltimore. Unless otherwise noted these documents provide the bases for the reconstruction of the slave families on the Carroll estate. For another analysis of the Carroll lists see Allan Kulikoff, "The Beginnings of the Afro-American Family in Maryland," in Aubrey C. Land et al., eds., *Law, Society, and Politics in Early Maryland* (Baltimore, 1977), pp. 179–89.

[2]Edwin M. Betts, ed., *Thomas Jefferson's Farm Book* (Princeton, 1953), reprints the censuses on pp. 5–9, 15–18, 24, 30, 57, and 128–29, and the partial lists on p. 60 of the farm book facsimile. Birth and death records and food and clothing distribution lists are scattered throughout the volume. Additional material of importance to reconstructing slave families on the Jefferson plantations is also located in Edwin M. Betts, ed., *Thomas Jefferson's Garden Book, 1776–1824* (Philadelphia, 1944). Unless otherwise noted, these sources provide the bases for information about slave families owned by Jefferson.

[3]Typescript of Carter's deed of manumission in the Robert Carter Papers, Duke University, Durham, N.C., and periodic inventories by quarter

holdings in a manner that revealed earlier domestic connections. C. C. Pinckney pieced together his South Carolina estate after 1808, but the bondsmen and women that he
inherited, acquired through marriage, or purchased had been
born and often married decades earlier.[4] Richard Bennehan,
an ambitious clerk who established one of the largest plantations in North Carolina, began his slave birth register in
1776.[5] These lists do not comprise all the systematic evidence
of eighteenth-century black family life, but they reveal its basic patterns and suggest its regional variations, its development over time, and, most significantly, its meaning.[6]

By the eve of the American Revolution, black people, generally just a generation or two removed from African enslavement and the harrowing experience of the Middle
Passage, had constructed a family life in mainland North
America. Of the nearly 400 slaves Charles Carroll of Annapolis owned in 1773, some 325 lived in immediate families
(parents and children), and the members of these immediate
families generally resided together on the same quarter (table
1). Young children nearly always lived with their fathers and
mothers (table 2). On the Jefferson plantation, which can be
viewed over time through successive censuses, parents and
children also lived together and marriages were nearly always lifelong. The single exception of Barnaby and Lilly, who
divorced and remarried about 1812, confirmed this general
rule (and demonstrates that the Jefferson censuses reflected
the reality of plantation life and not bookkeeping protocol).
Barnaby and Lilly's divorce also suggests that slaves usually
chose their own marital partners and that slaveowners played
little role in slave courting. Like other masters, Jefferson

---

in the Robert Carter Journals, 1784–89, Library of Congress; Edward Lloyd
Family Papers, Md. Hist. Soc.

[4]C. C. Pinckney Plantation Journal, L.C.

[5]Birth Registers, Bennehan-Cameron Family Papers, Southern Historical Collection, University of North Carolina, Chapel Hill.

[6]For additional evidence of slave family formation in the eighteenth
century, see Herbert G. Gutman, *The Black Family in Slavery and Freedom,
1750–1925* (New York, 1976), pp. 169–84 and 327–60.

SLAVERY AND FREEDOM

Table 1: Types of immediate families among Carroll slaves, 1773–74

Type of household	Number	Percent	Number of households with one or more members on a different quarter
Husband-wife	3	3.8%	1
Husband-wife-children	47	59.5%	9
Father-children	4	5.1%	1
Mother-children	25	31.6%	4
Total	79	100.0%	15

SOURCE: "A List of Negroes on Doohoregan Manor," Dec. 1, 1773, Charles Carroll Account Book, microfilm, Maryland Hall of Records, Annapolis.

grumbled about slaves who "imprudently married out of their respective families"—that is, off the home plantation; and he rewarded those who married within the plantation "family," usually with small gifts. "There is nothing I desire so much as that all the young people on the estate should intermarry with one another and stay at home," Jefferson noted. "They are worth a great deal more in that case than when they have husbands and wives abroad."[7] Yet despite their master's entreaties, many of the Jefferson slaves took partners from the neighboring farms and plantations, as did the slaves of other Virginia slaveowners.

Slave women generally married young, bore children soon after reaching sexual maturity, and usually settled into stable relationships by their early twenties.[8] As among nineteenth-

[7]Betts, *Farm Book*, pt. 2, pp. 25–26; Betts, *Garden Book*, p. 450.

[8]On the Jefferson plantation, which has the most complete records, the average age of mother at first birth for children born after 1774 was 18.2, with nineteen women having children at ages 15–17, sixteen at age 18, and twenty-two at 19–23. For the period for which there are full records, no woman appears to have borne a first child at age 24 or older. An investigation of intervals for all second and subsequent births for which months were noted (a total of 208) demonstrates that the slave women on the Jefferson estates came close to producing that one child every two years that their master regarded as ideal: fully 70 percent of the births came within three years of the one immediately preceding, 53 percent within thirty months, and 28 percent in twenty-four months or less. Conversely, only

Table 2: Household status of Carroll slaves under the age of
fifteen, 1773–74

Status	Under 5	5–9	10–14	Total
		Age		
Living with mother and father	55	38	29	122
Living with mother	13	10	10	33
Living with father	0	1	2	3
Living with siblings	1	4	4	9
Living with grand-parent(s)	2	5	1	8
Living alone; parent(s) on another quarter	0	5	6	11
Living alone; no kin connection	0	1	2	3
Total	71	64	54	189

SOURCE: "A List of Negroes on Doohoregan Manor," Dec. 1, 1773, Charles
Carroll Account Book, microfilm, Maryland Hall of Records, Annapolis.

century Afro-American slave women, childbirth before marriage (generally in their late teens) occurred with some frequency. On numerous occasions Jefferson listed young women
along with one or two children before he identified them, in
a subsequent census, with husbands. Sometimes it can be sur-
mised that their eventual husbands were the fathers of the
earlier children, in which case Jefferson's careful records may
reveal only his ignorance of life in the quarter. Molly, for
example, named her first children Phill (b. 1768) and Phyllis
(b. 1771), though she was not formally listed as the wife of
Phill Waggoner until 1783. But most such instances are not
so clear. It is impossible to tell whether Will Smith was the
father of Abby's first two children, Judy and Jesse, or whether
Jame Hubbard fathered Cate's daughters Hannah and Rachael, although they later had six children together. Furthermore, Jefferson's records never linked some women and their
children with adult men, and some men were always listed

28 percent of the births occurred after an interval of three years, with the
vast majority of these falling between thirty-six and forty-eight months.
For evidence on age of slave mothers at birth of first child in the nineteenth century, see Gutman, Black Family, pp. 50, 114, 124, 171.

singly. These cases may be indications of marriage off the plantation, of casual sexual liaisons, of women who bore children and never married, or a combination of these possibilities. They may also be nothing more than artifacts of the way Jefferson kept his records. For example, he often listed artisans as a group apart from their immediate families, making it difficult to identify their wives and children.

Although some slaves married outside their master's holdings and some masters physically separated family members, most plantation families resided together on the same quarter. The resident household allowed slave parents to regulate their day-to-day domestic affairs and to raise their children with little direct interference from their master. On the Carroll estate almost two-thirds of the slaves under the age of fifteen and over three-quarters of those under five lived with both parents. Most of the remainder resided with either their father or, more commonly, their mother. Only a small minority lived in the household of a more distant relative. For most plantation children, their parents, not their owner, provided the court of first and generally last resort.

Naming practices reveal both the degree of autonomy slaves had established for their family life by the end of the eighteenth century and the importance of the slave's immediate family. On the Carroll estate a significant proportion (fully one-fourth) of the slave children who were under the age of ten in 1773 and had been named for kin were named for a parent, usually the father. Similarly, twenty-three of the children and eight of the firstborn children on Jefferson's plantations carried a parent's given name. None of the slaves on either plantation shared their master's name.

Slavery evolved differently in the eighteenth-century Carolina lowcountry than it did in the Chesapeake region. South Carolina planters held larger numbers of slaves, lived away from their estates, and imported Africans long after Chesapeake masters had established a self-sustaining slave force. Following the rice revolution of the early eighteenth century, deaths exceeded births among lowcountry blacks until the 1770s. Nonetheless, some lowcountry slaves established families during the eighteenth century and cemented those ties by a tight pattern of kin naming. The descendants of Old

Anthony, progenitor of the slaves inherited by C. C. Pinckney from his father, provide one example. The son of Molly and Isaac, Old Anthony had two daughters, Rinah and Molly, the latter named for her grandmother. Rinah named one of her sons Anthony, for her father, and the other son Little Sam, for her husband. The son of the other daughter, Molly, and her husband January bore the name of his great-grandfather, Isaac, born early in the eighteenth century. The precedent established by Old Anthony in the Revolutionary era continued down to the Civil War and doubtless beyond. Twenty-six of the twenty-nine slave families who resided on Pinckney's estates named children for their parents or other blood kin, and more than half the children born after 1800 carried kin names. Many of these were African or were derived from African names, reflecting the continuing slave trade, the black majority, and the large degree of autonomy slaves enjoyed in the lowcountry. But despite the difference in the names themselves, the pattern of naming was no different from that in the Chesapeake.

In the Carolina lowcountry, as in the Chesapeake, family bonds became the most important mechanism slaves wielded to improve the lives of their loved ones. Slave parents commonly used family lines to bequeath their most valuable property: their skill. Pinckney's Carpenter Sam, who occasionally hired his own time, passed his trade on to his eldest son, Anthony, and saw his second son and namesake, Little Sam, receive a place in Pinckney's house. Both sons of Cooper Joe on the Carroll estate continued their father's trade of barrelmaking. Just as sons received their fathers' skills, so daughters learned their mothers' trades. Like her mother (Old Bess, born in 1730), Old Flora, born in 1760, served as midwife on the Pinckney estate. Family-based skill transfer concentrated privileged positions within a few families, with important, if still unexplored, consequences for the development of slave society. In all, about half the tradesmen under age twenty-five on Carroll's quarters had kin who were also skilled mechanics,[9] and all but one of the forty-two

[9]Kulikoff, "Beginnings of the Afro-American Family," p. 186, makes a similar point.

tradesmen and skilled house servants on Jefferson's plantations in 1810 came from eight extended families, with more than half of them from just three families. Four of the eight families, moreover, were linked by marital ties. Such skill transfers provide material evidence of the creation of intergenerational links—passageways that transmitted culture and forged cultural consciousness. Like naming practices, skill transfer indicates the presence of cultural connections through which black people could move backward and forward in time to retain or modify their traditions and customs. Generational linkages enabled slaves to maintain ties with an African past and to incorporate that past into a diverse and evolving American experience.

Immediate families—husbands and wives, parents and children—marked only the beginning of slave family life. By the time of the Revolution, slave families had radiated outward from these intimate ties of blood and marriage to form a thicket of family connections that enveloped every member: aunts and uncles, nephews and nieces, cousins, and, occasionally, grandparents. This tight web of kin connections can be seen most clearly on the largest quarters of the great plantations. For example, all but 30 of the 128 residents of Riggs, the home quarter of Carroll's sprawling 10,000-acre Doohoregan Manor, belonged to two extended kin groups. Similarly, Jefferson's Bear Creek Quarter in Bedford County, Virginia, was occupied in 1810 by Cate and her husband Jame Hubbard; their daughters Eve, Maria, Sarah, and Rachael; Rachael's husband James; all the children of Cate and Jame's daughters, with the exception of two teenaged boys who lived at Monticello; their adopted son Armistead; two of their adolescent grandsons by Cate's daughter Hannah, who lived in another quarter; and a son of Hannah's sister-in-law. The only persons on the quarter apparently unrelated to Cate and Jame Hubbard were Sal, Gawen, and their five young children. Conversely, the only direct descendants of Cate and Jame who did not reside at Bear Creek were Hannah, her family, and Cate and Jame's adopted son (all of whom lived at Poplar Forest, another Bedford County quarter); two grandsons (whom Jefferson had moved to Monticello); and an adult son, Phill (on Tufton Quarter in Albemarle County). In 1815, after

Phill married, he successfully petitioned Jefferson to allow him to move to Bear Creek to live with his family.

Naming patterns also confirm the importance of extended kin ties. On the Carroll plantation, of the sixty-one slaves named for blood relatives, nineteen bore the given names of grandparents; sixteen, those of uncles and aunts; and nine, those of great-grandparents and great-uncles or great-aunts. Limited knowledge of the seventeenth-century ancestors of Carroll slaves truncates an understanding of extended-kin naming practices and means that these totals represent the minimum number. If a full genealogy could be constructed, the count would doubtless be much larger. A similar pattern of kin naming could be found on the Jefferson quarters, although his censuses reveal even less about the pre-Revolutionary family histories of his bondspeople. Thirty of the children on Jefferson's plantations carried the names of uncles and aunts; twenty-five, those of grandparents; two, those of great-uncles; and four, those of great-grandparents.

By naming their children for kinfolk, slave parents welded the black population of the plantation into a single community. Special evidence of this can be found in necronymic practices among Jefferson slaves. Three newborn Jefferson slaves bore the names of recently deceased siblings. Sometimes a blood cousin carried the name of a dead kinsperson. Lovilo, youngest child of Davy and Isabel, died in 1815; three years later their oldest son, James, and his wife, Cretia, named a son Lovilo. When Lilly and Barnaby's four-year-old child, Anderson, died at Tufton Quarter, both Sally Hubbard (who lived at Bear Creek) and Nanny and Daniel (at Poplar Forest) named sons born that same year "Anderson"—a name unique on the plantation to those three children. Other naming practices served to reinforce family connections. For example, the sisters Flora and Sal married the brothers Austin and Gawen. When Flora and Austin had their first child, a boy, they named him Gawen for Austin's brother, who at the time had four daughters but no sons to bear his name. Thus the first child in that generation bore the name of an uncle without sons, which suggests how blood and marriage lines crossed to influence naming patterns and make kinship and community bonds one.

Table 3: Age and sex of Jefferson slaves, 1773–74

Age group	Male	Female	Total
Under 5			71
5–9			64
10–14			54
15–19	20	21	41
20–29	26	34	60
30–39	19	16	35
40–49	15	14	29
50+	13	16	29
Total	93	101	383

SOURCE: Edwin M. Betts, ed., *Thomas Jefferson's Farm Book* (Princeton, 1953), pp. 5–9, 15–18, 24, 30, 57, and 128–29.

Masters allowed and sometimes even encouraged the development of slave family bonds because such ties reflected their own ideal of family life, stabilized social relations within the plantation, and, perhaps most important, produced valuable offspring. Whenever possible, slaveowners tried to maintain an equal sexual balance on the plantation. Thomas Jefferson explicitly instructed his overseers to keep "gangs of half men & half women" (table 3).[10] Planters viewed young people without mates as particularly troublesome and a possible source of insurrectionary sentiment. The promise of a partner, on the other hand, could be used to stir greater exertions or stifle unrest. While some planters offered the promise of family security as a carrot to encourage accommodation, others wielded it as a stick. In 1803, while casting about for an appropriate punishment for Cary, a young bondsman who had maliciously injured another slave, Jefferson hit upon the severest of all punishments, the severance of family ties. Such a venture would be expensive for the always hard-pressed president because he would be forced to sell Cary below the slave's real worth. But Jefferson understood that if Cary "was sold in any other quarter so distant as never more to be heard of among us, it would be to the others as if he were put out of the way by death." Therefore, he told his son-in-law, "I should regard price but little in com-

[10]Betts, *Garden Book*, pp. 184, 196, and 200; Betts, *Farm Book*, pt. 2, pp. 46 and 43.

parison with so distant an exile of him as to cut him off completely from ever again being heard of." Jefferson knew that to the slaves on his quarters perpetual exile from the plantation family would be equivalent to death.[11]

Social stability was but one benefit that masters drew from settled slave families. Also significant was their recognition that regularized family relations best assured the continued growth of an indigenous slave force. Since mainland slaveholders, especially in the Chesapeake, depended on natural increase to supply their slaves, this was of particular importance. Planters not only tried to keep the sexes carefully balanced on their estates, but also removed women from field work during the last months of pregnancy and allowed them time to care for their children. Jefferson reminded his steward that he considered "the labor of a breeding woman as no object." Like Jefferson, many masters came to hold "a woman who brings a child every two years as more valuable than the best man on the farm. What she produces is an addition to capital, while his labor disappears in mere consumption."[12]

If the value of an increasing slave force strengthened planter interest in the slave family, it also set the limits of that commitment. Profits to be gained by selling young men and women were such that few masters, including Jefferson, could resist them. Thus, no matter what value slaveowners found in the stability that family provided and no matter how fully it reflected their own domestic ideal, they could not be relied upon to preserve the integrity of the black family. For that, slaves had only themselves to depend on.

To keep their families together, slaves manipulated their masters in their own interest. They commonly petitioned owners to allow co-residence. In a memorial typical of many others, James, a slave on Robert Carter's Capricorn Quarter, requested that his wife be moved from another part of Carter's estate so they could live together. Carter's Carpenter George asked that his motherless daughter Betty be sent to live with his second wife. On another occasion Carter re-

[11]Betts, *Farm Book*, pt. 2, p. 19.

[12]Betts, *Garden Book*, pp. 184, 196, and 200; Betts, *Farm Book*, pt. 2, pp. 46 and 43.

ceived a similarly motivated request and exchanged two young children between quarters so that they might live with their parents. Since slaves frequently married off the plantation despite their masters' objections, they also memorialized their owners to purchase their loved ones. Jefferson felt compelled to purchase the wife and three children of Moses, a Monticello blacksmith, even though he doubted that she could be profitably employed.[13]

Jefferson, Carter, and other slaveholders complied with their slaves' requests because they understood that failure to respect slave family ties provoked problems. When separated from kinsfolk, slaves complained, sulked, and refused to work. More unsettling still, some took direct action to restore familial relations. Many ran away to be with relatives. For this reason, masters searched among the slaves' most distant familial connections when looking for fugitives. Such escapes made masters chary about separating families and selling loved ones. All too often the planter's raw economic interest overruled these concerns, but occasionally they had the desired effect. Much to the distress of one Maryland master, his slave mechanic continued to run away to visit his wife on a distant estate. Unwilling to sell this valuable hand, he at last informed the offending fugitive (through his overseer) "that his pardon depends upon his future behavior, that if he behaves well, and endeavours to make amends for his past behavior I will when I return purchase his wife if her master will sell her at a reasonable price."[14]

Slaves struggled against their masters to maintain the integrity of their family life. Masters sold slaves at will and sometimes for trivial cause, and they moved bondspeople from quarter to quarter for reasons of economic efficiency, social stability, or mere whim. Slaves intervened successfully in these decisions only at the sufferance of the master. Thus no matter how cleverly or forcefully slaves made their case, slave-

[13]Robert Carter to Fleet Cox, Jan. 2, 1788, Carter to Samuel Carter, Mar. 10, 1781, Carter to Forest Quarter Overseer, July 19, 1782, Robert Carter letterbook (typescript), Robert Carter Papers; Betts, *Farm Book*, pt. 2, pp. 12, 20, 21, 32, and 25–26.

[14]John Hanson to ?, Jan. 29, 1782, John Hanson Papers, Md. Hist. Soc.

holder demands shaped slave family life in significant ways. For example, social relationships within the quarter depended, in some measure, on its size and composition. Depending on their function, Carroll's twelve quarters were staffed differently. Their size varied widely from 130 slaves at Riggs to 8 at Captain Ireland's. The sexual, age, and occupational composition of the slave force also differed from place to place. As a result distinctive family configurations and familial relations emerged on different quarters. For example, several large related families dominated Riggs Quarter. The most significant familial relations were between siblings—Ned, Kate, Harry, and Bob—all the children of Old Fanny; uncles and aunts were the dominant figures there.

James's Quarter, on the other hand, was composed of a single multigenerational family headed by James and Beck. All but one of James and Beck's nine children resided on James's Quarter. Will, the sole exception, labored at Riggs Quarter, but his new wife Moll and her three young children lived with Will's parents on James's Quarter. Three of James and Beck's daughters had started families in the 1760s, but their husbands did not live among them. James, at sixty-five, was the only adult male in the enlarged kin group on the quarter. As founding father and mother of the clan, James and Beck dominated James's Quarter and its family.

Family relations took still another form at the Carroll house in Annapolis, where thirteen children and young adults labored without familial connections. Only fragments of families—sibling and cousin relations—existed there, and slaves seemed to look back to the quarters of their origin, where their respective parents, spouses, or siblings lived, for their family life. A similar fragmentation could be found at Jefferson's home quarter, Monticello, and may reflect a common familial pattern among privileged bondspeople. Jefferson drew house servants and tradesmen from a few selected families. But because he brought them to his home quarter as individuals, not families, the Monticello slaves lived without close kin ties except at holiday time when Jefferson granted them leave for family reunions.

The diverse patterns of family relations among the Carroll quarters suggest how nonplantation life affected the development of the black family. Most Chesapeake slaves and many lowcountry ones lived in small, farm-size units. Their circumstances doubtless necessitated other strategies to maintain their domestic relations. But by the time of the Revolution they shared the same kin-related values as plantation slaves. Graphic evidence of this development may be drawn from the experience of the slaves of Richard Bennehan, who began purchasing slaves in the 1770s and eventually became one of the South's great planters. Bennehan acquired his bondspeople in small numbers and in a nonplantation setting, Orange County, North Carolina. Farms dominated the region, and in 1780, shortly after Bennehan began his climb into the planter class, only 3 percent of the county's slaveholders held more than twenty bondspeople. By 1790 Bennehan was the largest planter in the county, with twenty-four slaves. Like him, most of his slaves were newly arrived in the area, and there is no evidence that any had previous plantation experience. No nearby estates existed that might house complex kin networks similar to those in the Chesapeake or the Carolina lowcountry. Yet by the turn of the century, within less than a generation of the founding of Bennehan's dynasty, his slaves had established patterns of marriage, childbearing, and naming that were similar to those of the bondspeople on the Carroll, Pinckney, and Jefferson estates. Although plantations shaped black life in many ways, the plantation did not generate the slave family.

The broad network of family connections that informed all aspects of black life by the end of the eighteenth century allowed black people to take advantage of the opportunities provided by the Revolutionary crises. Most prominently, kinship ties smoothed the way for black people to move from slavery to freedom. Thomas Jefferson and Robert Carter, like other masters, lost large numbers of slaves as a result of British raids on their plantations. As they did elsewhere, blacks frequently left in family groups.[15] The strategy that had ear-

---

[15]Betts, *Farm Book*, p. 29; Louis Morton, *Robert Carter of Nomini Hall: A Virginia Tobacco Planter of the Eighteenth Century* (1941; reprint ed., Charlottesville, Va., 1964), pp. 110–11.

lier bound black people to their owners had a very different effect in the confusion of the Revolutionary War.

The war and the ideology that accompanied it fostered the growth of the free black population, perhaps the most significant structural change in colonial black society since the legalization of slavery more than a century earlier. As some black people gained their freedom, they used their new status to help loved ones out of bondage and thus give greater security to their family life. Since most newly freed blacks were poor, buying the liberty of a kinsperson demanded years of austere living. It was not unusual for a free Negro to save for five to ten years in order to liberate a single slave. Despite these obstacles, some free blacks dedicated much of their lives and fortunes to help others escape bondage. Graham Bell, a Petersburg, Virginia, freeman, purchased and freed nine slaves between 1792 and 1805. In 1792 Bell emancipated five slave children (probably his own) whom he had bought three years earlier. In 1801 he purchased and freed a slave woman, who later paid him £15 for the service. The following year, noting "that God created all men equally free," he emancipated two more slaves, and in 1805 he manumitted his brother. Bell's persistence was exceptional but not unique. In New Bern, North Carolina, John C. Stanly, a successful free Negro barber, purchased and emancipated his wife and children in 1805 and two years later freed his brother-in-law. During the next eleven years Stanly ransomed another eighteen slaves. Aletha Tanner of Washington equaled Stanly's benevolence. After purchasing her own freedom, she bought and liberated twenty-two relatives and friends[16]

Other free Negroes, anxious to reunite their families or friends, lacked the patience, money, or inclination to buy liberty. Instead, they plotted to aid fugitives from bondage. So often did newly freed blacks rescue their families from servitude that masters looked first to them when slaves ran away.

[16]Luther P. Jackson, "Manumission in Certain Virginia Cities," *Journal of Negro History* 15 (1930):285–86; John Hope Franklin, *The Free Negro in North Carolina, 1790–1860* (Chapel Hill, N.C., 1943), pp. 31–32; Constance McLaughlin Green, *The Secret City: A History of Race Relations in the Nation's Capital* (Princeton, 1967), p. 16.

When Jonathan fled slavery, his owner noted that he was "related to a family of negroes, who lately obtained their freedom"; Bet's mistress believed she "went off in company with a mulatto free fellow named Tom Turner, who follows the water for a living and calls her his wife"; and Sam's master thought he would go to Baltimore where he had "several relations (manumitted blacks), who will conceal and assist him to make his escape." Little wonder that slaveholders, determined to stop the growing number of fugitives, demanded legislative restraints on free blacks because of the "great number of relations and acquaintances they still have among us, and from the harbours and houses such manumitted Negroes" afforded runaways. Although slaveowners found free blacks easy scapegoats for slave unrest, their presumption proved true often enough to sustain their generalized suspicions. Once liberated from bondage, former slaves did not forget those left behind.[17]

The importance of kin networks and the assistance they gave blacks in the struggle to gain freedom is nowhere more evident than in the spate of freedom suits that accompanied the Revolution. The events of the Revolutionary era liberalized the regulations for such legal actions and encouraged black people to seek their liberty by judicial means. In Maryland, for example, admission of hearsay evidence greatly increased the number of slaves who sued for liberty on grounds of descent from a white person. The most famous case involved the descendants of Eleanor Butler, an Irish servant woman who had accompanied Charles Calvert to Maryland and later married a black slave named Charles. When her descendants, William and Mary Butler, sued for freedom nearly a hundred years later, their case rested on their ability to demonstrate descent from "Irish Nell." They did this and more. Their testimony mentioned over a hundred kinspeople, reporting who owned them, what work they did, and when "some salt water negroes [entered] into their count."

---

[17]Richmond *Virginia Gazette*, Dec. 11, 1793; Baltimore *Maryland Journal*, June 25, 1793; Annapolis *Maryland Gazette*, May 6, 1790; Petition from Accomack County, Jan. 3, 1783, Virginia Legislative Papers, Virginia State Library, Richmond.

They recounted the details of the wedding ceremony, the priest's name, and Nell's rebuke of Charles Calvert when the proprietor of Maryland attempted to dissuade her from marrying the slave: "she rather go to bed to Charles than his Lordship."[18] The case wended its way through the Maryland courts for over two decades, but in the end, William and Mary Butler won their freedom.

The success of the Butlers demonstrates how the generational links forged in the years before the Revolution allowed black people to take advantage of the new opportunities generated by the war and independence. The free black population grew rapidly, and newly liberated slaves worked feverishly to reconstruct their family life in freedom. Yet most blacks remained locked in bondage, and within a generation many of them would be hurled across the South by the forces unleashed by the cotton revolution. Yet for those left in bonds, as for those freed, family connections would guide their lives as it had their parents'. Nineteenth-century slaves retained strong attachments to their families and a knowledge of lines of descent reaching back into the colonial years. Among Carroll slaves, for example, naming patterns reveal ties between the slaves Charles Carroll of Carrollton willed to his heirs in 1832 and those his grandfather had purchased in the waning years of the seventeenth century. Along the cultural passageways slaves had forged flowed the collective experience of African peoples on mainland North America.

[18]Charles County Provincial Court Judgments, D.D., vol. 17, pp. 233–44, Md. Hall of Rec. The authors would like to thank Ross M. Kimmel for directing attention to the Provincial Court Judgments.

ALBERT J. RABOTEAU

The Slave Church
in the Era of the
American Revolution

IN MAY 1774 the governor and general court of Massachusetts received a petition from "a Grate Number of Blackes of
this Province, held in a state of Slavery within the bowels of
a free and Christian Country." Linking their cause to the
Revolutionary crisis, these black petitioners appealed for their
liberty on the same grounds that white Americans agitated
for theirs: "We have in common with all other men a naturel
right to our freedoms without Being depriv'd of them by our
fellow men as we are a freeborn Pepel and have never forfeited this Blessing by any compact or agreement whatever."
Slavery, they went on to argue, violated not only natural law
but also the fundamental commandment of Christianity.
"There is a grat number of us sencear members of the Church
of Christ how can the master be said to Beare my Borden
when he Beares me down with the Have chanes of slavery?"[1]
The official response to this petition, one of the earliest assertions by black Americans that slavery contradicted the basic ideals that constituted the nation's identity, remains
unknown. After the War for Independence, however, the liberty sought by the petitioners did come, but it came only
gradually, partially, and, for the vast majority of slaves, not
at all.

During the era of the Revolution, another social upheaval
held out the promise of liberation. A series of religious reviv-

[1]To Gov. Thomas Gage and the Massachusetts General Court, May 25,
1774, *Collections of the Massachusetts Historical Society*, 5th ser. 3 (1877):432–
33.

als, known collectively as the Great Awakening, swept over the colonies during the 1740s and, after abating in the North, continued to inundate parts of the South until the 1790s. The egalitarian impulse implicit in the evangelical Christianity of the revivals occasionally became explicit. The ideal of Christian equality preached in this revolution would prove as incomplete as the ideal of liberty proclaimed in the other, but the evangelical movement would give birth to an institution over which slaves exercised control and in which they asserted independence.

The Great Awakening divided American society, simultaneously calling into question the validity of ecclesiastical structures, the piety of duly ordained clergy, and eventually the very concept of an established church. Christian congregations splintered, fellowship gave way to rancor, and authority lost respect, all in the name of "experimental" or experiential religion. Even the methods of the evangelicals were disorderly. At their meetings, emotional preachers, some of them untrained and unlettered, encouraged the congregations to engage in enthusiastic exercises. Indeed, "the very Servants and Slaves pretend to extraordinary inspiration" and run about uttering nonsense, complained one Anglican cleric who was disturbed by the disruptive effect of the Awakening on society.[2] Revivals threatened the standing order. Nowhere was evangelicalism's potential for troubling an ordered society more graphically illustrated than in the Chesapeake region of the South, where, by the end of the century, it had literally changed the color of Christianity. The inclusion of black slaves in the brotherhood of Christian communion by Baptist and Methodist evangelicals reordered colonial society in Maryland and Virginia.[3] Compared to the formality and distance

[2]Lorenzo J. Greene, *The Negro in Colonial New England* (1942; reprint ed., New York, 1968), p. 276. See also Clarence C. Goen, *Revivalism and Separatism in New England* (New Haven, 1962); Edwin S. Gaustad, *The Great Awakening in New England* (New York, 1957); and Wesley M. Gewehr, *The Great Awakening in Virginia, 1740–1790* (Durham, N.C., 1930).

[3]Rhys Isaac, "Preachers and Patriots: Popular Culture and the Revolution in Virginia," in Alfred F. Young, ed., *The American Revolution: Explorations in the History of American Radicalism* (DeKalb, Ill., 1976), pp. 127–

characteristic of the old Anglican order, the shared emotion and ecstatic behavior of evangelical meetings brought blacks and whites closer to equality. Before the power of God, internalized in the liminal experience of conversion, all persons were leveled in the dust, and blacks as well as whites rose up to pray, exhort, preach, and even pastor.

Evangelicals threatened the social fabric because they dissented from establishment and, more generally, because they disturbed the peace. In eighteenth-century Virginia, Anglicans turned to both legal and mob action to harass the Separate Baptists, perceived as the most radical of the lot. During the 1760s and 1770s, rowdy groups of Virginians kicked, clubbed, and dunked Baptist preachers; interrupted their sermons with insults; and disrupted their baptismal services by riding horses through the water. Virginia magistrates sentenced Baptists to jail terms for preaching in public, some of the miscreants repeatedly enduring confinement for weeks or months at a time.[4]

Significantly, the Anglican clergy chose to counter the Baptists by linking them with the sixteenth-century Anabaptists of Münster, who long had served in polemical literature as *the* example of religion run to fanatical excess. Even the plain dress and physical appearance of the early Baptists set them apart from gentle folk. Men cut their hair "like Cromwell's roundheaded chaplains, and the women cast away all their superfluities so that they were distinguished from others."[5] People generally perceived the early Baptists as different in an unsettling sort of way: "There was a company of them in the back part of our town, and an outlandish set of people they certainly were," remarked one elderly woman to the Baptist historian David Benedict. "You yourself would say so if you had seen them. . . . You could hardly find one among

---

56, and idem, "Evangelical Revolt," *William and Mary Quarterly*, 3d ser. 31 (1974):348–53.

[4]Robert B. Semple, *A History of the Rise and Progress of the Baptists in Virginia*, ed. George W. Beale (Philadelphia, 1894), p. 30; Gewehr, *Great Awakening in Virginia*, pp. 119–21.

[5]John Leland, "Virginia Chronicle," in *The Writings of the Late Elder John Leland*, ed. L. F. Green (New York, 1845), p. 117.

them but was deformed in some way or other." And it was these outsiders, "hardly any of [whom] looked like other people," who claimed to live according to the true ordinances of the gospel.[6]

The appearance of fanaticism bred distrust. So did the evangelicals' success among the slaves. During the political struggle for disestablishment in Virginia, the colony's elite depicted dissenters as "subversive of the morals of the people and destructive of the peace of families, tending to alienate the affection of slaves from their masters." A pro-establishment petition warned the Virginia assembly in 1777 that "there have been nightly meetings of slaves to receive the instruction of these teachers without the consent of their masters, which have produced very bad consequences."[7] Tense confrontations between masters and slaves affirmed the subversive impact of evangelical religion. Jupiter, "a great Newlight preacher," fled his owner when the master scarred him for "stirring up the Negroes to insurrection." Complaints about other black preachers rang through the press. In 1772 the *Virginia Gazette* listed as runaway "a likely Virginia born Mulatto Lad named Primus, about nineteen or twenty years of Age," who "has been a Preacher ever since he was sixteen Years of Age, and has done much Mischief in his Neighborhood."[8] Similarly, Thomas Jones, owner of an escaped slave named Sam, informed the public exactly how religion had ruined his slave: "He was raised in a family of religious persons, commonly called Methodists, and has lived with some of them for years past, on terms of perfect equality; the refusal to continue him on these terms, the subscriber is instructed, has given him offence, and is the sole cause of his absconding. . . . He has been in the use of instructing and exhorting his fellow creatures of all colors in matters of religious duty." According to runaway notices in a Baltimore newspaper, Jem, a twenty-eight-year-old artisan, "is or pre-

[6]David Benedict, *Fifty Years among the Baptists* (New York, 1860), pp. 93–94.

[7]Charles F. James, ed., *Documentary History of the Struggle for Religious Liberty in Virginia* (Lynchburg, Va., 1900), pp. 84–85.

[8]*Virginia Gazette* (Purdie and Dixon), Oct. 1, 1767, and Feb. 27, 1772.

tends to be of the society of Methodists, he constantly attended the meetings, and at times exhorted himself"; and Jacob, thirty-five years of age, "professes to be a methodist and has been in the practice of preaching of nights." Slaves preaching, attending night meetings, living on terms of equality with whites—clearly evangelicalism posed a threat, a threat that could get out of hand. In 1789 the sheriff of King William County, Virginia, had to notify the governor that black and white evangelicals had resisted when members of a patrol tried to seize the slaves in attendance at a late night prayer meeting. The sheriff requested assistance in restoring law and order.[9]

The egalitarian impulse of Christianity drove some individual evangelicals and their churches to take a stand against slavery. Among the Baptists the most outspoken opponents of slavery were elders David Barrow and John Leland. Barrow freed his slaves in 1784 because he was convinced that slavery violated the laws of God and the precepts of republican government. Leaving Virginia for Kentucky, he published a *Circular Letter* in 1798 in which he asked Christian slaveowners if they were "doing as they would others should do to them!" John Leland composed the antislavery resolution adopted by the General Committee of Virginia Baptists in 1789. The resolution condemned slavery as "a violent deprivation of the rights of nature" and recommended that Baptists "make use of every legal measure to extirpate this horrid evil from the land."[10]

Given Baptist polity, which held that each congregation govern itself, the antislavery resolution had no legislative authority. Neither did it express the moral sentiments of Baptists as a whole. In 1790 the Roanoke Baptist Association responded to the General Committee's resolution by declaring that the subject of slavery was "so abstruse" that no reli-

[9]*Maryland Journal and Baltimore Advertiser*, June 14, 1793; *Maryland Gazette*, Jan. 4, 1798, and Sept. 4, 1800; Luther P. Jackson, "Religious Development of the Negro in Virginia, from 1760 to 1860," *Journal of Negro History* 16 (1931):172–73.

[10]David Barrow, *Circular Letter* (Norfolk, Va., [1798]), pp. 4–5; Semple, *Baptists in Virginia*, p. 105.

gious society had the right to concern itself with the issue as a society. Each individual should be left "to act at discretion in order to keep a good conscience before God, as far as the laws of our land will admit." The association maintained "that it is the indispensable duty of masters to forbear and sur-press cruelty" and do that which is just and equal to their servants.[11] This exhortation proved to be the path of retreat that most churches took to escape internecine conflict over the issue of slavery: the concern of the church should be amelioration, not emancipation. In 1792 the Strawberry Association told the General Committee, in effect, to mind its own business. And in 1793, four years after passing the anti-slavery resolution, the General Committee capitulated, deciding "that the subject be dismissed from this committee, as believing it belongs to the legislative body."[12]

While the resolutions of the Baptist Association could only advise, the rulings of the Methodist Conference bound all members to comply. But the Methodist legislation against slaveowning ultimately proved no more effective than the recommendations of the Baptists. The founder of Methodism, John Wesley, and the early leaders of the American church, Francis Asbury and Thomas Coke, attacked the evil of slavery. Individual Methodist converts, such as Jesse Lee, Philip Gatch, and the aptly named Freeborn Garrettson, having experienced the liberation of conversion, found it repugnant to hold men in slavery. Garrettson, as he stood one day lining out a hymn, was struck by the thought that it was wrong to keep his fellow creatures in bondage. Interpreting the thought as the voice of God, he replied, "Lord the oppressed shall go free," and claimed that from that moment on he was "as clear of them in my mind, as if I had never owned one."[13] During the revival of 1787–88, Virginia Methodists reput-

---

[11]Gewehr, *Great Awakening in Virginia*, pp. 240–41.

[12]Ibid., p. 241.

[13]Nathan Bangs, *The Life of the Rev. Freeborn Garrettson* (New York, 1832), p. 39; John McLean, *Sketch of Rev. Philip Gatch* (Cincinnati, 1854), pp. 92–93; Gewehr, *Great Awakening in Virginia*, p. 242.

edly freed more than a hundred slaves at one session of the Sussex County court.[14]

Methodist Conferences in 1780, 1783, and again in 1784 strongly condemned slavery and tried "to extirpate this abomination," first from the ministry and then from the membership as a whole, by passing increasingly stringent regulations against slaveowning, slave-buying, and slave-selling. In the upper South, where Methodism grew most rapidly, the church's antislavery position met with strong, immediate, and, as the leadership quickly realized, irreversible opposition. For example, when Coke preached against slavery in Virginia in 1785, a mob threatened to whip him, and two counties indicted him for disturbing the peace. That same year the Baltimore Conference suspended the rule against slavery. As Coke explained, "We thought it prudent to suspend the minute concerning slavery, on account of the great opposition that had been given it, our work being in too infantile a state to push things to extremity." Although the conference reiterated antislavery sentiments, in practice the church retreated. Asbury admitted as much in his journal: "Would not an *amelioration* in the condition and treatment of slaves have produced more practical good to the poor Africans than any attempt at their *emancipation?* The state of society, unhappily does not admit of this."[15]

The evangelical challenge to slavery failed. The intransigence of slavery set the limits of the egalitarian impulse. Rapid growth of the Baptist and Methodist churches, rather than overthrowing slavery, instead forced an inevitable accommodation to slaveholding principles. At the beginning of the nineteenth century Robert Semple described the change among Virginia Baptists after 1791: "Their preachers became much more correct in their manner of preaching. A

[14]Gewehr, *Great Awakening in Virginia*, p. 249, n. 71.

[15]Donald G. Mathews, *Slavery and Methodism: A Chapter in American Morality, 1780–1845* (Princeton, 1965), pp. 293–99; Jackson, "Religious Development of the Negro in Virginia," p. 173; Gewehr, *Great Awakening in Virginia*, pp. 244–48; Francis Asbury, *The Journal and Letters of Francis Asbury*, ed. Elmer T. Clark, J. Manning Potts, and Jacob S. Payton, 3 vols. (Nashville, 1958), 2:284.

great many odd tones, disgusting whoops and awkward gestures were disused. . . . Their zeal was less mixed with enthusiasm, and their piety became more rational." Semple attributed such modifications to the broadening of the Baptist membership: "They were much more numerous, and, of course, in the eyes of the world, more respectable. Besides, they were joined by persons of much greater weight in civil society; their congregations became more numerous. . . . This could not but influence their manners and spirit more or less."[16] What Semple described is, in Weberian terms, the routinization of charisma, an inevitable institutional process.

Success and respectability changed the evangelicals, but the evangelicals also changed society. By the inclusion of both blacks and whites in close communities of small, voluntary, religious societies, the Baptists and Methodists far outstripped the old Anglican parish in rationalizing the relationships, the "daily walk and talk," of their biracial memberships. Though the churches accommodated slavery, in their attempt to measure life by the rule of gospel order, they were still forced to face the disquieting contradiction between Christian fellowship and human bondage. Two issues in particular drew attention to the inconsistency of calling slaves "brother" and "sister." One was slave marriage, the other slave control.

In October 1796 the Dover Baptist Association of Virginia (one black delegate attending) received a query: "Is there no restriction on believing masters in the chastisement of their servants?" The association's answer was general rather than specific, but it did make clear that treatment of slaves fell within the discipline of the church: "There is no doubt but masters may, and sometimes do exercise an unreasonable authority; but as it is very difficult and perhaps impossible to fix a certain rule in these cases we think, the churches should take notice of such as they may think improper and deal with the transgressor, as they would with offenders in other crimes." Such pronouncements were not mere rhetoric, but attempts to address real problems facing individual congregations. For example, in 1780 Nero, the slave of one John Lawrence,

[16]Semple, *Baptists in Virginia*, p. 59.

brought charges of "misconduct" against his master, and Lawrence was found guilty by the South Quay, Virginia, Baptist congregation and expelled. Similarly, James Johnson was expelled from the Black Creek, Virginia, Baptist church in 1792 "for beating a Negro." In September 1793 Shadrach Roberts and his wife Sarah, charged with beating Nancy Sims, had to come forward and give satisfaction before the congregation of Wheeley's Baptist Church in North Carolina.[17]

The question of slave marriage proved even more vexing to church order. The failure of the churches to lobby for the protection or recognition of slave marriage indicated the extent of the accommodation of Christian ideals to the system of slavery. The specific issue with which the churches had to wrestle was clearcut: could slaves involuntarily separated from their spouses be permitted to remarry, or should they be expelled for adultery if they took a new mate? On a practical level the issue could often be solved by compromise, as in the case of Sam, a slave member of the Flat River Primitive Baptist Church in Person County, North Carolina. Sam's wife had been removed by her owner to South Carolina, and Sam sought permission from the church to marry again. The church's decision was sympathetic, "this being a trying case where a man and his wife is parted by their owners, who being in bondage cannot help themselves, as such we have come to this conclusion that it shall not brake fellowship with us if Sam should git another wife."[18]

On a theoretical level, however, the problem of slave marriage was much more difficult to solve, as the Portsmouth Baptist Association acknowledged in 1793 when it took up the query "Is it lawful, and agreeable to the Word of God, for a black Manservant, (or Slave) who has been Married, and his Wife removed from him a great distance, without his or her consent to marry another Woman during her Life or

---

[17]*Minutes of the Dover Baptist Association, Oct. 8, 1796* (Richmond, 1797), pp. 3–4; W. Harrison Daniel, "Virginia Baptists and the Negro in the Early Republic," *Virginia Magazine of History and Biography* 80 (1972):63; Wheeley's (Wheeler's)Baptist Church Minutes, 1790–98, Southern Historical Collection, University of North Carolina, Chapel Hill.

[18]Flat River Primitive Baptist Church Records, Nov. 1790, S. Hist. Coll.

not?" After long debate the delegates agreed to withdraw the query and appointed a committee to substitute another in its stead. The committee returned with a reformulated query that went directly to the heart of the issue: "What ought Churches to do with Members in their Communion, who shall either directly, or indirectly separate married Slaves, who are come together according to the custom as Man and Wife?" After another long debate the delegates simply declared the matter "to be so difficult that no answer could be given it."[19] The length of the debate and the passion that apparently accompanied it indicate that the separation of married slaves troubled the Portsmouth Association, and yet the association could not mount a successful attack upon a practice so obviously contrary to gospel ordinances. Such frustration reveals the incomplete nature of the evangelical revolution; for slaves it brought neither freedom nor protection of the most basic Christian values, including the sanctity of marriage.

Despite such failings, slaves perceived the egalitarian dimension implicit within Christianity, a dimension articulated by evangelicalism at least some of the time. The identification of evangelicals with the poorer sort, their persecution as dissenters and disturbers of the peace, their willingness to license blacks to exhort and preach, and the antislavery views and deeds of a few undoubtedly made their version of Christianity seem a "gospel of freedom" to many slaves. For example, fifteen years after the Methodists had rescinded their antislavery rule, the slaves involved in Gabriel's insurrection plotted to massacre all whites except Methodists, Quakers, and Frenchmen "on account of there being friendly to liberty."[20] Moreover, within the institutional structure of the evangelical congregations, particularly the Baptist, slaves achieved new status as active and frequently founding members of churches. They participated in the monthly or quarterly meetings in which the covenanted community attempted to regulate all spheres of life. The church recognized their

[19]*Minutes of the Virginia Portsmouth Baptist Association* (Norfolk, Va., 1793), p. 4.

[20]Gerald W. Mullin, *Flight and Rebellion: Slave Resistance in Eighteenth-Century Virginia* (New York, 1972), pp. 158–60.

"gifts" and gave them "liberty to exercise" them as exhorters and preachers. Most important of all, evangelical Protestantism not only allowed blacks to participate actively with whites in church life, it provided them the opportunity to found and pastor their own churches as well. In the church, slaves developed a unique, if limited, channel to secure their autonomy in the midst of slavery.

Due to their strong emphasis on the experience of conversion, Methodists and Baptists did not insist upon advanced education as a qualification for preaching. If an individual was converted and had the gift, then he preached, even in the absence of "gentle" standing. Deficiencies in educational and social status mattered little at evangelical prayer meetings. There, as revivalist Devereaux Jarratt recalled, "the poorer sort, who at first may be shy in speaking, soon wore off their shyness and spoke as freely as others."[21] Race offered no greater barrier to vocal participation than class. As one critical Anglican remarked in 1776, the "most illiterate among them are their Teachers even Negroes speak in their meetings."[22] Blacks, slave as well as free, took advantage of the opportunity to exercise their talents as exhorters and preachers. By the end of the eighteenth century a significant group of black preachers had emerged. Mainly Baptist, since the congregational independence of the Baptists gave them more leeway than any other denomination, most of these pioneer black preachers remain anonymous. But occasional glimpses of their lives and their ministries fortunately survive.

The eloquence of black preachers aroused the curiosity and sometimes the admiration of white audiences. In 1782 Lewis, a slave of a Mr. Brokenborough of Essex County, preached in Virginia's Northern Neck to crowds as large as four hundred people. According to one white observer who heard him preach on several occasions, Lewis spoke "with the greatest sensibility I ever expected to hear from an Ethiopian," and his "gift exceeded [that of] many white preachers." Harry

[21]Quoted in Gewehr, *Great Awakening in Virginia*, p. 252.

[22]Quoted in Marcus W. Jernegan, "Slavery and Conversion in the American Colonies," *American Historical Review* 21 (1916):515.

Hosier, another black preacher, frequently accompanied Methodist itinerants Asbury, Garrettson, and Whatcoat as they traveled the Maryland and Virginia circuits in the 1780s and 1790s. Although particularly popular among the slaves, "Black Harry" preached effectively to whites as well and consistently attracted large audiences to Methodist meetings.[23]

In a few cases the "liberty" given a slave preacher to exercise his gift was physical as well as spiritual. For example, local Baptists gave money to Jacob Bishop, a slave preacher from Northampton County, Virginia, to purchase his freedom. "His preaching," according to contemporary report, "was much admired by both saints and sinners." After the resignation of the pastor of the predominantly black Portsmouth church, the congregation employed Bishop in 1795 to preach to them. Bishop later moved north and became pastor of the Abyssinian Baptist Church of New York City. In 1792 delegates to the Roanoke (Virginia) Baptist Association decided to purchase the freedom of a slave named Simon because, in their words, "we think him ordained of God to preach the gospel." In the same year, white Baptists freed "Uncle Jack," an African-born slave who preached for over forty years in Nottoway County, Virginia.[24]

Some white congregations turned to black preachers to fill their pulpits. After the death of their pastor, the white members of the Petsworth Church of Gloucester "did what it would hardly have been supposed would have been done by Virginians"; they "chose for their pastor William Lemon, a man of color." Lemon served the church until his death and represented the Petsworth congregation at the Dover Association in 1797, 1798, and 1801. At the turn of the century two free black preachers actually led in the foundation of Baptist and Methodist churches in locales where none had existed

[23]Richard Dozier, quoted in Garnett Ryland, *The Baptists of Virginia* (Richmond, 1955), p. 155; Jackson, "Religious Development of the Negro in Virginia," p. 176.

[24]Semple, *Baptists in Virginia*, p. 458; Lemuel Burkitt and Jesse Read, *A Concise History of the Kehukee Baptist Association* (Halifax, N.C., 1803), pp. 258–59; Ryland, *Baptists of Virginia*, p. 155; Rev. William S. White, *The African Preacher* (Philadelphia, [1849]).

before. Henry Evans, a shoemaker by trade, was licensed by the Methodists in the 1790s as a local preacher and organized the first Methodist church in Fayetteville, North Carolina. While preaching to blacks, Evans attracted the attention of several prominent whites who soon pushed the black members of his congregation from their seats. Another free black, Joseph Willis, pioneered in the spread of the Baptist message in southwestern Mississippi and Louisiana.[25]

Blacks preaching to, converting, and even pastoring whites signaled that evangelicalism offered a path to status and authority that was available nowhere else to black men. The rise of black exhorters and preachers in the last quarter of the eighteenth century also meant that black participation and even leadership shaped American evangelicalism during its formative years. The influence of black preachers upon white evangelicals was significant, but of greater significance for the development of religious autonomy among the slaves was the fact that black preachers took it upon themselves to minister to their own people, with or without license from whites. As an early historian of the Baptists observed, much of this ministry was informal and extraecclesiastical: "among the African Baptists in the Southern states there are a multitude of preachers and exhorters whose names do not appear on the minutes of the associations. They preach principally on the plantations to those of their own color, and their preaching though broken and illiterate, is in many cases highly useful."[26]

It would be difficult to overestimate the importance of these early black preachers for the development of Afro-American culture. In effect they mediated between Christianity and the experience of the slaves, interpreting the stories, symbols, and

[25]Semple, *Baptists in Virginia*, p. 170; Ryland, *Baptists of Virginia*, p. 156; *Minutes of the Dover Baptist Association*, 1797, 1798, and 1801; John Spencer Bassett, *Slavery in the State of North Carolina* (Baltimore, 1899), pp. 57–58; Walter H. Brooks, "The Evolution of the Negro Baptist Church," *Journal of Negro History* 7 (1922):103; David Benedict, *A General History of the Baptist Denomination in America*, 4th ed. (New York, 1850), p. 779.

[26]David Benedict, whose *General History of the Baptist Denomination* first appeared in 1813, quoted in Charles Colcock Jones, *The Religious Instruction of the Negroes in the United States* (Savannah, 1842), p. 58.

events of the Bible to fit the day-to-day lives of those held in bondage. And whites, as they well knew, lacked complete control of the "accuracy" of the interpretation. Nurturing Christian communities among slaves and free blacks, these pioneer preachers began to build the black church in the last quarter of the eighteenth century. As sociologist Robert Park correctly observed, "With the appearance of these men, the Negroes in America ceased to be a mission people. At least from this time on, the movement went on of its own momentum, more and more largely under the direction of Negro leaders. Little Negro congregations, under the leadership of Negro preachers, sprang up wherever they were tolerated. Often they were suppressed, more often they were privately encouraged. Not infrequently they met in secret."[27] In some instances their organization antedated the white congregations.

Before 1800 black Baptists had formed several separate "African" churches. Typically, their congregations consisted of both slave and free members. They were independent to the extent that they held their own separate services; ran their own business meetings; admitted, disciplined, and dismissed their own members; called their own pastors; and joined with white congregations in sending delegates to associational meetings. In some cases separate white and black churches resulted from division of previously mixed congregations. In other instances "African" churches were founded as separate institutions from the start. For example, Virginia blacks established the African Baptist Church of Williamsburg independently, and it thrived in spite of severe initial persecution. By 1810, when a Baptist historian wrote the following account, it was already an established institution.

> This church is composed almost, if not altogether, of people of colour. Moses, a black man, first preached among them and was often taken up and whipped, for holding meetings. Afterwards Gowan, who called himself Gowan Pamphlet . . . became popular among the blacks, and began to baptize, as well as to preach. It seems, the association had advised that no person of colour

[27]Robert E. Park, "The Conflict and Fusion of Cultures with Special Reference to the Negro," *Journal of Negro History* 4 (1919):120.

should be allowed to preach, on the pain of excommunication; against this regulation, many of the blacks were rebellious, and continued to hold meetings. Some were excluded, and among this number was Gowan. . . . Continuing still to preach and many professing faith under his ministry, not being in connexion with any church himself, he formed a kind of church out of some who had been baptized, who, sitting with him, received such as offered themselves; Gowan baptized them, and was moreover appointed their pastor; some of them knowing how to write, a churchbook was kept; they increased to a large number; so that in the year 1791, when the Dover association was holden . . . they petitioned for admittance into the association, stating their number to be about five hundred. The association received them, so far, as to appoint persons to visit them and set things in order. These, making a favourable report, they were received, and have associated ever since.[28]

This chronicle illustrates the determination of blacks to control their own religious life. Rebelling against white ecclesiastical control, they insisted upon their claim that congregational independence belonged by right to black as well as white Baptists.

Several other independent black churches emerged in Tidewater Virginia during the Revolutionary era. In Charles City County black members of the mixed church established a short-lived separate congregation rather than obey a rule denying them permission to preach.[29] After the white pastor of Allen's Creek Church in Mecklenburg County moved away in 1790, the congregation, "having a considerable number of black people in their society of whom there were some preachers of talents," continued to administer the sacraments, although none of the black preachers had been ordained. Persecuted by some whites in the community, the church was defended by others and rapidly increased in size. In only a few years more than one hundred black converts joined the church and received baptism. Eventually the former pastor returned and "attempted to settle them in order," with mixed success. Some black members rejoined him and

[28]Semple, *Baptists in Virginia*, p. 148.

[29]Ibid., p. 145.

chose to be rebaptized by a duly ordained preacher, but "many refused to give up their independent state."[30] Another independent black church, numbering 200 members, was organized in York and James City counties in 1781 with Gowen (probably the same Gowan associated with the Williamsburg church) as pastor and Joseph Mead as itinerant.[31]

The rise of black preachers and separate black churches in the Chesapeake region undoubtedly benefited from the dramatic increase in the free black population at the end of the eighteenth century. The ideals of the Revolution, the fervor of evangelical revivals, and changing economic conditions encouraged emancipation in the upper South. Furthermore, the inclusion of slaves in the "close communion" of evangelical churches was feasible because Chesapeake blacks, unlike those living farther south, regularly came into close contact with whites. In lowland Georgia and South Carolina, the vast majority of slaves toiling on the rice plantations remained isolated from whites and their culture. Lowland planters were absent for long periods, blacks far outnumbered whites, and slaves worked in large units under the supervision of black foremen. Here more than anywhere else in the new nation, African customs and beliefs continued to influence the language, folklore, singing, dancing, naming practices, burial rites, and religion of Afro-Americans. Forming a "nation within a nation," the slaves of the lowcountry transmitted the religious traditions of Africa to their children and grandchildren. Long after emancipation the Christian prayer meetings of their descendants still reflected African styles of spirit possession and ecstatic dance.[32]

In the lowcountry the only slaves likely to come into regu-

---

[30]Ibid., pp. 290–91.

[31]John Asplund, *The Universal Register of the Baptist Denomination* (Boston, 1796), p. 68.

[32]Ira Berlin, *Slaves without Masters: The Free Negro in the Antebellum South* (New York, 1974), especially ch. 1, and idem, "Time, Space, and the Evolution of Afro-American Society on British Mainland North America," *American Historical Review* 85 (1980):44–78; Georgia Writers' Project, Work Projects Administration, *Drums and Shadows: Survival Studies among the Geor-*

lar contact with whites were those who lived in the vicinity of cities like Charleston and Savannah. These urban slaves took advantage of their access to religious privileges and organized separate black churches. The earliest separate congregation, founded between 1773 and 1775, was established in Silver Bluff, South Carolina, a few miles from Savannah. Its significance rested not only in its chronological priority but also in the careers of George Liele, David George, and several other black preachers associated with it. The church originated among the slaves of George Galphin, a successful trader and merchant at Silver Bluff. A white Baptist minister named Palmer converted eight slaves, among them David George, his wife, and Jesse Galphin (or Jesse Peter). Gathered as a church, they held meetings at Galphin's mill. David George had a gift for exhorting, and with the approval of Palmer the small congregation appointed him elder. During the Revolution the British occupied Savannah and its environs, interrupting the congregation's access to itinerant ministerial care. In the absence of Palmer, David George assumed the responsibility of preaching to the congregation, which soon increased to over thirty members.[33]

The Revolution not only pushed black churchmen into positions of authority, but, by scattering them across the landscape, it spread their influence to other parts of the black community. When the British seized Savannah in 1778, Galphin fled, leaving his slaves to seek refuge within British lines. David George spent some time in Savannah and Yamacraw, where he preached with George Liele, and then moved on to Charleston, South Carolina. When the British evacuated Charleston in 1782, George emigrated with them to Nova Scotia. There he continued to preach in several places and established a church for black émigrés in Shelburne. In 1792

---

gia Coastal Negroes (1940; reprint ed., Garden City, N.Y., 1972); Albert J. Raboteau, *Slave Religion: The "Invisible Institution" in the Antebellum South* (New York, 1978), pp. 67–73; Lorenzo D. Turner, *Africanisms in the Gullah Dialect* (Chicago, 1949).

[33]John Rippon, *The Baptist Annual Register for 1790–1793* (London, [1794?]), pp. 473–76.

George migrated with a colony of black settlers to Sierra Leone, where he founded yet another Baptist church.[34]

George Liele, a slave who occasionally preached at Silver Bluff, had been a childhood friend of David George and was influential in George's conversion to Christianity. Liele himself had been converted around 1733 and several years later received license to preach in the Savannah area. When the British evacuated the lowcountry, Liele, like George, decided to leave the country, even though his master had freed him. In 1784 he emigrated to Jamaica and, with four other black émigrés from North America, founded at Kingston the first Baptist church on the island. By 1791 Liele's church had grown to a membership of 350, most of them slaves.[35] Thus, by 1792 black American Baptists had sent their first missionaries to other lands.

On the mainland Jesse Galphin, a founding member of the Silver Bluff church, also took up the Baptist ministry. By 1793 he formed the First African Church of Augusta, Georgia, with a congregation of about sixty. In addition, Galphin preached at several churches in the countryside. A white Baptist clergyman described Galphin to John Rippon, the English church chronicler, in flattering terms: "His countenance is grave, his voice charming, his delivery good, nor is he a novice in the mysteries of the kingdom."[36]

Before sailing for Jamaica in 1782, George Liele had converted an ambitious slave named Andrew Bryan. Upon Liele's departure Bryan began to preach to blacks and whites in Savannah and Yamacraw, where Liele had been active. Bryan's successful ministry earned the disapproval of local authorities, who imprisoned him, his brother Sampson, and many of his followers on two separate occasions, and severely whipped about fifty people, including the Bryan brothers. The intercession of Andrew Bryan's master and several other prominent white citizens secured the slaves' release, as well as permission to gather for worship during the hours after

---

[34]Rippon, *Baptist Annual Register*, pp. 476–83.

[35]Ibid., pp. 332–37.

[36]Ibid., pp. 541 and 545.

sunup and before sundown. In 1788 Abraham Marshall, a white Baptist minister, accompanied by the slave preacher Jesse Galphin, visited Bryan's congregation, baptized about forty people, and licensed Andrew Bryan to preach. Shortly thereafter, following the death of his master, Bryan managed to purchase his own freedom. By 1790 his church numbered 225 full communicants and about 350 converts. His assistants included four deacons and his brother. In 1803 members of the First African Church organized a second, and several years later founded a third. Black men pastored both new congregations.[37]

The persistence of black preachers and black congregations, despite persecution from whites, demonstrates not only the appeal that evangelical Christianity held for them, but also their ability to distinguish the Gospel of Christ from the version of Christianity lived by whites. Nowhere was the determination of black Americans to make Christianity their own more fully realized than in the career of Richard Allen. Born a slave in Philadelphia in 1760, Allen as a child was sold to an owner in Delaware, where he experienced conversion to Methodism at the age of seventeen and began to exhort others to seek the Lord. His master, convinced by Freeborn Garrettson that slaveholding was wrong, allowed Allen to purchase his freedom. Once free, Allen traveled through Delaware, Pennsylvania, and New Jersey, supporting himself by manual labor and preaching all the while.

In 1785 Francis Asbury asked Allen to accompany him on a preaching tour. But Allen, unlike Harry Hosier, did not find his niche as an itinerant. He declined the bishop's invitation when he learned that he would not be permitted to "intermix with slaves" and, while in slave country, would have to sleep in Asbury's carriage. Allen's ministry instead developed in the North, where the "first abolition" provided more leeway to organize black Methodists than he would have had in the South. In 1786 he returned to Philadelphia. Preaching twice and even four or five times a day, he quickly built up a society of forty-two members. His success convinced him that

---

[37]Ibid., pp. 340–43 and 540–41; James M. Simms, *The First Colored Baptist Church in North America* (Philadelphia, 1888), pp. 56–59.

the time was ripe to erect a church for black people, since they were "considered a nuisance" by whites. When several black members of St. George's Church were forced from their places to make room for white parishioners, the blacks withdrew from the church en masse. By 1794 Allen and his followers had built and dedicated Bethel African Methodist Church. Legal battles between black and white Methodists for control of Bethel dragged on for several years before the Supreme Court of Pennsylvania decided in favor of the black litigants. Similar experiences led black Methodists from Maryland, Delaware, New Jersey, and Pennsylvania to gather at Bethel in 1816 to organize the first Afro-American denomination, the African Methodist Episcopal Church, under the episcopal leadership of Richard Allen.[38]

When narrating his own life, Allen did not hesitate to condemn the hypocrisy of white Methodists who ignored the church's discipline to play the tyrant over black people. Yet Allen did not reject Christianity or even abandon Methodism. In answer to those who left the Methodists after the experience at St. George's, Allen maintained that "the Methodists were the first people that brought glad tidings to the colored people." Allen defended his loyalty to Methodism by praising the effective simplicity of its preaching. On a symbolic and more profound level, Allen's most effective defense of Methodism in particular and evangelical Christianity in general was his own ministry. By refusing to allow Christianity to be identified as a white religion, Allen—and the other early black preachers as well—made it acceptable to blacks. At the same time, the churches they created stood in eloquent, if mute, judgment on the failure of the evangelical revolution.[39]

During the early decades of the nineteenth century, black preachers and churches would face severe restriction, particularly in the aftermath of slave insurrections. Black churches weathered proscription, nonetheless, and continued to gather members. The number of separate black churches increased, and it was not unusual for them to be the largest congrega-

---

[38]Richard Allen, *The Life Experience and Gospel Labors of the Rt. Rev. Richard Allen*, ed. George A. Singleton (New York, 1960), pp. 15–35.

[39]Ibid., pp. 29–30.

tions in their denominational associations. Although viewed by some defenders of the slave system as dangerous anomalies, black preachers, slave and free, continued to pastor their people. It was to the church that Afro-Americans turned to understand their past, define their present, and project their future. In the church they kept alive the deferred promises of revolution.

III

The Impact of the American Revolution on Slave Societies and Their Ideologies

DUNCAN J. MACLEOD

Toward Caste

THE GROWTH OF antislavery apart, the history of American slavery has rarely been written with an eye to chronology and in terms of change and continuity. Recent work on the history of colonial slavery, in the context of the much greater body of literature on the nineteenth-century institution, now makes such a task possible. A temporal perspective underscores the significance of the Revolutionary era for the development of black life in America. It also suggests a new periodization for the study of slavery in the colonial era. The first phase of this chronology of Afro-American life begins with enslavement and ends in the 1720s; the second extends from the 1720s to the era of the American Revolution; and the third, from the Revolution into the early nineteenth century. Although some aspects of the development of black life in the British mainland colonies transcend these divisions and the divisions apply more satisfactorily to some regions and to some parts of the story than to others, nonetheless this periodization provides insight into the nature of Afro-American society.

From initial arrival until the 1720s, the black population of Britain's North American mainland colonies increased along a common trajectory. During the first three-quarters of the seventeenth century, the black population of all the colonies grew slowly. The situation changed abruptly at the end of the seventeenth century. The black rate of growth accelerated between the 1690s and the 1720s and everywhere came to exceed that of the white population. From 1680 to 1720 the number of blacks in New England rose by more than 50 per-

An earlier version of this essay appeared in A. C. Hepburn, ed., *Minorities in History* (London, 1978). Acknowledgment is made to the publisher, Edward Arnold, for permission to reprint.

cent each decade, and by 1750 blacks comprised over 3 percent of the total population. In the middle colonies growth of the black population peaked during the first two decades of the eighteenth century. By 1720 blacks made up more than 10 percent of the region's population, and in New York they equaled over 15 percent of the whole. The demographic history of the upper South followed a similar pattern. From 7 percent in 1680, the number of blacks grew until in 1720 they represented nearly a quarter of the total. The black population increased even more dramatically in South Carolina. Although blacks had been an important element of the population there from the first days of settlement, comprising some 17 percent of the early settlers, by 1720 they outnumbered whites by more than two to one. Although the absolute and proportionate magnitude of the black population differed from region to region, growth everywhere in the colonies followed a similar path. Between 1680 and 1720 the percentage of increase in the black population was parallel in the colonies of New England, the middle region, and the upper South.[1]

[1]The percentages are derived from U.S. Bureau of the Census, *Historical Statistics of the United States: Colonial Times to 1970*, 2 vols. (Washington, D.C., 1975), ser. Z 1–19, 2:1168. Assuming that natural increase in the slave population was proportional to the number of slaves, one can derive figures for importation in each region. The following table was derived using the midpoint of each twenty-year period as the base for calculation. It expresses importations in terms of the total population and thus measures, however crudely, their impact upon the labor market.

Importations of slaves per 1,000 residents

	1700–1720	1720–1740	1740–1760	1760–1780
New England	9.3	11.6	1.9	−6.5
Middle colonies	66.7	11.4	20.3	1.6
Upper South	146.8	148.8	170.6	72.2
Lower South	890.6	374.6	263.7	178.5

It is clear that during the first half of the century the experiences of the middle region and the upper South diverged sharply as the middle colonies came to approximate the behavior of New England. Even this measure, then, helps to confirm the *shape* of my argument. The accuracy of the figures should not be too readily assumed, but there is no reason to doubt the relative orders of magnitude they suggest.

The increase in the size of the black population prompts three questions. Why did it occur? What effects did it have on the treatment and status accorded blacks? Did it lead blacks to change the way they conceived of their role and social position?

The near universality of the black population increase suggests an answer to the first question. Whatever else slavery may have been or became, it was a labor system developed in response to a chronic and general shortage of labor in the colonies. The settlement of semitropical regions in the southernmost mainland colonies and the growth of tobacco plantation agriculture farther north increased the demand for agricultural workers in both regions. In the middle colonies and New England, the growth of commerce and the consequent development of port cities similarly multiplied the need for laborers. And, of course, corresponding increases in the wealth of planters and merchants created a greater demand for house servants. The burgeoning economic development of the colonies everywhere led to a generalized concern about securing an adequate work force.

A decline in the supply of white labor in the late seventeenth and early eighteenth centuries aggravated fears of a labor shortage. Although the reasons for this sudden contraction are obscure, the evidence permits some reasoned guesses. The stagnation of England's population growth beginning in the 1660s and a general leveling of grain prices reduced some of the pressures upon land and upon the rural poor, diminishing the impulse to emigrate. In any case emigration became more difficult as a result of European wars of the period. This disruption of the labor supply from traditional sources, combined with an increase in demand, led American planters and merchants to seek alternative sources of workers. Perhaps only naturally they seized upon African slaves, the normal and long-standing source of labor for other societies of the Western Hemisphere, as substitutes for white servants.

White indentured servants had traditionally included in their number many skilled and semiskilled artisans and craftsmen. The growing shortage of necessary skills—relative, that is, to the opportunities for deploying them—compelled slaveowners to train slaves in similar skills. Craftsmen were especially needed in the cities. Slavery in the early eighteenth century had a strong urban component in the middle and New England colonies, but also in Charleston, South Carolina. In 1690 blacks constituted about one-third of Charleston's population. By 1709 they nearly equaled the white population of that city, and they maintained parity through the Revolutionary era. Indeed, they monopolized many of the skilled trades, a fact that white artisans bitterly lamented. New York City also witnessed an explosion in the size of its black population. From about 750 in 1700 the number of blacks rose to nearly 2,300 at mid-century. During the first two decades of the century the growth in their numbers far exceeded that of whites; by 1720 blacks constituted nearly one-quarter of the city's population. Thereafter the influx of whites exceeded that of blacks, so that by mid-century blacks represented only 16 percent of the total. The rise in Newport, Rhode Island, occurred a little later, but by mid-century blacks there numbered over 1,000, also about 16 percent of the population. Boston's black population grew scarcely less conspicuously. Rising in number from about 400 in 1708 to 2,000 in 1720, blacks in the latter year equaled one-sixth of the city's population. Over the next three decades they suffered a proportionate decline, however, so that by mid-century their share of the total stood at only 8 percent.[2]

The decline in the significance of slavery in the middle colonies and New England, particularly urban bondage, began after the Peace of Utrecht. No longer interrupted by European wars, white immigration once more resumed its earlier course. Moreover, conditions in Britain again worsened, increasing the desire of poorer Englishmen and women to emigrate. Of even greater significance, new sources of immigrants opened in Ireland, Scotland, and Germany. After 1715, for example, there were three Irish immigrants for every black imported into Boston. While black slaves remained impor-

---

[2]Carl Bridenbaugh, *Cities in the Wilderness: The First Century of Urban Life in America, 1625–1742* (Oxford, 1971), pp. 95, 200, 201, 249, and 409; idem, *Cities in Revolt: Urban Life in America, 1743–1776* (Oxford, 1971), pp. 88 and 333.

tant in the social and economic life of the middle and New England colonies, the institution of slavery had passed its peak. Only in Rhode Island did it continue to grow. Elsewhere, the black proportion of the total population fell, and slavery declined in economic importance. At the same time, the material conditions of blacks as a group apparently worsened as blacks lost their foothold in the skilled trades.[3]

In the upper South a different picture emerged. Continued expansion of tobacco, the region's major crop, fueled demand for new laborers. But two factors operated in this region to aggravate the general colonial shortage of English servants. Pressure upon the English rural poor lessened in the later years of the seventeenth century, but that upon the smaller freeholders increased, inducing many of the latter to emigrate. The dynamics of this migration had an entirely different effect on American life than had the earlier arrival of impoverished servants. Englishmen who wished to preserve small freeholdings or who sought to turn modest mercantile wealth into landed property found it increasingly difficult to do so. Yet neither the economic importance of land ownership nor the status and, to a limited extent, power attached to it diminished as land became less accessible. While £400 or £500 might not go far in England, that amount would go a considerable distance in Virginia or Maryland. In the colonies of the upper South such a sum would buy a decent plantation, complete with slaves. Thus at the precise moment that the supply of white labor began to dry up, men with capital eager to invest in colonial agriculture arrived in the upper South.[4]

Internal factors also predisposed Virginia and Maryland employers toward slave labor. During the seventeenth century the emerging planter class had sought to maximize its control of labor and its profits by extending periods of service on the flimsiest grounds—for example, by creating an

[3]Bridenbaugh, *Cities in the Wilderness*, pp. 201, 250, and 409.

[4]F. M. L. Thompson, "The Social Distribution of Landed Property in England since the Sixteenth Century," *Economic History Review*, 2d ser. 19 (1966):505–17; J. P. Cooper, "The Social Distribution of Land and Men in England, 1436–1700," *Economic History Review*, 2d ser. 20 (1967):419–40.

artificial scarcity of land which drove people back into a species of servitude and by inflicting severe penalties for killing
hogs, which might make work unnecessary. Servants resisted
exploitation, but brutal conditions of bond labor assured that
few lived long enough to register their protest. As conditions
improved, mortality rates declined and more bondsmen survived to become freemen; overt conflict between landlords
and laborers increased and, as in Bacon's rebellion, sometimes boiled over into outright warfare. Slavery provided an
alternative to the growing resistance of white servants and
freemen. The labor barons of the 1620s and the land and
labor barons of the 1660s and 1670s treated their servants
with sufficient brutality to render unlikely any squeamishness regarding chattel bondage. But the enslavement of English people required actions unlikely to be approved by
Parliament and certain to close the supply of labor. Buying
African slaves was a less hazardous matter. Furthermore, some
had labored in the colony since the 1620s and had proved
their ability to master the tobacco economy. African slavery
provided well-to-do Chesapeake planters with a means of
continuing their engrossment and exploitation of labor that
did not at the same time generate uncontrollable social and
political discontent. For this reason, expansion of staple crop
agriculture made it easy for freemen to prosper but did not
lead to a reversion to white labor when such workers again
became plentiful.[5] In the middle and New England colonies,

[5]Edmund S. Morgan, *American Slavery, American Freedom: The Ordeal of
Colonial Virginia* (New York, 1975). This discussion follows closely the argument in Morgan's chapters 11–18. The delay in the expansion of slavery
arose for a number of reasons. Slaves cost more than servants at the same
time that the high mortality rate made it unlikely that more work could be
extracted from them. It was not, moreover, until about 1660 that the comparative costs of sugar and tobacco converged sufficiently to make it more
profitable for traders to sell slaves in Virginia than in the British West
Indies. While the Dutch were happy to oblige, at that time they were in-
terdicted from so doing by the Navigation Laws, and it was only in later
years, when the Royal African Company and private interlopers stepped
in, that a stable supply of slaves could be guaranteed. A more reliable
supply situation coincided with increasing possibilities for slaves to produce profits from the cultivation of tobacco. Their working lives grew longer,
and lower mortality rates enhanced the relative advantages to employers

dependence upon black labor had been a stop-gap measure; in the upper South colonies, on the other hand, internal considerations made it more desirable than white labor. Thus while the growth of the black population had peaked in the middle colonies by the 1720s, the initial period of population growth in the upper South proved to be but a prelude to the sustained development of a thoroughgoing slave society. The middle colonies became increasingly distinct from those of the upper South less because they lacked slavery than because their slavery peaked early. Continuation of a substantial slave trade into the upper South generated the divergence; the initial impetus toward slavery was not a southern phenomenon alone but an American one.

The labor shortage that spurred the development of slavery throughout the British mainland colonies took still another form in the lower South. In South Carolina the early settlers had arrived from Barbados as often as from England, and they frequently brought their slaves with them. With so many of the white colonists firmly rooted in a slave society, it was natural that they should have recourse to slavery, especially since Barbados was the nearest source of supply. But the unattractiveness of South Carolina's climate to many whites accentuated the labor shortage. Production for a market under conditions of a limited supply of free labor and a plentiful supply of slave labor could, in the context of time and place, produce only one result. By the third decade of the eighteenth century blacks greatly outnumbered whites, by as much as a hundred to one in some lowland areas.[6]

Although slavery took different forms in different colonies, it grew rapidly everywhere in the mainland British colonies before 1720. Not surprisingly, colonial legislatures accommodated themselves to the new institution by estab-

---

of black slaves over white servants. And since the proportion of women carried in the slave trade was greater than that in the servant trade, the prospects for capital gains arising from a natural reproduction of the slave force began to grow even better.

[6]The best treatment of slavery in early South Carolina is Peter H. Wood, *Black Majority: Negroes in Colonial South Carolina from 1670 through the Stono Rebellion* (New York, 1974).

lishing legal codes more similar than dissimilar. This legislation reflected the problems inherent in any attempt to define persons as things. Confusion existed as to whether slaves should be considered as real or as personal property, and doubts continued about the extent of an owner's legitimate powers over his property. The slave codes entered piecemeal onto the statute books everywhere except in South Carolina, where Barbadian precedents were enacted with some coherence. But they universally recognized that slaves were property of some kind, that their management was largely the prerogative of their owners, but that the state could intervene between owner and slave in certain circumstances. The codes were harsh, especially in the southern colonies, but so too was the legislation concerning white servants and apprentices.[7]

Two features of the codes deserve special emphasis. First, they defined the position of a laboring class in terms designed to secure the interests of the employers. Second, although they reflected long-standing racial prejudices, they did not codify those prejudices. Put another way, the racial features of the codes were incidental to their regulation of labor. Of course, slavery could not have been developed so easily, or such laws have been passed, without the existence of racial prejudices, but the object of the codes was not so much to define social distinctions based upon race as to establish class distinctions based upon function. The codes formulated between 1690 and the 1730s remained largely unrevised until the Revolutionary era, when legislation began consciously to concern itself with racial and class considerations on more or less equal terms.

Labor competition apparently provided much of the context for relations between blacks and whites. White craftsmen in Charleston and in northern cities fought against black penetration into their trades and, in the former case, the

---

[7]See the discussions in Winthrop D. Jordan, *White over Black: American Attitudes toward the Negro, 1550–1812* (Chapel Hill, N.C., 1968), pp. 103–10, and David Brion Davis, *The Problem of Slavery in Western Culture* (London, 1970), pp. 274–88.

monopolization of many trades by blacks. In Charleston the conflict remained a central one into the Revolutionary era; elsewhere it was muted within a more pervasive ethnic consciousness. In Boston and Newport, Philadelphia and New York, black competition often seemed of minor importance to established craftsmen, compared with the new immigration of Scotch-Irish, Scots, and Germans. But it persisted nonetheless. John Adams later claimed that the abolition of slavery in Massachusetts in the 1780s reflected the hostility of whites to the protection accorded slave artisans; without a formal abolition, he suggested, white workers would have taken matters into their own hands.[8]

Labor conditions also provided the context within which blacks responded to changed circumstances as far south as South Carolina, where they resented the deterioration of the rough functional equality with whites that had characterized the early frontier experience. Peter Wood has argued that after about 1720 South Carolina slaves became more assertive of their position. An alternative reading of his evidence suggests that the process was more defensive than innovative: slaves resisted the erosion of their former more favored position that resulted from the spread of the plantation.[9]

Before 1720 slavery was but one of a number of subordinate statuses in colonial America. Blacks worked alongside white indentured servants, transported criminals, and apprentices, and all were subject to the discipline and whims of their masters and mistresses. Blacks reacted adversely to the debasement of their position in relation to other subordinate groups, but that debasement was less a function of slavery as such than of the increasing concentration of slaves upon plantations. It was thus more evident in the South than elsewhere.

The second period, the middle decades of the eighteenth century, witnessed a continued shift toward plantation agri-

---

[8]Bridenbaugh, *Cities in Revolt*, pp. 88, 274, and 286; Massachusetts Historical Society *Collections*, 5th ser. 3 (1877): 401–2.

[9]Wood, *Black Majority*, ch. 7.

culture in the upper and lower South which accounts for the southern focus of most Afro-American history. Even within the South, however, the process was not uniform. The lower South developed highly specialized plantations of considerable size with widespread absentee ownership, while Charleston provided an urban setting for much of the region's cultural and political development. Elsewhere, especially in the upper South, the plantation developed as a diversified economic unit which also served as a surrogate for towns. The demographic structure of the slave population also differed regionally. In the lower South the proportion of African-born slaves was higher than elsewhere, and that African-born contingent was more heavily concentrated geographically. As a result, a framework emerged within which African cultural forms and values could more easily be preserved. In the upper South, African-born slaves were rarely concentrated together in such numbers. Indeed, the large planters who often acted as agents for slave traders tended to disperse imported Africans by sale in small groups. As a consequence these blacks were isolated linguistically and culturally in a manner not experienced by their counterparts in the lower South.[10]

The tobacco plantation reached the apogee of its development in the mid-eighteenth century. In its most complete form it was a petty autarchy, self-sufficient in food, cash crops, and the skills needed for it to function effectively as an independent entity. Its independence was partly a matter of geography. The great plantations of Virginia sprawled along the banks of the York, Rappahannock, James, and Potomac rivers, which divided the Tidewater into great peninsulas. Ocean-going ships tied up at their wharves, and the planters acted as agents for both their less fortunately located brethren and the ships' captains. They dealt directly with English merchant houses. In creating their modern baronies they responded to social and political motives as well as economic ones. And their actions had economic, social, and political consequences, affecting the manner in which owners thought

[10]See the discussion in Michael Mullin, ed., *American Negro Slavery: A Documentary History* (New York, 1976), pp. 8–33. See also the account by Wood, *Black Majority*, and Morgan, *American Slavery, American Freedom*.

of their slaves and the ways in which slaves reacted to their situation.[11]

The search for autarchy produced a society in which control of and concern for the poor was decentralized: it devolved upon individual slaveholders. Planters thereby experienced a substantial increment in their functions and powers. Regarding his plantation as a total entity, the great slavemaster perceived it as an extended family, just as the nobility of England considered its servants and apprentices as family members and controlled their destinies. If slavery was ever characterized by paternalism, this was the time and place. The plantation provided a setting within which blacks could adjust to the American experience in a variety of ways, because its very autarchic nature compelled diversification. It also served as a surrogate for towns by becoming a center of colonial culture and political life. Because plantations required skilled workers and because they controlled the economic life of the region, slaves came to control the skilled trades. And because their owners dominated the political and cultural life of their colonies, some slaves also came into contact, albeit tenuously, with the main intellectual currents of the larger society.[12]

Nevertheless, the situation of plantation slaves was inferior in some important respects to that of their urban counterparts. Since cities were entrepôts through which ideas flowed as freely as goods, urban slaves operated within a more cosmopolitan context. Thus the plantation fragmented the laboring class: it offered diverse opportunities at the expense of isolating one group of slaves from another. Blacks had limited opportunities for developing larger horizons and generating a broad class or racial perspective regarding their own position. Moreover, the paternalism of the slavehold-

[11]The autarchic nature of the tobacco plantation in the eighteenth century is well understood and is most succinctly suggested in Mullin, *American Negro Slavery*, Morgan, *American Slavery, American Freedom*, and by Daniel J. Boorstin, *The Americans: The Colonial Experience* (London, 1965), pp. 118–69.

[12]Mullin, *American Negro Slavery*, pp. 14–33; Morgan, *American Slavery, American Freedom*, pp. 363–87.

ers—paternalism that should not be confused with kindness—was suffocating. It demanded loyalty, gratitude, and duty from the slaves just as it required obligations on the part of the masters. Slaves might materially enhance the ease and comfort of their lives by conforming to their masters' demands, but only by resisting them could they maintain their dignity and psychic well-being. A recent study has suggested that it was the more acculturated slaves who found this situation most difficult to accept. They were more likely to resist the authority of their masters and mistresses and more likely to flee the plantation. While they provided the majority of support for Gabriel Prosser's rebellion in 1800, they ordinarily resisted in an individualistic manner. They ran away singly or in pairs; they tried to pass themselves off as free or hired themselves out. Only rarely did they act collectively and seek to establish outlying communities such as those created by the maroons of Suriname and Jamaica. In part, of course, this pattern was a product of differences in geography, in part a matter of demography. But it was also a function of the unique process of North American acculturation. The greater their degree of assimilation into American society, the more likely blacks were to resist slavery without rejecting the total society of which it was a component part.[13]

In the lower South the situation was different. The rice plantation was more specialized and provided less opportunity for the development of a wide range of skills than its Chesapeake counterpart. Since whites did all they could to escape the lowcountry's insalubrious climate, the concentration of blacks was also greater. There could be no paternalist ethos in a context of widespread absenteeism. Just as the pressures toward assimilation were less, so the opportunities for collective behavior were greater. Large numbers of slaves from similar regions of Africa worked and lived together. When they sought to flee the confines of slavery, they often did so in groups; their aim was usually to establish outlying communities or to escape to the Spanish settlements to the

[13]Gerald W. Mullin, *Flight and Rebellion: Slave Resistance in Eighteenth-Century Virginia* (Oxford, 1972).

south. The Stono rebellion of 1739 was just such an attempt. The work of Angolan slaves, its object was a group escape from slavery. In many important respects the experience of the lower South approximated that of the West Indian islands, where unassimilated slaves sought collective escape.[14]

The middle period, then, was one in which the status of blacks as slaves was firmly established. It witnessed the transformation of the southern colonies from societies with slaves into slave societies. It also saw the development of two possible modes of black resistance. In the lower South blacks seem to have been able and desirous of developing along a path that was consonant with their African past. But the attempt to define themselves in terms of a separate culture was an option that depended upon the existence of large specialized plantations, a substantial African-born element in the population, and widespread white absenteeism. After the end of the eighteenth century these circumstances no longer coexisted or even individually defined large areas of the South. In the upper South, blacks—or at least those for whom evidence exists from which their responses can be inferred—increasingly assimilated the dominant cultural forms of the society in which they found themselves; they sought less to resist or evade them than to participate in them more fully. As members of an oppressed group, they endeavored to escape oppression in order to enjoy the same rights as those enjoyed by their oppressors.

The middle years of the eighteenth century saw a decline in the social and economic importance of slavery in New England and the middle colonies; the establishment of a slave society in the upper South, a region where blacks were becoming increasingly assimilated; and the rapid growth of a slave society in the lower South, where blacks predominated in numbers and remained largely unacculturated. Nowhere, however, did whites systematically attempt to conceptualize the meaning of the existence of a large black minority in America. Slavery had been defined and this definition spilled over into some uncoordinated treatment of blacks as such,

---

[14]Wood, *Black Majority*; Mullin, *American Negro Slavery*.

but still the institution was regarded as only one among many forms of servitude. No firm concept of a black racial minority as opposed to a slave class had yet been developed.

Long before the final quarter of the eighteenth century—the last period in this chronology of Afro-American life—all the ingredients existed for a thoroughly racist society in America and were reflected in the colonial slave codes. Slavery and the color line largely coincided. Free blacks were far from numerous, and many spent a considerable portion of their lives in effective slavery, either as indentured servants or bastards serving until the age of thirty-one. But the slave codes were not justified or rationalized in racial terms; instead they were advanced and accepted as methods of social and economic control, as pragmatic measures. In short, the slave laws were discriminatory but not sacred. Developments during the Revolutionary era changed all this and produced a coherent racist doctrine that became a sacred, significant totem in American society.[15]

Four distinct developments account for this change. The first was the ideology of the Revolution. Interpreting the imperial conflict as an attempt by Britain to make them slaves, the colonists inevitably made the chattel slavery that they themselves practiced an issue. With no compelling reason to resist the logic of Revolutionary rhetoric, the northern states abolished slavery, although considerations of property rights slowed the process of abolition. In the southern states powerful economic and social circumstances pointed to a different course. Property rights were more extensively involved, of course, and slaveholders reasonably feared economic catastrophe if so fundamental an alteration were made in existing patterns of labor relations. But these arguments were politically inadequate. Few slaveholders doubted the legitimacy or even the justice of slavery, and they apprehended dangers from the actions of their leaders. The dangers were of two kinds. First, Revolutionary leaders caught up in the ideology of the Revolution might act directly against slavery,

---

[15]What follows is based on the account in Duncan J. MacLeod, *Slavery, Race and the American Revolution* (Cambridge, England, 1974).

as Jefferson seemed to do in his draft Declaration of Independence. Second, the routine operation of sound American principles might undermine slavery. In a decision paralleling that of the Massachusetts Supreme Court, George Wythe, a justice in the Virginia Court of Chancery, ruled that the Virginia Bill of Rights had effected a general emancipation. Although a higher court overturned Wythe's action, the original decision revealed the potential for disaster. But slaveholders were compelled to fashion a defense of slavery not only to protect themselves from such contingencies but also to convince themselves and others of their true attachment to American principles; otherwise they must stand branded as hypocrites. Usually, although not always, they acknowledged the ultimate iniquity of slavery while affirming its present necessity. Such arguments were not exclusively racist. The existence of an extensive landless proletariat was, for instance, incompatible with the idea of republicanism as Americans then defined it. And what else could the mass of freedmen be if a general emancipation were accomplished? More fundamentally, however, southerners developed the argument that black and white could not live freely together because of racial differences. Blacks, they asserted, were inferior in intellect, in their capacity for survival in a competitive economic society, and in that observance of moral values upon which civilized society ultimately depends. The phrase "All men" in the Declaration of Independence had to be interpreted as all *white* men.

From this line of thinking emerged the clear outlines of a hostile stereotype of blacks. They were deemed to be lacking in intelligence; to be idle, dishonest, and savage; and to be sexually promiscuous, a threat to white womanhood and the purity of the white race. The need to repel attacks on slavery from outside the region stimulated southern whites to develop such systematic views. But, more significantly, these arguments also arose from the tension generated by articulating libertarian ideals within a slave society. In seeking to reconcile these contradictory tendencies, southern whites preserved their commitment to republicanism by formally reading blacks out of the polity, thereby separating black slavery from white freedom.

The creation of a new political framework reinforced this distinction. Southern control over southern institutions had not been complete during the colonial period, and independence from Great Britain accentuated rather than resolved the problem. Now the southern states found themselves linked in union with quite dissimilar states, whose commitment to freedom led them to abolish slavery within their own confines. The sense of a special American destiny to establish freedom-oriented goals and structures made this new linkage potentially dangerous for the South.

Relations between North and South were from the beginning bedeviled by the existence of slavery. Any central government would have to represent in some admixture the population, wealth, and power of its constituent parts. How was slavery to enter into the calculation? This was a problem during debates over the Articles of Confederation; it was an even bigger problem in drafting the Constitution in Philadelphia. The compromises inherent in that document seemed to guarantee southern interests, but the scruples that prevented the terms *slave* or *slavery* from appearing in it, the heat of debate generated by the issue, and the willingness and ability of northerners to interpret the document in an antislavery sense, all raised doubts. During the following years whenever the new Congress raised the question of slavery in any form, the debate was acrimonious and laden with threats to the Union. Moreover, it was apparent from the beginning that sectional balance within the Union depended upon a more or less equal division of western territories between the North and the South, between slavery and freedom. Further, the South refused to concede that it had surrendered any of the powers necessary to maintain autonomous control over its own institutions. But legalistic arguments of this nature were not wholly effective. Merely professing self-interest would hardly repel assaults made in the name of American principles in a satisfying or permanent way. Southern whites responded instead by elaborating the dangers of a general emancipation. Their arguments centered upon the nature of blacks and the depredations they could be expected to commit upon any society foolish enough to liberate them prematurely.

Third, the threat of a revolutionary solution to the problem of slavery was not lost upon any of the parties. No one doubted that the example of the American Revolution was relevant to the slaves. Lord Dunmore, royal governor of Virginia, rammed the point home by enlisting slaves under his loyalist banner with the promise of freedom. Of course, slave societies had become inured to the idea of revolt. Slave revolts were everywhere feared and they were also expected, but few slaveholders doubted that they could be suppressed. The age of revolutions, and especially the French Revolution, altered these optimistic perceptions of revolt. Welcomed in its early stages as evidence of the influence of American ideals, the French Revolution turned sour for most white Americans as the Terror unfolded and as Napoleon's imperial ambitions emerged. But events in France alarmed southern whites less than events in the French West Indies. The slave revolts in Martinique, Guadeloupe, and Saint-Domingue injected a new order of magnitude into modern slave rebellions. Saint-Domingue eventually secured its independence and became Haiti, the first autonomous black republic in the Western Hemisphere, but it did so only after a decade and a half of bitter, bloody fighting and constant massacres. In a three-cornered fight among blacks, mulattoes, and whites, all parties were guilty of horrendous cruelties, although the horrors perpetrated by blacks most impinged upon the white imagination.

For white southerners one lesson seemed to stand out above all others. The revolt appeared to have stemmed from actions taken in Paris. Saint-Domingue, the richest colony in the hemisphere, had been thrown into ruin through the ill-considered actions of those determined to interfere in the relations between black and white without being fully appraised of the realities of the multiracial situation. Antislavery—not slavery—was the source of slave revolt.

Finally, the feature of the Haitian imbroglio that impressed itself most fiercely upon southern consciousness was the role of the free mulattoes. The claims of this caste for the same political rights enjoyed by whites, and its eventual willingness to ally with the slaves, explained the inferno. Did the United States have such a caste? Many historians, most notably Carl Degler, have argued that American slavery was differentiated from that in other Western Hemisphere countries by the difficulty of securing freedom. Manumission was legally circumscribed in the southern mainland colonies. Degler has argued, furthermore, that as a result of the greater assertiveness and equality of English women, compared with their Latin counterparts, interracial sex was less openly enjoyed by their husbands. Anglo-American masters might fornicate with slave women, but they were less likely to make the relationship overt by liberating or giving special privileges to their mistresses and offspring. While at the outset of the American Revolution slavery and the color line corresponded closely, and those who were free were predominantly mulattoes, the Revolution promoted important changes.[16]

After the Revolution the same forces that secured abolition in the New England and middle states temporarily loosened manumission laws in the South. From an estimated population of between 3,000 and 5,000 in 1780, the number of free blacks rose to 60,000 in 1790 and over 180,000 in 1810. The great majority resided in the upper South and in the middle states. The coincidence of slavery and color had been broken, as had the overwhelming predominance of mulattoes among the free colored community. Whites viewed this new class with increasing fear and distaste: as potential aides to slave insurrection, promoters of unrest and discontent among the slaves, receivers of goods stolen by slaves from the plantations, and a poor, work-shy, criminal element that constituted a drain upon society. Soon after the turn of the century, southern lawmakers renewed restrictions upon private manumissions.[17]

Reconciliation of Revolutionary pretensions with southern slavery, defense of the southern position within the Union,

[16]Carl N. Degler, *Neither Black nor White: Slavery and Race Relations in Brazil and the United States* (New York, 1971), pp. 235–39.

[17]MacLeod, *Slavery, Race and the American Revolution*, pp. 162–69; Ira Berlin, *Slaves without Masters: The Free Negro in the Antebellum South* (New York, 1974).

resistance to antislavery, and fears about the fastest growing sector of the population—the free blacks—all acted to focus attention upon Negroes who were free. Their character was scrutinized and found wanting: they were poor, idle, and vicious. They seemed to refute the charge that similar vices observed upon the plantations were the consequences of slavery and were adduced as evidence that such vices were innate to blacks. Discrimination against blacks would henceforth follow an explicitly racist orientation as well as a class one; indeed, where slavery no longer existed, the rationale for discrimination followed a wholly racial line. Whites had come to define blacks as a minority that differed from themselves in biological and cultural characteristics.

Minorities can be variously defined, and the term is here used to denote patterns of subordination rather than of numbers. Blacks had long experienced subordination, and they had for a long time been victims of racial prejudice and discrimination; but they had never before been so clearly defined as different and inferior, nor had their place in society ever before been so coherently and systematically deduced from those differences. A useful way of classifying minorities is in terms of their objectives. Do they seek assimilation in the majority but are rejected? Or do they seek to preserve a separate status or culture from erosion by the majority?[18] Without dispute, white racial ideologies closed the door to assimilation. In this sense, whites both created and defined the black minority in America. From the black perspective the picture is, initially at least, not so clear. Again beyond dispute, a great number of blacks—at least those about whom much is known—sought assimilation into white society to the extent that they insisted upon the inclusiveness and universalism of the Revolutionary message. They wished to be, and to be considered as, Americans. That some soon established separate black churches and other institutions as rejoinders to white discrimination does not negate this argument. Nevertheless, Ira Berlin has recently enriched understand-

---

[18]For a useful, brief introduction to the subject, see A. C. Hepburn, ed., *Minorities in History* (London, 1978), pp. 1–10.

ing of black cultural developments in the eighteenth century by emphasizing their variety.[19] He has insisted upon the impropriety of perceiving black Americans as a single cultural entity. His distinctions are clearly important to an understanding of the eighteenth century but would appear to have been losing their sharpness and significance with the passage of time. As creolization progressed, the African element was inevitably diluted and absorbed. It would be difficult to substantiate a view of blacks in the late eighteenth or early nineteenth centuries as being dominated by a concern to resist the erosion of their culture by whites, despite the evident assault upon that culture. This is neither to argue that separate cultural values and norms were nonexistent nor to suggest that those which did exist were merely defensive or unhealthy. It is to say that, considered as a minority group, the principal political concern of blacks was to establish their right to participate as free men in the American polity. Minority status was forced upon blacks and was not freely chosen. It was forced upon them by whites as allegedly essential to the fulfillment of white social and political goals. Blacks did not seek the preservation of their minority status within a pluralistic society. On the contrary, they desired full incorporation into the extended American society.

[19]Ira Berlin, "Time, Space, and the Evolution of Afro-American Society on British Mainland North America," *American Historical Review* 85 (1980): 44–78.

FRANKLIN W. KNIGHT

The American Revolution and the Caribbean

ALTHOUGH THE PEOPLE of the Caribbean were unaware of it at the time, the American Revolution signaled the beginning of the end of the conventional structure of their slave systems. Its significance, however, lay not in any frontal attack or any overt threat to the imperial interests of the diverse Europeans in the Caribbean. The successful Declaration of Independence did not jeopardize the political, economic, or social structure of the Caribbean societies. Nor was American political independence an immediate threat to the Caribbean system of slavery. Indeed, the southern section of the independent United States became one of the last bastions of slave society in the Americas. But the American Revolution was a watershed because it set in motion an intricate, interrelated series of changes that surreptitiously undermined the socio-economic basis of Caribbean slave society and attacked the mercantilist principles along which the eighteenth-century empires were more or less conducted.[1] Like the development

I would like to thank Ida Altman, Philip D. Curtin, Robert Forster, William Freehling, Louis Galambos, Jack P. Greene, Richard Kagan, Ingeborg Bauer Knight, David Spring, and the members of The Seminar in the Department of History of The Johns Hopkins University for their helpful comments on an earlier draft of this essay. I have tried to answer all their queries, but I remain solely responsible for remaining defects and shortcomings.

[1] The later eighteenth century saw a rapid breakdown in the theory and the practice of mercantilism as the principles of free trade increased in popularity (Frances Armytage, *The Free Port System in the British West Indies* [London, 1953]; Allan Christelow, "Contraband Trade between Jamaica

and maturation of the institution of slavery itself, the process of disintegration was a long-term one, manifesting an inordinate degree of paradox and ambiguity.[2] Above all, the Caribbean in 1776 was not a uniform area, where the slave system was equally pronounced. Some colonies, like French Saint-Domingue or British Barbados, Antigua, and Jamaica, were fully developed plantation structures. Others, like Spanish Cuba and the newly acquired British colonies of Trinidad, Saint Lucia, Berbice, Demerara, and Essequibo in the Guianas, were just embarking on full-scale development. Still others, like French Saint Martin, Dutch Curaçao, Saba, and Saint Eustatia, Danish Saint Thomas and Saint Croix, or British Bermuda, were no longer practical examples of plantation societies.

The impact of the American Revolution, therefore, varied according to the imperial system, as well as among the individual Caribbean colonies. Even as it diminished slaveholding in the northern section of British North America, the American War of Independence spurred the expansion of

---

and the Spanish Main, and the Free Port Act of 1776," *Hispanic American Historical Review* 22 [1942]:309–43; and Seymour Drescher, *Econocide: British Slavery in the Era of Abolition* [Pittsburgh, 1977], pp. 15–37).

[2]See, for example, Winthrop D. Jordan, *White over Black: American Attitudes toward the Negro, 1550–1812* (Chapel Hill, N.C., 1968); David Brion Davis, *The Problem of Slavery in Western Culture* (Ithaca, N.Y., 1966); idem, *The Problem of Slavery in the Age of Revolution, 1770–1823* (Ithaca, N.Y., 1975); Edmund S. Morgan, *American Slavery, American Freedom: The Ordeal of Colonial Virginia* (New York, 1975); Suzanne Miers and Igor Kopytoff, eds., *Slavery in Africa: Historical and Anthropological Perspectives* (Madison, Wis., 1977); Elsa V. Goveia, *Slave Society in the British Leeward Islands at the End of the Eighteenth Century* (New Haven, 1965); Edward Brathwaite, *The Development of Creole Society in Jamaica, 1770–1820* (Oxford, 1971); and Lowell J. Ragatz, *The Fall of the Planter Class in the British Caribbean, 1763–1823* (New York, 1928). Two excellent examples of general reviews of the field of studies concerning slavery are: Vera Rubin and Arthur Tuden, eds., *Comparative Perspectives on Slavery in New World Plantation Societies* (New York, 1977) and Michael Craton, ed., *Roots and Branches: Current Directions in Slave Studies* (Waterloo, Canada, 1979). An excellent qualitative review of the literature may be found in John V. Lombardi, "Comparative Slavery Systems in the Americas: A Critical Review," in *New Approaches to Latin American History*, ed. Richard Graham and Peter H. Smith (Austin, Tex., 1974), pp. 156–74.

slavery in the Bahamas, especially the outer islands where some defeated loyalists settled with their slaves.[3] Other slave-owners and their slaves emigrated to Jamaica and Barbados, while still others moved to Trinidad.[4] The independent North American state offered a fillip to the development of plantation society in Spanish Cuba and Santo Domingo during the late eighteenth and early nineteenth centuries.[5] Nor should it be forgotten that the full flowering of the continental variant of the slave system developed after 1776, under the auspices of the expanding cotton interests in the South.

The American Revolution enormously complicated the principles and practices then prevailing between the European metropolises and their Caribbean colonies. A politically free United States of America established the basis for a new, competing economic metropolis for the export-oriented Caribbean producers of tropical staples. As the Revolution began the disintegration of the European empires in the Americas, it also exposed the unstable economic, social, political, and ideological foundations on which the various Caribbean slave systems operated. By baring their vulnerability, their anomaly and ambiguity, the American Revolution contributed to the process of their disintegration. The North American declaration of 1776—much like the calling of the States-General of France in 1789—did not begin the period of difficulty and change for the Caribbean colonies. It did, however, eventually prove to be patently portentous, if not definitely calamitous, for Caribbean slavery. For it began the age

---

[3]Michael Craton, "Changing Patterns of Slave Families in the British West Indies," *Journal of Interdisciplinary History* 10 (1979):1–35. Also see James E. Smith, *Slavery in Bermuda* (New York, 1976), pp. 140–47.

[4]B. W. Higman, "African and Creole Slave Family Patterns in Trinidad," in *Africa and the Caribbean: The Legacies of a Link*, ed. Margaret E. Crahan and Franklin W. Knight (Baltimore, 1979), pp. 41–64.

[5]Manuel Moreno Fraginals, *El Ingenio: Complejo económico social cubano del azúcar*, 2d ed., 3 vols. (Havana, 1978); Franklin W. Knight, *Slave Society in Cuba during the Nineteenth Century* (Madison, Wis., 1970); and Roland T. Ely, *Cuando reinaba su majestad el azúcar: Estudio histórico-sociológico de una tragedia latino-americana: el mono-cultivo en Cuba Origen y evolución del proceso* (Buenos Aires, 1963).

of revolutions and the legitimation of secular political attacks on monarchical and metropolitan parliamentary authority.[6]

The American Revolution affected the Caribbean in three interrelated ways. First, the wars of 1776–83 brought the Caribbean within the theater of conflict, directly damaging and dislocating Caribbean society. Second, the Revolution had profound economic effects which will be examined in more detail. As integral components of European mercantilistic policies (somewhat relaxed by free-trade agreements beginning in 1776), Caribbean colonies faced readjustments to the emerging world of the nineteenth century in which the United States of America became an expanding economic power. Finally, it unleashed a political ideology with which the European colonists of the Caribbean had to contend. Yet, as powerful as they were, these forces were not alone in affecting Caribbean society. The impact of the American Revolution mixed unevenly with that of the French Revolution, the abolition of the slave trade, the rise of nationalism, and the increase of free-trade sentiment in Great Britain. The Caribbean region found itself adjusting not only to the new reality created by the success of the American Revolution but also to drastic changes within its own societies and within the Atlantic community. Consequently, it is extremely difficult to pinpoint at precisely what stage the impact of the American Revolution ended and the wider changes began.

Certainly the most obvious immediate effect of the American Revolution was to expose the divergent patterns of empire emerging throughout the Americas. Before 1776 the American hemisphere contained two sets of colonies. On the one hand were settlements that reflected the full range of European societies and cultures and were predominantly European in their populations. British North America and the mainland colonies of Spain and Portugal fell within this group. On the other hand were the colonies that, whether they began as settlements, were converted into exploitation

[6]Robert R. Palmer, *The Age of the Democratic Revolutions: A Political History of Europe and America, 1760–1800*, 2 vols. (Princeton, 1959). For the influence of the North Americans on Spanish-American nationality and politics, see John Lynch, *The Spanish American Revolutions, 1808–1826* (New York, 1973), pp. 28–30.

zones of predominantly dependent economic enterprises.[7]
Both types of colonies incorporated some common aspects
of European social and economic thought. Furthermore, en-
claves of settlers could be found even in Cuba and Puerto
Rico, Martinique and Guadeloupe, Barbados and Saint-Domingue until the end of the eighteenth century. As tropical,
staple-producing plantations came to dominate these islands,
the need for food and other necessities of production forged
a powerful symbiotic economic and trading relationship between the primarily exploitation tropical colonies and the
predominantly temperate or subtropical settler colonies. This
relationship grew extremely strong, especially after the An-
glo-French Seven Years' War of 1756–63.[8] American colonists from the contrasting types of colonies commonly accepted
the reciprocal relationship as though the socioeconomic com-
plexes that facilitated it were no more than the two sides of a
common coin. Nothing could have been less true. Indeed,
the two types of colonies represented almost completely different worlds. Settler colonies in the temperate zones were
organic microcosms of European society, evolving sui ge-
neris. They were capable of propagating within themselves a
more homogeneous world view and a more generalized sense
of a common identity than were the exploitation colonies.
The exploitation colonies were essentially artificial constructs
engineered in the interest of profit and productive efficiency,
with little or no conscious intention by their European architects to create conditions that the rebellious colonists of British North America could describe in 1776 as conducive to
"life, liberty, and the pursuit of happiness." The two divisions
of predominantly settler and predominantly exploitation colonies explain in part the contrasting appeals of independence. It was not merely the extent of their vulnerability that

[7]See Franklin W. Knight, "Patterns of Colonial Society and Culture: Latin
America and the Caribbean, 1492–1804," *South Atlantic Urban Studies* 2
(1978):3–23.

[8]David H. Makinson, *Barbados: A Study of North American–West Indian
Relations, 1739–1789* (London, 1964); Richard B. Sheridan, *Sugar and
Slavery: An Economic History of the British West Indies, 1623–1775* (Baltimore,
1974), pp. 306–58.

made the appeal of political independence weak among the white island colonists. It was their tenuous relationship to the land and the societies.

Ignorance of the fundamental differences in the genesis of these two types of colonies created monumental frustration for the revolutionary British North Americans. No one expressed both the frustration and the intellectual myopia more clearly than John Adams. Dismayed at the low level of opposition to the Stamp Act of 1765, Adams wrote: "But can no punishment be devised for Barbados and Port Royal in Jamaica? For their base desertion of the cause of liberty? . . . Their mean, timid resignation to slavery? . . . They deserve to be made slaves to their own Negroes. But they live under the scortching sun, which melts them, dissipates their spirits and relaxes their nerves. Yet their Negroes seem to have more of the spirit of liberty, than they. . . . I could wish that some of their Blacks had been appointed Distributors and Inspectors over their Masters. This would have but a little aggravated the indignity."[9] Later, at the end of the war, and conscious of the economic interdependency between his new nation and the Caribbean—but obviously not fully aware of the near fatal degree of Caribbean dependency—Adams wrote from Paris on June 23, 1783: "The commerce of the West Indian Islands is a part of the American system of commerce. They can neither do without us, nor we without them. The creator has placed us upon the globe in such a situation that we have occasion for each other. We have the means of assisting each other, and artful contrivances cannot separate us. Wise statesmen, like able artists of every kind, study nature, and their works are perfect in proportion as they conform to her laws. Obstinate attempts to prevent the islands and the continent, by force or policy, from deriving from each other those blessings which nature has enabled them to afford, will only put both to thinking of means to come together."[10] Adams's

[9]*The Diary and Autobiography of John Adams*, ed. Lyman H. Butterfield, 4 vols. (New York, 1961), 1:285, quoted in Davis, *Slavery in Western Culture*, p. 442.

[10]Charles F. Adams, ed., *The Works of John Adams . . .* , 10 vols. (Boston, 1850–56), 8:74, 75, quoted in Ragatz, *Fall of the Planter Class*, p. 174.

thought already contained the dormant seeds of Manifest Destiny, but his words were, happily, still devoid of the arrogance and blatantly narrow self-interest that were to characterize the foreign policy of the United States during the centuries that followed. Besides, his words contained much truth and reason. The economic relationship with New England was an important aspect of the viability of the Caribbean slave society, and the War of Independence in the North American colonies increased costs and diminished the supplies of the Caribbean.

In the decades immediately preceding the outbreak of the American Revolution, the large Caribbean islands had turned increasingly to monocultural production of sugar. Open fields of sugar cane were incompatible with maintenance of the original hardwood forests for which they had been celebrated. Barbados, Antigua, Saint Kitts, and Cuba rapidly depleted their forests to provide more land for sugar cane. The thirteen colonies of North America came to supply most of the horses and cattle for transport; the shingles, boards, and timber for construction and fuel; the barrels and barrel staves for shipping sugar; and corn, bread, flour, salted beef, pork, and fish for feeding the slaves and the free laboring masses. With the rise of competition among the various island producers, the system of *conucos*—or provision grounds—decreased as planters and slaveowners found it more economical to import food than to produce it locally.[11] As Bryan Edwards, a Jamaican writer and planter, confessed, "It is true economy in the planter, rather to buy provisions from others, than to raise them by his own labor. The product of a single acre of his cane fields will purchase more in Indian

[11]*Conucos* were parts of the estate lands set aside for the cultivation of food crops and provisions for the slaves and for the free local markets on the various Caribbean islands. North American–Caribbean relations are extensively dealt with in Ralph Davis, *The Rise of the Atlantic Economies* (Ithaca, N.Y., 1973), pp. 250–87; also see William Woodruff, *Impact of Western Man: A Study of Europe's Role in the World Economy, 1750–1960* (New York, 1967), pp. 168–69, as well as Richard B. Sheridan, "The Crisis of Slave Subsistence in the British West Indies during and after the American Revolution," *William and Mary Quarterly*, 3d ser. 33 (1976):615–41; Drescher, *Econocide*, pp. 16–54.

Table 1: Estimated value of the British West India trade with North America in selected years, 1682–1774, at C.I.F. sterling values (annual averages in £1,000)

Years	Commodity exports	Commodity imports	Combined exports and imports
1682–83	55.0	65.0	120.0
1699–1701	100.0	110.0	210.0
1726–30	139.5	190.0	329.5
1748–50	241.5	313.5	555.0
1773–74	420.0	725.0	1,145.0

SOURCE: Richard B. Sheridan, *Sugar and Slavery: An Economic History of the British West Indies, 1623–1775* (Baltimore, 1974), p. 315.

corn than can be raised in five times that extent of land, and pay besides freight."[12] This commercial dependency was economical in the short run but dangerous over the long term. It bred a vulnerability, especially in the British Caribbean, that colored the thought and actions of the white colonists immediately before and during the American Revolution. The confidence of mainland colonists in their economic and political viability was not shared by whites on the islands.

Englishmen on the islands noted the degree of their dependence. The import and export trade with North America had increased from about £120,000 in the period from 1682–83, when it accounted for only about 3 percent of Anglo-American trade, to £1,145,000 (approximately 20 percent of the trade) in 1773–74. As Richard B. Sheridan points out, "British West Indian commodity exports to North America increased by some seven and a half-fold during the nine decades from 1682 to 1774."[13] This British North American trade, unlike that with the metropolitan countries, was usually conducted in cash instead of the conventional semibarter, and more often than not violated the spirit as well as the letter of imperial legislation. Cash operations permitted the North Americans to sell their commodities in the highest-priced markets, while purchasing their rum, molasses, sugar, cotton

[12]Bryan Edwards, *The History, Civil and Commercial, of the British Colonies in the West Indies*, 3d ed., 3 vols. (London, 1801), 2:378.

[13]Sheridan, *Sugar and Slavery*, p. 315.

Table 2: British West Indian share of total British trade, 1773–1832 (by value)

Years	Imports	Exports	Total
1773–77	28.7%	11.6%	19.7%
1778–82	29.3	13.4	21.0
1783–87	26.8	11.3	19.1
1788–92	24.3	12.0	17.8
1793–97	24.3	13.2	18.0
1798–1802	27.6	14.3	20.2
1803–7	30.5	13.1	20.8
1808–12	30.3	14.0	20.9
1813–17	27.6	11.9	17.6
1818–22	25.8	9.7	15.9
1823–27	21.1	8.6	13.8
1828–32	20.1	7.0	12.3

SOURCE: Seymour Drescher, *Econocide: British Slavery in the Era of Abolition* (Pittsburgh, 1977), p. 19 and source cited there.

wool, pimento, coffee, cacao, ginger, indigo, and exotic woods at the lowest prices. Not only was the Caribbean–North America trade heavily imbalanced in favor of the latter, but it drained off valuable and scarce specie from the planting classes of the Caribbean states.[14] According to Lowell J. Ragatz, "The American traders would accept nothing but genuine, unmutilated coins at face; all others were taken only by weight. Sound money was therefore regularly withdrawn from the British West Indies, and local trade came to be increasingly carried on by means of spurious and lightweight pieces passing at fictitious values."[15]

Regardless of the ledger-balance of their trade, the British West Indian colonists manifested profound sympathies with their fellow North American colonists before 1776. The local legislatures in Grenada, Barbados, Tobago, and Jamaica passed resolutions of support for the Americans in the great dispute leading up to the War of Independence.[16] The Jamaica House of Assembly petition spoke of "their oppressed brethren of

[14]Useful trade data for Jamaica and some of the British West Indian islands may be found in Bryan Edwards, *History*, 5th ed. (London, 1819), appendixes.

[15]Ragatz, *Fall of the Planter Class*, p. 90.

[16]Brathwaite, *Creole Society*, p. 60.

North America."[17] Bermuda and the Bahamas actively sided with the Americans until the British intervened directly in 1779.[18] Bermuda and the Bahamas were not, however, fully developed sugar colonies dependent on British imperial market preferences or on the support of British military forces to suppress their overwhelming number of African slaves in case of a revolt. A self-acknowledged vulnerability imposed a grating prudence on the large Caribbean colonies. Instead of going to war against the metropolis, the West Indians pressed for peace. In January 1775 a meeting held in London of "all persons having relations with the Caribbean colonies" drew up a petition to Parliament predicting widespread disaster in the Caribbean should war break out and disrupt American trade with the West Indies.[19] This prediction of disaster never materialized. The British West Indians grossly exaggerated their inconveniences.

The North American War of Independence undoubtedly resulted in some severe short-term dislocations in the British West Indies. But the inconveniences did not preface either immediate decline or disaster. Scarcity of basic foodstuffs was the greatest problem, especially after the failure of attempts to alleviate shortages by increasing imports from Canada and after the abrupt cessation of trade with the French and Spanish colonies when France and Spain entered the war in 1777–78. The situation appeared critical in the smaller Leeward Islands by 1778.[20] In Antigua, Saint Kitts, Dominica, and Montserrat, merchants remained without adequate provisions, prices for all commodities skyrocketed, and some people starved.[21] In Jamaica flour prices increased from fifteen shillings per hundredweight in 1774–75 to between twenty and fifty shillings in 1776. Rice selling before the war at between

[17]Robert Renny, *An History of Jamaica* (London, 1807), p. 70.

[18]Brathwaite, *Creole Society*, p. 68.

[19]Ragatz, *Fall of the Planter Class*, p. 143.

[20]Goveia, *Slave Society*, pp. 6–7; Ragatz, *Fall of the Planter Class*, pp. 146–47; George Wilson Bridges, *The Annals of Jamaica*, 2 vols. (London, 1828), 2:166–67.

[21]Ragatz, *Fall of the Planter Class*, p. 150.

thirteen and nineteen shillings per hundredweight com-manded prices ranging from forty to eighty shillings after-ward. In Barbados and the Leewards, prices increased correspondingly. After the war, prices declined, but they sta-bilized considerably above the prewar levels. Flour prices in Antigua stabilized after the war at thirty shillings per hun-dredweight, 65 percent above the immediate prewar level. In the same market rice stabilized at 55 percent and lumber at 60 percent above the prewar prices.[22]

Inflation of this sort placed the British West Indian sugar producer in a quandary. Rice, flour, and lumber were basic commodities that made up a significant part of production costs on a sugar estate. The war also brought increased freight and insurance rates, with the latter approaching 23 percent. In the 1780s came further unwelcome increases in the fixed import duty on sugar landed in Great Britain. Indeed, in the three years between 1779 and 1782, sugar duties rose from a little more than six shillings per hundredweight to more than twelve shillings per hundredweight—an increase of al-most 100 percent.[23] Moreover, with warfare constantly dis-rupting shipping and supplies, the sugar market became erratic. Gradual increases in the retail price of sugar led to a sharp reduction in demand, and along with the accumula-tion of a surplus on the European markets came a general clamor against the monopoly position of West Indian–pro-duced sugar on the British market. Even when prices fell, the antipathy to monopoly sugar remained strong.

The British West Indian planter felt the effects of the war more directly than did his Spanish West Indian and French West Indian rivals. British sugar producers shipped their cargoes to Great Britain on consignment and sold them via commission agents. Losses at sea, as well as increases in trans-portation costs, insurance rates, duties, and fees were borne directly by the planter. The British middleman merchant or agent had little to lose by fluctuating fortunes, prices, and taxes and could therefore manifest an indifference to the va-garies of war and politics that his colonial clients could not

[22]Goveia, *Slave Society*, p. 7.

[23]Ragatz, *Fall of the Planter Class*, pp. 164–66.

afford. The economic impact of the war was more pronounced among British Caribbean sugar producers than among their rivals, but, in a certain sense, they were all in the same precarious situation, since it was not an overt economic threat that they faced but the psychological reaction to a change they understood only imperfectly.

The wide range of price increases that Caribbean producers confronted when the war ended in the 1780s—and to which they pointed eloquently—disguised the true conditions of their economic prosperity. Over the long run, sugar prices rose steadily on the European markets until well into the 1820s and in general kept ahead (though at times only slightly ahead) of increases in costs of production. William Taylor, a Jamaican planter, estimated that his cost for slaves had increased by about 71 percent between 1775 and 1790; his number of slaves rose 48 percent, and his profits increased by about 75 percent.[24] Taylor's profits may have been above average, but they probably represented the general trend. A recent study of Worthy Park Estate in Jamaica demonstrates that the average income of the operation increased steadily throughout the eighteenth century, and at the end of the century the profit margin exceeded by 100 percent that of any date before 1750. At that time, in 1800, the estate was returning between 15 and 20 percent profit on its assessed value.[25] Production figures for the various islands, as well as for individual estates such as the Codrington estates in Barbados, do not reveal any significant downward trend in production or profits, despite the vagaries of war and weather in the years before the French Revolution. Whatever the profits, however, the Caribbean producer had good reason to be preoccupied with the new circumstances in which he found himself as the eighteenth century drew to a close. The American Revolution cracked the foundation on which his colonial economic relationship had existed. His colonial preference on the British market was in jeopardy. The system of colonial preference had worked for as long as it did

[24]Drescher, *Econocide*, pp. 43–44.

[25]Michael Craton and James Walvin, *A Jamaican Plantation: The History of Worthy Park, 1670–1970* (Toronto, 1970), pp. 116–18.

for two reasons: the unity of the British American empire disguised internal discrepancies, and the political influence of the West Indian sugar producers far exceeded their proportional representation in the British Parliament. After 1783 it was not only the empire which had begun to crumble; the political power base of the formerly formidable West India lobby had also begun its slide.[26]

What seemed important to the sugar producers and slave-owners at the end of the century, then, was less the actual decline of their economic position than their (and others') perception of this decline. This aspect of the problem has often been overlooked in the long debates over whether the West Indies were declining or improving economically at the beginning of the nineteenth century. Whether siding with Lowell Ragatz and Eric Williams, who perceive a decline, or Roger Anstey and Seymour Drescher, who argue the opposite, all scholars must admit that whatever the real conditions, what the West Indians and their trading partners thought about their situation was equally important. They believed they were losing their economic place in the Atlantic world, and they acted accordingly. Indeed, their actions reveal that they were also losing more than their economic standing. They were losing their self-confidence, and, to a lesser extent, they were losing control of the world of slaves and plantations that they had largely made. The damage to their psyche was greater after 1783 than the damage to their pocketbooks.

The war years certainly brought about some changes in the economic world of the Caribbean plantation. The experience of the war forced the Antillean producers to acquiesce in a series of measures that eventually catalyzed the forces making for the disintegration of the world of sugar and slavery. The exigencies of the war spawned a number of projects designed to minimize the vulnerability and dependence of the local Caribbean societies. Some schemes, for example, development of the cattle industry and local production of

---

[26]A contrary view may be found in Roger Anstey, *The Atlantic Slave Trade and British Abolition, 1760–1810* (Atlantic Highlands, N.J., 1975), pp. 286–363; and Drescher, *Econocide*.

oil, salt, and lumber, were sensible as well as promising. Others, such as the bounty offered in Jamaica for the introduction of buffaloes, were fanciful. During the 1780s and 1790s vigorous efforts were made to expand coffee production, refine sugar, and establish a tanning industry. With the exception of the coffee ventures, these projects were short-lived.[27]

More far-reaching and permanent were the attempts to establish self-sufficiency in foodstuffs. In order to feed their slaves, most sugar planters found it necessary to expand the area utilized for the cultivation of provisions. In some cases, land formerly planted in sugar cane was converted to grow food or raise stock.[28] The planters—whose control of the local legislatures in the British islands permitted them to exclude or restrict independent nonwhite production and sale of export commodities, such as rum, sugar, molasses, indigo, cotton, and coffee—welcomed nonwhite cultivation and sale of supplementary provisions to avert critical food shortages. Expansion of the *conucos*, which had declined with the growth of staple production, stimulated the development of an agricultural peasantry and the system of internal marketing noticeable during the nineteenth century.[29]

The colonial governments, too, responded to the recurring threat of starvation among the Caribbean populations during wartime. The British government introduced and encouraged the adoption in the local cuisine of the ackee (*Blighia sapida*) in 1778. The French carried the mango (*Mangifera indica*) from Mauritius to the West Indies in 1782, only to have the cargo fall into the hands of the British, who propagated it in Jamaica and, later, in the eastern Caribbean islands. In 1793 Commander William Bligh, a former lieutenant

[27]Brathwaite, *Creole Society*, p. 82.

[28]Ragatz, *Fall of the Planter Class*, p. 147.

[29]See Sidney W. Mintz, "Slavery and the Rise of Peasantries," in *Roots and Branches*, pp. 213–42; Mintz, "The Jamaican Internal Marketing Pattern," *Social and Economic Studies* 4 (1955):95–103; Alan H. Adamson, *Sugar without Slaves* (New Haven, 1972), pp. 34–41; W. K. Marshall, "The Establishment of a Peasantry in Barbados, 1840–1920," in *Social Groups and Institutions in the History of the Caribbean*, ed. Thomas Matthews (Rio Piedras, Puerto Rico, 1975), pp. 84–104.

of Captain Cook, was sent to Tahiti to collect samples of the breadfruit (*Artocarpus communis*), as well as other food plants, a project interrupted six years earlier by the mutiny on H.M.S. *Bounty*. Establishment of botanical gardens in a number of islands facilitated the cultivation and dissemination of these crops long before they were accepted into the popular diet.[30]

The new food crops and the new dependence on locally grown provisions brought the subordinate castes of free nonwhites and slaves more closely into the economic operations of the planters. Planters and merchants who formerly had all their transactions with outsiders now found that they had three principal sources of supplies and three sets of creditors: in their respective metropolises; in North America; and, locally, among their slaves and the free colored communities of their islands. This diversification of economic relations increased the demand for cash and allowed the free colored communities and the slaves to increase their shares of the scarce currency in circulation. Planters who found themselves indebted not only to the conventional foreigners but also to locals, whom they despised, could only feel an increasingly diminished command of their world and greater vulnerability to forces beyond their control. While the need for the new food crops was beyond question, the expansion of this sector of the local economies increased the competition for labor, which, after the abolition of the transatlantic slave trade in 1807, became even more expensive than before.[31]

The adverse economic impact of the American Revolution and the revolutionary wars that followed was not equally distributed throughout the Caribbean. Until the wars spread to involve France and Spain in 1778 and 1779, the French and Spanish colonies enjoyed a sort of economic miniboom. Movement of ships in and out of Havana harbor remained

[30]John Parry and P. M. Sherlock, *A Short History of the West Indies*, 3d ed. (New York, 1971), pp. 148–49.

[31]B. W. Higman, *Slave Population and Economy in Jamaica, 1807–1834* (Cambridge, England, 1976), pp. 224–26; Drescher, *Econocide*, pp. 157–60; Michael Craton, *Searching for the Invisible Man: Slaves and Plantation Life in Jamaica* (Cambridge, Mass., 1978), pp. 270–93.

relatively unaffected.[32] The opening of the Spanish free ports
in 1776 enabled British planters to supplement their provisions, while Spanish purchases of slaves in Jamaica and
Barbados provided additional specie for commercial under-
takings.[33] The outbreak of the American Revolution also
converted the previously illegal North American trade with
the French islands into a regular, legal traffic, since the new
American confederacy no longer comprised a part of the
British Empire. The Declaration of Independence liberated
North American entrepreneurs from the constraints of British imperial commercial laws and eventually enabled the
United States of America to develop a prominent merchant
marine during the nineteenth century.

British North American political ideas had considerably less
impact in the Caribbean than did the economic problems and
dislocations of the revolutionary wars. At the level of abstract
political philosophy, the British West Indian planter elite found
itself not far from its fellow North American colonists, as the
Jamaican assembly's "humble petition and memorial" of 1774
clearly indicated. The instruments of government—an appointed governor and elected assemblies—were similar on
some of the islands and on the mainland. The West Indians,
too, could legitimately grumble about "taxation without representation" and the tyranny of king and Parliament. But,

[32]Data tabulated from *Archivo General de Indias* (Seville) *Sección Audiencia
de Santo Domingo. Legajos* 1520–1523: "Relación de embarcaciones que han
entrado en y han salido del puerto de la Habana en el año de . . . " indicates the fluctuation of harbor traffic into and out of Havana.

Year	Number of Ships		
	Entered	Departed	Total
1774	222	226	448
1775	200	211	411
1776	241	230	471

With very few exceptions these ships came from or sailed for Spanish ports.
Of the 663 ships entering between 1774 and 1776, only 32 (4.8 percent)
declared their cargo to contain slaves—a suspiciously low percentage.

[33]Ragatz, *Fall of the Planter Class*, pp. 147–49; Armytage, *The Free Port
System*.

unlike the North Americans, the British West Indians needed the imperial connection. Imperial preference and mercantilist policies protected the Caribbean planters' metropolitan market for their tropical staples. The British Navy protected the islands from outside attack and provided psychological support for a superordinate minority of whites organizing, coercing, and exploiting a vast majority of African and Afro-American slaves. The West Indian colonists, therefore, got back some of their taxes in the necessary military defense, which could not be provided locally. For the West Indians on the sugar islands to have joined in the war against Great Britain, then, might have been politically, economically, and psychologically suicidal, and the later example of the destruction of the French colony of Saint-Domingue demonstrated how terrible the denouement of the Caribbean colonial predicament could be. The American wars of independence, beginning with the battle of Lexington and continuing to the surrender of the Spanish forces at Ayacucho, resulted from the development of a strong national self-consciousness throughout the settler colonies. The mainland wars were the manifestation, in part, of an incipient nationalism that did not evolve in the sugar islands.

Most European colonists in the Caribbean failed to grasp the sense of an *American* identity that prevailed on the mainland. The economic vulnerability and political ambivalence of the British West Indians were symptomatic of some essential differences between British North Americans and British West Indians. From the perspectives of the elites, British North Americans in 1776 formed an organic society with a clearly articulated world view, although whether this world view was identical in both North and South is debatable.[34] With the possible exception of Cuba, this sense of identity did not manifest itself in the Antilles. Regardless of the intelligence and the perceptiveness of an Edward Long or a Bryan Edwards, regardless of their attraction and love for Jamaica, they were not, and never could be, true Jamaicans. Along

[34]See Eugene D. Genovese, *The World the Slaveholders Made: Two Essays in Interpretation* (New York, 1969); W. J. Cash, *The Mind of the South* (New York, 1941).

with the other members of the local Caribbean assemblies, they were Englishmen in the tropics. Their views of the world remained the views of Englishmen, tempered only by their peculiar economic interests and their frontier experience. Their Caribbean world was a fragile, artificial construct, an economic necessity. The Caribbean was a place to make, maintain, or recover their fortunes, not to nurture their children or forge a new society.[35] The members of the Jamaican assembly spoke candidly, if somewhat unconsciously, when they admitted in their famous declaration of 1774 that they were "colonists, Englishmen, or Britons."[36] As integral parts of units that encompassed large numbers of settlers, the continental slave societies represented fundamentally different worlds from the Caribbean slave societies.

The success of the North Americans in establishing the autonomy of their world had some long-term, though indirect, repercussions on the world of the Caribbean slaveholders. The economic significance of slavery began to fade for Great Britain after the loss of the mainland colonies, although no direct relationship can be established between the two interests. British interest waned just as cotton production began to revitalize the institution of slavery on the North American mainland. Thus, when antislavery rose in Britain after 1800, the British West Indians had already lost some potentially powerful allies who might have played a prominent role in the British debates over slavery in the 1820s and 1830s. Had the United States failed to gain its independence, the effect of the cotton interests in the British Parliament would have been hard to calculate. "Loss of the American colonies," Elsa V. Goveia has argued, "caused a further weakening of the position of the British West Indies. The political rivalry of the two sets of colonies had not prevented them from sharing some common interests, and the departure of a large section of slaveholding colonies from the empire at this time, when the humanitarian movement was becoming more active and more confident, certainly impaired the effectiveness

[35]H. P. Jacobs *Sixty Years of Change, 1806–1866* (Kingston, Jamaica, 1973).

[36]Brathwaite, *Creole Society*, p. 70.

of the colonial resistance to humanitarian attack later on."[37]
Moreover, by 1800 British economic interests were becoming
far more diversified and did not have the same affinity for
the West Indian slave colonies as previously.

North American independence had a more salutary political effect on the elites of Spanish and French colonies. Spanish and French immigrants had accommodated more readily
to their Caribbean environment than had the British adven-
turers, and at the end of the eighteenth century they were
ambivalently poised between being Europeans and being
Americans. The white Cubans in particular did not allow the
unfortunate circumstances of French Saint-Domingue to inhibit their drive toward the establishment of a slave society,
and between 1774 and 1840 Cuba became the premier sugar-
producing territory in the world.[38] Subsequently, when the
British government pressed for abolition of the slave trade
and dismantlement of the system of slavery, the Cuban slavocracy looked to the example of the southern United States,
which exemplified to them the perfect compatibility of slavery and civilization. The expansion of slavery in the United
States, which had based its revolution on freedom, greatly
comforted the slaveowning elites of Cuba and Brazil during
the nineteenth century until the American Civil War forced
them to accept the inevitable.

The colonial elites of the Caribbean colonies, however, neither enjoyed the same dominance over their societies that
prevailed in North America nor controlled and restricted the
political ideas that emanated from the American Revolution.
In a society of masters and slaves, the slaves often heard the
same ideas as their masters, although they understood them
differently. Whatever encouragement the Caribbean elites
derived from the expansion of slavery in the South, therefore, was offset by the impact that the continuing debate in
the United States over the issue of slavery would have on
their own subordinate groups of the free and the unfree,
especially the maroons and the slaves.

[37]Goveia, *Slave Society*, pp. 5–6.

[38]Moreno Fraginals, *El Ingenio*; Knight, *Slave Society in Cuba*.

Talk of freedom always made slaves restive, but the maroon communities did not need the American Revolution to provide a rational or philosophical justification for freedom from bondage. For centuries the maroons had defied the existing order of the plantation slave societies.[39] From Cuba to Suriname, *marronnage* of one sort or other was endemic. In Jamaica the maroons had fought a series of wars during the eighteenth century that resulted in a mutually recognized modus vivendi with the colonial government, complete with formal peace treaty and territorial state within the colony. As far as the maroons were concerned, then, what the Americans had done after 1776 was merely what they had been trying to do for generations: establish their independence from British colonial authorities. For the maroons, however, liberty meant personal freedom as well as political independence. The good gentlemen of Boston, Philadelphia, and Charlottesville, on the other hand, did not consider Afro-Americans equally deserving of the "life, liberty, and the pursuit of happiness" that they deemed the goal of their new state. It was left to the slaves of the French colony of Saint-Domingue, under Toussaint Louverture, to implement the first thorough revolution in the Americas and to transform fundamentally and irrevocably the social basis of political power.[40] In Haiti, the new state established after 1804, the former slaves became the government, and the government would represent the majority in a way unequaled in the history of the Americas.

If the American Revolution did not initiate the concept of

[39]See Richard Price, ed., *Maroon Societies: Rebel Slave Communities in the Americas* (New York, 1973); and Eugene D. Genovese, *From Rebellion to Revolution: Afro-American Slave Revolts in the Making of the Modern World* (Baton Rouge, La., 1979).

[40]See C. L. R. James, *The Black Jacobins: Toussaint L'Overture and the San Domingo Revolution* (1938; reprint ed., New York, 1963); Philip D. Curtin, "The Declaration of the Rights of Man in Saint-Domingue, 1788–1791," *Hispanic American Historical Review* 30 (1950):157–75; Thomas O. Ott, *The Haitian Revolution, 1789–1804* (Knoxville, Tenn., 1973); Gabriel Debien, "Les Colons de Saint-Domingue réfugiés a Cuba (1793–1815)," *Revista de Indias* 55 (1954):559–605, and 56 (1955):13–36. Also see Charles Frostin, "St. Domingue et la Revolution Americaine," *Bulletin de la société d'histoire de la Guadeloupe* 22 (1974):73–113.

liberty among the slaves, the Revolution certainly gave the idea greater currency and reality. It mattered little that masters and slaves had different definitions of liberty. The topic of liberty agitated Caribbean slaveowners long before the French Revolution created the paranoia that afflicted all American slaveowners from Baltimore to Buenos Aires. Maroon autonomy, therefore, was only grudgingly accepted by the planters. The vicious response of the planters to maroon discontent in Trelawney Town, Jamaica, between 1791 and 1795, was calculated to intimidate the slaves as well as pacify the maroons.[41] The massive destruction of the maroon settlement, accompanied by the execution and transportation to Sierra Leone of those who surrendered, manifested the overreaction of a nervous and frightened elite. Its action brought only a temporary respite. Revolts and rumors of revolts kept the slave colonies on the verge of explosion, and the Haitian Revolution remained the continual nemesis of slaveholders throughout the Americas.

The great Haitian Revolution was the extreme example of political agitation in the colonies. Its antecedents ran through both the American and the French revolutions, with the latter being the trigger mechanism. The early stages of the French Revolution saw the French colonial planters, particularly those from Saint-Domingue, exploit their tenuous representation in the Constituent Assembly to espouse loudly the American political principles of the legitimacy of self-government and the sanctity of private property. When the Continental Congress had gathered in Philadelphia, the selective nature of the assembly permitted the eloquent ambiguity of an expression like "all men" without any challenge or dispute from those who were excluded. Moreover, the gathering in Philadelphia was sufficiently homogeneous to speak with a unified voice. But in 1790, when the French National Assembly, which represented both Frenchmen and French overseas colonists, substituted what they hoped would serve as a satisfactory compromise for the diametrically opposed views on who constituted "citizens" and on property restrictions for the franchise, their inelegant phrase "*toute les*

[41]Brathwaite, *Creole Society*, pp. 250–51.

personnes" merely fanned the smoldering discontent among the French representatives of the *grands blancs, petits blancs,* and *gens de couleur.* At no time was the contrast between mainland American and island American slaveowners sharper. The gathering in Philadelphia pretended to speak for a single class. The French members of the States-General had a common understanding of their corporate identity, and their class interests prevailed. But the French colonists from Saint-Domingue and the other Antilles represented antagonistic classes as well as races. Their representatives in France all joined the Third Estate, but the unyielding insistence of the *petits blancs* on the abolition of property qualifications and the fanatic insistence of the *gens de couleur* upon such qualifications as the basis of their legitimate claims to the franchise destroyed the prospect of harmony among the Antillean colonists. The nuances of colonial racial and caste conflict were lost on most of the metropolitan audience. Indeed, the conflict in the States-General was greatly exacerbated by the blatant attempt of the predominantly white Société des Amis des Noirs to attack slavery indirectly by supporting the issue of the equality of the *gens de couleur.*[42] In their attempts to outmaneuver their respective antagonists, each side tried desperately to be orthodox revolutionaries and loyal Frenchmen at the same time that they were conservative, orthodox members of the society of Saint-Domingue. The position was untenable. The ensuing war among the free classes in Saint-Domingue opened the way for class suicide. In the clash of arms, the slaves quickly appropriated the revolutionary ideology and gave a new, and surprising, definition to "*toute les personnes*": liberty and equality became inseparable.

When the North Americans enthusiastically espoused the cause of freedom in the 1770s and 1780s, they thought only narrowly of a bourgeois concept of man and citizen.[43] Theirs

[42]Davis, *Slavery in the Age of Revolution,* pp. 137–48; Ott, *Haitian Revolution,* pp. 28–72. Also see Jack P. Greene, "All Men Are Created Equal: Some Reflections on the Character of the American Revolution," Oxford Inaugural Lecture, Oxford University, Feb. 10, 1976.

[43]For an intelligent discussion of the term *bourgeois* and its application in the seventeenth and eighteenth centuries, see Robert Forster, "The Middle

was a revolution by men of property. Their equality was one shared within a certain class. Equality for non-propertyholders and slaves never entered their minds. The case of Haiti created anxiety and ambivalence. As David Brion Davis acknowledged, "The United States had been closely involved with the fate of St. Domingue. The American Revolution had not only opened the way for a brisk trade that supported the sugar boom of the 1780s, but had given military experience to St. Domingue mulattoes fighting with the French armies. In the late 1790s, during the undeclared naval war with France, American ships supplied and openly aided Toussaint. It is doubtful whether Haitian independence could have been achieved without American arms and provisions."[44] The United States, despite this assistance, failed to recognize the independent state until 1862. How can the American attitude be explained? Winthrop D. Jordan suggested an answer: "The reaction of Americans to the shocks of revolution which swept through France and the West Indies was mixed. They hoped for the triumph of liberty in the world but not for a complete one. They delighted to talk of freedom but wished their slaves would not. They assumed that their slaves yearned for liberty but were determined not to let them have it. To trace the spread of Negro Rebellion in the New World and to examine American responses to what they saw as a mounting tide of danger is to watch the drastic erosion of the ideology of the American Revolution."[45]

The American Revolution evoked admiration as well as fear among Caribbean elites. Before the events in Saint-Domingue became an obsession, it was the most profound political event in their history since the establishment of the plural, plantation society. But the Americans lost an opportunity to exert moral leadership in the Caribbean because their attitudes toward the people of the Caribbean betrayed either an unwillingness or an incapacity to think through the practical

Classes in Eighteenth Century Western Europe: An Essay," in *Wirtschaftskräfte und Wirtschaftswege: Beiträge zur Wirtschaftsgeschichte*, ed. Jürgen Schneider (Nuremberg, 1978), pp. 15–36.

[44]Davis, *Slavery in the Age of Revolution*, p. 152.

[45]Jordan, *White over Black*, p. 375.

consequences of the rhetoric as well as the reality of the world of 1776. Given the plural nature of Caribbean societies, political revolution could not be separated from social revolution. If colonialism and imperialism violated man's natural rights, as the American Declaration of Independence implied, then so too did slavery. The attempt to restrict the ideology of the Revolution in the nineteenth century was an attempt to turn the clock back, to avoid reality. It tarnished the view of America held by other aspiring political elites in the rest of the Americas. Nevertheless, the impact of the American Revolution on the slave societies of the Caribbean could not be contained. Its most pronounced immediate effect was to catalyze disorder among the upper levels of the social system. The American Revolution legitimized political protest and created disorder. This disorder and dissatisfaction seriously eroded the carefully constructed veneer of political and military invincibility that the Caribbean elites tried to maintain in order to discourage social unrest among their slaves and the lower orders of free society. In mainland America the white groups existed in sufficient numbers to permit internal division and even civil war while containing their subordinated slaves. A different, far different situation existed in the Caribbean. There the hopelessly outnumbered white upper sector simply did not have enough manpower to defend itself for any extended period of time. They needed military assistance. Forced to ally themselves with the legally recognized maroons, as in the case of Jamaica, or with their slaves, as in the case of Saint-Domingue, the whites contributed in a major way to the eventual disintegration of their own slave system, a disintegration that was fueled by the long-term effects of the American Revolution. The success of the American Revolution considerably weakened the economic interests supporting slavery in the British Empire, altered the political power associations within the British Parliament, and encouraged revolutionary sociopolitical engineering among all colonial peoples. The quest for a new society and the will to fashion it constituted the irresistible political force of the American Revolution. This was the strong political wind that blew throughout the rest of the Americas in the early nineteenth century and eventually came to rest in the Caribbean, somewhat delayed but with fury undiminished. Wherever men sought to be free or to constitute a new state, they invariably began with the justification and the words of the men of Philadelphia in 1776, the architects of the Declaration of Independence.

DAVID BRION DAVIS

American Slavery and the American Revolution

THE IDEOLOGICAL CONNECTIONS between American slavery and the American Revolution have been carefully studied and fully documented by numerous historians.[1] There is no need to repeat the story they have told or to dwell further on the notable inconsistency between American ideals and American practice. Yet a broader understanding of the connections between the Revolution and the fate of black slavery can perhaps be furthered by engaging in some highly speculative reasoning. I hesitate to use the fashionable term *counterfactual*, which suggests that mathematical precision can be given to a fantasy. At the outset, however, I frankly acknowledge that this is an experiment in disciplined fantasy—disciplined because its plausibility and ultimate value depend on reasoned inferences and analogies based on empirical knowledge, and a fantasy because it departs from reality and arbitrarily assumes that certain events could have been dif-

---

[1]Benjamin Quarles, *The Negro in the American Revolution* (Chapel Hill, N.C., 1961); Arthur Zilversmit, *The First Emancipation: The Abolition of Slavery in the North* (Chicago, 1967); Winthrop D. Jordan, *White over Black: American Attitudes toward the Negro, 1550–1812* (Chapel Hill, N.C., 1968); Betty Fladeland, *Men and Brothers: Anglo-American Antislavery Cooperation* (Urbana, Ill., 1972); Duncan J. MacLeod, *Slavery, Race and the American Revolution* (Cambridge, England, 1974); Donald L. Robinson, *Slavery in the Structure of American Politics, 1765–1820* (New York, 1971); David Brion Davis, *The Problem of Slavery in the Age of Revolution, 1770–1823* (Ithaca, N.Y., 1975); Robert McColley, *Slavery and Jeffersonian Virginia*, 2d ed. (Urbana, Ill., 1973); A. Leon Higginbotham, Jr., *In the Matter of Color: Race and the American Legal Process* (New York, 1978); John Chester Miller, *The Wolf by the Ears: Thomas Jefferson and Slavery* (New York, 1977).

ferent without altering every other variable. It will be assumed, for example, that the North American colonies remained part of the British Empire but that this counterfactual change did not prevent the French Revolution or the wars against France by the various European coalitions. The intention is to question some of the tacit assumptions historians often make about the effects of the American Revolution on slavery and abolition—for example, that emancipation would have come earlier within a united British Empire.

Suppose, then, that the American Revolution failed and that the British succeeded early in the conflict in suppressing armed resistance and in vindicating Parliament's constitutional supremacy. In this scenario there is no compromise settlement leading to semiautonomy within a confederated empire, but henceforth Parliament would be more sensitive to the prerogatives of the chartered or legislative colonies, refraining from overt intervention in domestic affairs. This was in fact the case, at least through the 1820s, with respect to the chartered colonies in the British West Indies. Assume also that the skirmishes and ultimate showdown of the mid-1770s did not involve a total disruption of colonial society or the intervention of foreign powers; and that the broad social, economic, and intellectual trends of the pre-Revolutionary period were little affected by the abortive struggle for independence.

The most striking consequence of this fantasy for the future of slavery would have been an enormous strengthening of the British slave system, especially when compared to that of Britain's chief rival, France. In 1770 there were 379,000 slaves in the French Caribbean and 428,000 in the British Caribbean. By 1790, after years of wartime depression, the slave population in the British islands had increased only slightly, to 480,000; but in the French colonies, thanks to provisions from the United States and to the great sugar boom in Saint-Domingue, the number had soared to 675,000. If there had been no war for American independence, the French would still have gained the advantage of a larger labor force in the sugar colonies, but the British would have retained nearly 700,000 slaves in North America—not even allowing for the tens of thousands of blacks who died, escaped, were carried off, or were freed as a direct result of the war. In such a case the British New World colonies would have contained by 1790 roughly twice as many slaves as the French colonies.

Moreover, as Stanley L. Engerman has recently emphasized, the American Revolution led initially to "a significant impairment of the economic conditions in the southern states," signified by a dramatic decline in the southern share of the nation's wealth and exports.[2] One can argue that by maintaining beneficial commercial ties with Britain, the upper South in particular would have avoided much of the economic decline of the 1780s and 1790s, and the South as a whole would not have lost to the Middle Atlantic states its regional dominance over American wealth and exports.

Imperial unity would also have meant that Britain would retain possession of Florida and of the Gulf coast extending to Spanish Louisiana. Assuming that the North American colonies would have participated in the war against France and then Spain, following the precedent of earlier imperial conflicts, it seems likely that Britain could easily have added Louisiana to Trinidad and other New World conquests. Even if the British and French armies would have failed to subdue the rebellious blacks of Saint-Domingue—as was in fact the case—Britain would have entered the nineteenth century as the unrivaled master of the New World's slave colonies and of virgin lands, ideal for plantation agriculture, extending from Guiana to eastern Texas.

The scenario from this point is now clear-cut if one accepts the assumptions of Eric Williams and his followers. According to this school of thought, the American Revolution hastened the inevitable decline and fall of the British West Indies. It gave a temporary though self-destructive advantage to the French colonies, and enabled British capitalists to see the light and to begin disengaging themselves from the burned-out cornucopia that had originally financed the Industrial Revo-

---

[2]"Notes on the Patterns of Economic Growth in the British North American Colonies in the Seventeenth, Eighteenth and Nineteenth Centuries," in Paul Bairoch and Maurice Lévy-Leboyer, eds., *Disparities in Economic Development since the Industrial Revolution* (London, 1981), pp. 51–52.

lution. Henceforth, they could afford the moral luxury of condemning the sin of slaveholding while investing in the expansion of slavery in Brazil, Cuba, and the United States, regions where the institution was still economically indispensable and which supplied British industry with essential raw materials, especially cotton. If American independence marked the political separation of an ascending and profitable slave system from one that was declining and already becoming an economic burden, then the retention of the North American colonies would logically have weakened the motives for antislavery. The first and telling reversal of actual British policy would have been the successful defense and continuation of the British slave trade, which Parliament outlawed in 1807.

But this line of reasoning is untenable. First of all, Britain did enter the nineteenth century as the leading "Slave Power" in the New World. By 1805, with the victory at Trafalgar, Britannia literally ruled the waves. As a result of its strategic conquests and virtual monopoly of the African slave trade, Britain enjoyed unprecedented control over the labor supply of Caribbean and Latin American plantation societies that had not begun to achieve a self-reproducing labor force. While American independence infuriated British slave merchants, who complained bitterly about unpaid debts and the temporary ban on slave imports even by Georgia and South Carolina, British ships, merchants, and capital continued to dominate the post-Revolutionary slave trade to the latter two states. Between 1790 and 1807 the United States imported more African slaves than during any twenty-year period of the colonial era. Yet in 1806, a year before Congress moved to outlaw this trade, Parliament prohibited British subjects from transporting African slaves to any foreign markets, including those of the United States.

The argument that Britain sought by this prohibition to cripple foreign competitors hardly applies to the southern United States, which never posed an economic threat to the British West Indies. There is little reason to think that Parliament would have been less eager to suppress the African slave trade if the United States had remained part of the empire. On the contrary, it may reasonably be supposed that a variety of American interests, prejudices, and aspirations would have reinforced the growing public sentiment in Britain for outlawing the slave trade. For it was in America that this sentiment first crystallized. The motives, to be sure, were not altogether humanitarian. As Gary B. Nash has recently shown, social and economic conditions following the Seven Years' War brought a marked protest against all forms of bound labor in Boston, New York, and Philadelphia, as well as an extraordinary decline in slave imports and in the proportion of black slaves in the North. A largely artisan insistence on free white labor drew support from racial prejudice and from fear that an Africanized population would feed the conceits and power of a colonial aristocracy. In the Chesapeake colonies tidewater planters had long profited from the rapid natural increase of their slave population and from the sale of slaves to the south or west. A desire to retain a monopoly in supplying this interregional trade, coupled with fears of black demographic density and surplus labor, intensified opposition to further imports of African slaves. Moreover, Americans of every colony resented British vetoes on legislative acts to tax or restrict the importation of slave labor.[3]

To note such American opposition to further slave importation is by no means to endorse the hypocritical argument, repeated both during and after the Revolution, that the perfidious British had imposed an unwanted burden of black slavery upon the American colonists. The United States Constitution not only barred Congress from prohibiting the importation of slaves before 1808 and from imposing a tax of more than ten dollars upon "such persons," but specifically exempted this provision from the power of amendment. New Englanders and New Yorkers long continued to outfit slave ships; and in 1803, following the purchase of Louisiana and the promise of unlimited demand for labor in the Southwest, South Carolina legalized a short-lived but prodigious slave trade from Africa.

[3]*The Urban Crucible: Social Change, Political Consciousness, and the Origins of the American Revolution* (Cambridge, Mass., 1979), pp. 109–10, 320–21, and 343–45. It is also true that continuing prosperity in the Chesapeake colonies might have muted opposition to the slave trade in the decades before cotton became a major American export.

Yet there can be no doubt that even by the 1780s Americans overwhelmingly opposed the continuation of the African slave trade. In 1794 Congress forbade Americans from selling slaves in foreign markets. By 1798 even Georgia permanently outlawed further slave imports. South Carolina's defiant action at the end of 1803, based on the expectation of a national prohibition in 1808, shocked and outraged the rest of the nation. Despite the agitation of southern extremists in the 1850s, reopening the slave trade was never a realistic option even for the Confederate States of America. Given this unmistakable commitment, reinforced by interest, prejudice, and humanitarian values, it can reasonably be predicted that a unified empire would not have delayed the abolition of the slave trade beyond 1807. Even if South Carolina had allied with Jamaica and the other West Indian islands, British public opinion would have been incalculably strengthened by the division among slaveholding colonies. The North American colonies would have proved that a British-governed population of black slaves was capable of rapid natural growth, presumably as a result of humane treatment and planter foresight, although today we know that slave demography involved many complex variables. For some decades British abolitionists were in fact inclined to applaud the putative enlightenment of the southern states; as British colonies, they would have been far more forceful models of the advantages of the so-called breeding system. Since Parliament came close to abolishing the slave trade in the 1790s, the example and support of Virginia, Maryland, North Carolina, Pennsylvania, and other northern colonies might well have hastened the decision by a decade or more.

It is not really paradoxical to add that imperial unity would have removed a major barrier to subsequent British efforts to suppress the illegal slave trade to foreign markets, especially Cuba and Brazil. For in defiance of American law, American ships continued to play a crucial role in this traffic, and the American flag often protected foreign ships from British search and seizure. It was not that the American government covertly encouraged smugglers; the United States simply lacked the will and the naval power to enforce its own laws. Moreover, the Revolution and the War of 1812 be-

queathed a hypersensitivity to any pretexts for British polic-
ing of the high seas. If, however, Britain had retained an
increasingly effective control of imperial trade, most Americans probably would have approved the trial and punishment of fellow subjects who persisted in such a widely
reprobated crime. Even had other nationals taken up some
of the smuggling abandoned by the Americans, it is almost
certain that in the nineteenth century fewer African slaves
would have been transported to Cuba and Brazil.

But thus far only the African slave trade has been considered. How would the robust expansion of British North
American slavery have affected the supposedly declining fortunes of the British West Indies? In the first place, Seymour
Drescher has marshaled considerable evidence to show that
the British slave system was actually expanding well into the
nineteenth century, at least in terms of its capital value and
its share in Britain's overseas trade.[4] It is also true that for
decades the West Indians complained about the hardships
entailed by American independence and by subsequent British restrictions on trade with the North American mainland.
It can therefore be assumed that a flow of cheap foodstuffs
and other essential commodities from a still British North
America, as well as access to North American markets for
muscovado sugar, molasses, and rum, would have further accelerated West Indian economic growth. There is no point in
speculating here on the needed and perhaps unlikely adjustments in British mercantile policy. It is sufficient to empha-
size that preservation of the Old Empire would have united
within a single polity two prosperous, expanding, and com-
plementary slave systems. If this would have diminished the
relative importance of the Caribbean system—at the turn of
the nineteenth century it constituted the most important
market, outside Europe, for British imports and exports—
the British West Indies could only have gained from a relatively noncompetitive alliance with North America.

By 1790, however, it was easy to caricature Britain's remaining New World colonies as a fringe of clearings in the
Canadian woods and a cluster of sugar islands owned by ab-

---

[4]*Econocide: British Slavery in the Era of Abolition* (Pittsburgh, 1977).

sentee proprietors and populated essentially by African slaves. Jamaica and the new state of Virginia each contained over a quarter million slaves, but there were no more than 20,000 whites in Jamaica while in Virginia they numbered 442,000. The survival of the Old Empire would have retained over three million whites in the British colonial population, a fact that profoundly complicates every colonial issue as well as the very meaning of colonial labor. In British America, even taken as a whole, free white laborers would always outnumber black slaves.

From what is known of the growing shortage of productive land along the Atlantic seaboard, the central political issue would clearly have been the rich, uncleared lands of the West. In one sense, the independence of the United States freed Britain from the dilemmas of formulating and enforcing a western land policy, except in the ultimately self-defeating role of a foreign adversary lending support to Indians and other resisters. In 1763 the British government drew a "proclamation line" intended to close the transappalachian West to white settlers; this general policy of protecting the Indians and the Indian fur trade, confirmed by the Quebec Act of 1774, was one of the causes of the American Revolution. While the imposition of such a barrier was actually vague and relatively unenforceable, presumably Britain would have persisted, in our counterfactual scenario, in trying to thwart or at least restrict the advance of American squatters and speculators.

Faced with such restraints, westerners might have forged an alliance with Spain or France. Even disregarding this option, it is clear that in the Mississippi Valley Britain would have had less administrative control than in the newly conquered territories of Trinidad and Guiana, which will be considered shortly. On the other hand, a wise restrictionist policy, especially if it could have been separated from the claims of the Catholic population in Quebec, would have drawn increasing support from northeastern Protestant groups who feared that westward migration would increase their labor costs and weaken their communities, who expressed outrage over the despoliation and removal of the Cherokees and other so-called civilized tribes, and who protested bitterly the ad-

mission of Missouri as a new slave state. The discrediting of
the Federalists as an essentially un-American party contributed to the image of cramped, mean-spirited Anglophiles who
selfishly tried to preserve their labor supply while thwarting
the manifest destiny of the West. But these same groups might
have appeared more liberal and even humanitarian if allied
on the winning side with Parliamentary leaders like William
Wilberforce and with Colonial Office officials intent on protecting Indians, restricting the expansion of slavery, and en-
suring a gradual and orderly settlement of designated regions
of the West.

If this is an idealized view of British policy, it is nevertheless instructive to look at the forces that encouraged or opposed development of the Carolina backcountry in the era
of the Revolution. From the 1760s onward, the South Carolina Regulators and patriots represented a rising planter class
eager to consolidate landholdings, establish commercial ties
with Charleston, and guarantee the security of slave property in a backcountry still populated with Indians, white
hunters, fugitive slaves, and outlaws of various kinds. Tories
and British officers enlisted the support not only of Cherokees but of various antiplanter groups of woodsmen and
bandits, some of whom included white women, free blacks,
and escaped slaves. Such British allies posed a temporary ob-
stacle to the kind of planter-class expansionism later symbolized by Andrew Jackson. Indeed, it is worth noting that
Jackson's obsessive Anglophobia arose from his boyhood experiences with the guerrilla warfare on the South Carolina
frontier; his famous invasion of East Florida in 1818, osten-
sibly to end British-instigated Indian raids and remove a fugitive slave refuge, was foreshadowed in the early 1780s when
patriots invaded East Florida in pursuit of tories and interracial outlaw gangs.[5]

This is not to say either that the British and the tories were
inclined toward abolitionism or that restrictions on westward
expansion would have condemned slavery to an inevitable

---

[5]This and the following paragraph are much indebted to Rachel Klein,
"The Rise of the Planters in the South Carolina Backcountry, 1767–1808,"
Ph.D. diss., Yale University, 1979.

economic death. With regard to the first point, it is true that after capturing Charleston in 1780 Sir Henry Clinton issued a proclamation promising freedom to those slaves who deserted their rebel owners and took up arms for the king. But Clinton scrupulously returned fugitive slaves to tory owners; and even in the Caribbean, where the British later enlisted thousands of African troops with promise of freedom upon discharge, British commanders restored slavery in the conquered French islands where it had earlier been abolished. The question of restricting slavery's expansion is far more complicated. Historians have tended to accept the nineteenth-century dogma, championed by the Free Soil and Republican parties, that slavery could not survive economically without being rejuvenated by constant expansion into undepleted western lands. This assertion always evoked significant dissent in the South, and it has been challenged by modern economists who contend that the slave economy would have benefited from less rapid geographic expansion. It is therefore conceivable that British restrictions on western settlement actually would have promoted the economic growth of the Cotton Kingdom, especially if British policies had been increasingly guided by the central interests of the cotton textile industry.

But economic questions should not be divorced from political ones. Although John Randolph of Roanoke bitterly opposed continental expansion as a threat to the slaveholders' world, he also understood that a political power that could restrict the expansion of slavery could eventually be used to emancipate slaves. British policies with respect to the conquered and ceded colonies in the West Indies, especially Trinidad and the Guianese colony of Demerara, in fact bore out Randolph's fears. These policies should be taken into account when considering a hypothetical Anglo-American empire, in order to appreciate that economic interests would have been complicated by administrative, strategic, political, and humanitarian objectives. While the fertile and undeveloped lands of Trinidad promised almost unlimited supplies of cheap sugar, the Demerara frontier was especially prized for cotton, which became the latter colony's initial and most valuable export to Britain during the early years of the nineteenth century, before the United States emerged as a major producer. Beginning in the late 1790s, investors, speculators, planters, and merchants exerted intense pressure for the rapid sale of these frontier lands and for unlimited supplies of African slave labor. Nevertheless, Britain denied these colonies the legislative form of self-government enjoyed by the older West Indies, delayed the sale of crown lands, prohibited in 1805 the further importation of slaves from Africa, and in 1806 imposed effective restrictions on the flow of slave labor from the older colonies. It would range too far afield to debate the motives of policies that unquestionably curbed production of British sugar, cotton, coffee, and other tropical staples. It should be noted, however, that various orders-in-council were designed to make Trinidad in particular a model for ameliorating the condition of black slaves.

Extending this model to North America suggests that such new states as Alabama, Mississippi, Florida, and Louisiana might have been governed as crown colonies and subjected to free-labor experiments on crown lands. According to this scenario, they would have been ruled by successive secretaries of state who relied on the expertise of a permanent abolitionist bureaucrat, James Stephen the younger. In 1813 Stephen became legal counsel to the Colonial Office; his influence over the details of administration increased until, first as assistant undersecretary and then as permanent undersecretary in the 1830s, he helped to rationalize and reorganize the entire colonial system. In 1833 it was Stephen who drafted the government's bill for slave emancipation.

Of course such policies could not have been pursued in North America without provoking revolution. In 1810, to choose a potentially explosive year, the power of a few thousand West Indian planters and speculators was hardly comparable to that of two million southern whites. But the examples of Trinidad and Guiana show that the British government was capable of restricting and regulating the expansion of black slavery, even to the probable detriment of imperial economic interests. From 1812 to the end of slave apprenticeship in 1838, the slave population of British Guiana dropped from 100,000 to less than 83,000. By 1841, when most freedmen had deserted regimented plantations for the relatively free but subsistence agriculture of backwoods villages, officials estimated the effective labor force at a mere 25,000. Sugar production fell accordingly. In a disciplined fantasy of imperial unity, such policies would doubtless have been modified in response to southern and British industrial demands. Yet it still seems probable that the future Cotton Kingdom would have assumed a different form, less characterized by rampant speculation and "herrenvolk democracy." In the likely event of an Anglo-American war against Spain and France, the West Indian analogy also suggests a widespread dependence on black troops, large-scale manumission, and an imperial policy prescribing at least minimal civil rights for freedmen.

The point of this theorizing is not to idealize British authority, which could be as tyrannical in America as in suppressing British workers or Irish peasants. What needs to be emphasized is that the American Revolution freed southern slaveholders from various imperial restraints, opening the way for Indian removal and for a westward expansion of slavery that met no serious opposition until the rise of the Republican party in response to the Kansas-Nebraska Act of 1854. The United States Constitution gave slaveholders privileges and powers that exceeded the wildest dreams of the beleaguered West Indian whites, who had to deal with official "protectors of slaves" and with imperial reorganizations intended to assure that colonial governors would represent the crown. Guaranteed state autonomy within a federal system, southern slaveholders could count on disproportionate national power as a result of slave representation, federal assistance in the recovery of fugitive slaves or the suppression of insurrections, and noninterference in matters relating to race and labor. Perhaps even more important was the political neutralization of the natural opponents of an expanding slavocracy. Fearful of being stigmatized as tories and "Anglomen," as Jefferson called them, these potential opponents quickly discovered that concessions on slavery were indispensable for winning southern votes on such pressing questions as credit and the public debt. As Howard A. Ohline has recently shown, the Congressional debates over slavery in 1790, decisive in establishing a framework of basic consensus, were governed by the northern desire to win southern support for Hamilton's financial program.[6] From 1790 onward, at least to the late 1850s, it became increasingly clear that any effective national coalition depended on appeasing slaveholder demands. Within the South, Federalists and Republicans, Whigs and Democrats, represented conflicting local interests and also competed to present the most convincing defense of black slavery.

Because the structure of American politics served so many vital needs and interests, even at the cost of reinforcing the local and national power of slaveholders, it is difficult to imagine the realignments that might have emerged within a single British empire. As late as the 1830s and 1840s, when abolitionism in both countries had enlisted wide popular support and had become intertwined with various radical causes, American politicians could still successfully stigmatize the movement as a popular front for antirepublican despotism. It is hardly cheering to think of America being ruled by men whose power would have depended on the patronage of Pitt, Liverpool, Castlereagh, Canning, and Wellington. Yet it is conceivable that under British rule, implemented mainly by the men who led the Federalist and Whig parties, southern slaveholders would have been unable to "make" the autonomous, paternalistic world which Eugene D. Genovese has empathetically described.

But a disciplined fantasy of this kind should lead to questions, not answers. It should not only generate contradictory scenarios but point to intermediary zones which blur and confuse accepted categories of historical understanding, just as actual historical events confound conventional labels and expectations. Therefore, before suggesting a tentative choice among various possibilities, a few extreme but not impossible options can be explored. First, one can imagine a revitalized British West Indies joining the South in a fused American Revolution and Civil War, precipitated by British and northern attempts to restrict the expansion of slavery. Second and less conventional, one can picture an irreconcilable conflict

---

[6]"Slavery, Economics and Congressional Politics, 1790," *Journal of Southern History* 46 (1980):335–60.

in which land-hungry northern farmers and artisans, galvanized by racial prejudice and by the republican ideology which Eric Foner has eloquently described, would have pitted themselves against a constraining, conservative alliance of southern planters, northern cotton-textile magnates, and British industrialists and landed gentry. In this scenario it would have been the northern and northwestern radical Republicans, led perhaps by Lincoln, who would have seceded from a multiracial British empire based on slave-grown cotton, factory production, centralized government, and control of world markets. It is worth emphasizing, in this respect, that Britain's global hegemony depended in large measure on the manufacture and export of cotton textiles, and that after the 1820s the entire British economy became dependent on low-cost, slave-grown American cotton, much as modern Western economies have become dependent on Mideastern oil. During the pre–Civil War decades of soaring demand, and despite frantic searches for alternative sources of supply, Britain relied on the South for over 70 percent of all its cotton imports. America's national independence meant that British statesmen never had to face the political implications of this economic dependence. Within a united empire, such a compelling national interest would surely have led to drastic political realignments. One can imagine, for example, southern and West Indian proprietors abandoning some of their states rights and agrarian doctrines and forging a Junker-like alliance with leading Anglo-American industrialists. Or there might have been a reactionary swing on the part of British capitalists, faced now with the political consequences of their American investments and dependence on American cotton, and with the need for suppressing antislavery along with other forms of radicalism. This script could have led finally to a revolutionary alliance of Anglo-American workers, slaves, and abolitionists, with minds inflamed on both sides of the Atlantic, as in the French Revolution, by the exploits of a John Brown or Toussaint Louverture.

Thus far, however, these speculations have omitted reference to the ideology of the American Revolution and to its continuing influence on history. It is clear that antislavery arguments, taken in the abstract, preceded the Revolution. One can even argue that the Revolution cut off and then fragmented the antislavery efforts of the Quakers, who led the way in translating abstract ideals into personal decision and organized pressure on central and local governments. Both British and American Quakers deplored the imperial conflict as a violation of their pacifist principles and as a rupture of their transatlantic fellowship; American Quakers, including prominent abolitionists, suffered a loss of political influence and even imprisonment as suspected tories. Anthony Benezet, unsure of the war's outcome, sent copies of his antislavery pamphlets to General Howe as well as to the Continental Congress.

Nevertheless, the Declaration of Independence was the touchstone, the sacred scripture for later American abolitionists, for blacks like David Walker as well as for whites like Benjamin Lundy and William Lloyd Garrison. It was no less important for tories and British critics who scoffed at the arrogance of slaveholders who preached the inalienable rights of man. Less directly, the words of the Declaration inspired French and Latin American champions of emancipation. The 1791 manifesto of the French Amis des noirs was more explicit than Jefferson's Declaration: "We hold that all men are born free and with equal rights, regardless of their color, their nationality, or the condition of birth. We hold that no man can give up his freedom, and no man can seize the freedom of his fellow man, and that no society can legitimate such crime."[7]

As early as A.D. 869 thousands of black slaves had risen in revolt against their masters, in that case against the Arabs of Mesopotamia. But such earlier slave revolts had never challenged the justice of slavery as an institution. It was a wholly unprecedented ideology that led American blacks of the early 1770s to petition for their freedom on the grounds of natural rights. Never before in human history had slaves challenged the general principles justifying slavery. If the American Revolution is eliminated from these calculations, the pride of

[7]*Adresse de la Société des Amis des Noirs, à l'assemblée nationale* . . . , 2d ed. (Paris, 1791), pp. 107–8.

subsequent generations of free blacks whose ancestors had won freedom by fighting for the rebel cause, and who looked back upon the War of Independence as a struggle betrayed, is also lost.

The Revolution was also of crucial psychological importance in combining the secular philosophy of individual rights and political equality with a millenarian vision of national mission and retributive justice. The history of religion provides innumerable examples of millenarian and revitalization movements, many of which have attacked secular sins and impurities. There were no precedents, however, for the clerical condemnations of slaveholding that suddenly erupted during and after the American Revolution. These apocalyptic warnings and denunciations, which merged an affirmation of natural rights with threats of divine judgment, flowed from southern Baptists, Presbyterians, and Methodists, as well as from the New England followers of Jonathan Edwards. If the rhetoric of such jeremiads inevitably allowed for later declension and accommodation, the testimony could not be forgotten. Historians have too often slighted the clerical founding fathers who established a prophetic tradition that later American abolitionists, both black and white, revived and reformulated to suit their needs.[8]

Without such a tradition American antislavery might have been more moderate and institutionally oriented. Yet the Revolution was directly responsible for the most striking example of such conservative reform: the acts of gradual emancipation in Pennsylvania, Connecticut, Rhode Island, New York, and New Jersey. These laws were designed to free only the future-born children of slaves, at ages ranging from twenty-one to twenty-eight. Robert W. Fogel and Stanley L. Engerman, computing some eighteen variables, such as maintenance expenditure and "the ratio of the value of the childbearing capacity of a woman of a given age to her price at that age," conclude that these earliest emancipation laws imposed little if any capital losses on northern slaveholders.

---

[8]This subject is ably explored by James David Essig, "Break Every Yoke: American Evangelicals against Slavery, 1770–1808," Ph.D. diss., Yale University, 1978.

In effect, the labor of northern slaves subsidized the costs of emancipation. Moreover, many northern owners seem to have reaped substantial capital gains by selling their slaves in the South.[9] It is almost certain, however, that even this grudging and self-serving emancipation would have been infinitely delayed without the spur of Revolutionary ideology and the heightened consciousness of political self-determination.

The example of Canada raises a possible objection to this argument, because in 1793 the House of Assembly and Legislative Council of Upper Canada passed an emancipation act resembling Connecticut's law of 1784. While this measure conflicted with the Imperial Act of 1790, which permitted free importation of black slaves and other chattel property into British North America, it received the crown's assent. It appears, however, that Upper Canada was decisively influenced by the example of the northeastern United States and by the desire of loyalist refugees to prove their own liberality. If the states south of Maryland had remained within the empire, it seems highly probable that the British government would have vetoed all such emancipation acts in the interest of imperial unity and security. Restraints might even have been applied on the judges who actually succeeded in undermining slavery, without benefit of positive law, in Massachusetts, New Hampshire, and the eastern provinces of Canada. Certainly British courts gave no encouragement to the idea of extending to the colonies the common-law principles of the famous Somerset case of 1772, which denied legal support for slavery in England. As late as 1827 Lord Stowell ruled in the Court of Admiralty that the Somerset decision implied no more than a suspension of colonial slave codes during a slave's residence in England. Far from affecting the status of slaves in the colonies, Somerset could not even prevent the reestablishment of slave status for a black who had voluntarily returned to the colonies from England. The most revealing point, however, is that despite the example of some northern states which by the 1820s had totally outlawed slav-

[9]"Philanthropy at Bargain Prices: Notes on the Economics of Gradual Emancipation," *Journal of Legal Studies* 3 (1974):377–401.

ery, black slavery remained legal in all parts of British America until August 1, 1834.

It is impossible to imagine Parliament passing the celebrated Emancipation Act of 1833 if the United States had remained part of the empire. Cotton was by then far more vital for British industry and trade than sugar had ever been. Moreover, both contemporary British observers and later historians agree that no emancipation plan was politically feasible unless it included monetary compensation from the British government to West Indian proprietors. Parliament finally assented to the staggering figure of £20 million because of the pressing need to win the cooperation of slaveholders, to affirm the sanctity of private property, and to guard against other and more threatening forms of expropriation. But this twenty million-pound grant, which the so-called black apprentices were to supplement for a period of six years with forty-five hours of unpaid labor for their masters out of a sixty-hour working week, was clearly an upper limit for British taxpayers. Slave prices tended to be higher in the United States than in the British colonies. But even at the same average compensation per slave, the more than two million slaves in the southern states would have increased the taxpayers' bill by another £51 million.[10] It is true that the addition of the United States would have increased the number of taxpayers, but if British leaders had managed to preserve the empire for fifty-seven additional years, they presumably would have been sensitive to American feelings about taxes. As Thomas Jefferson put it in 1824, after making somewhat similar calculations of the costs of African colonization, "it is . . . impossible to look at the enterprise a second time."[11]

Where, then, does this leave us? On the one hand, contin-

---

[10]Ibid. The figure would be £42.6 million if one allows for the discounted late payments calculated by Fogel and Engerman. Even when the British subsidy is discounted to the value of £16.6 million, Fogel and Engerman estimate that it amounted to 49 percent of the actual value of the emancipated slaves, whose continuing labor covered most of the balance.

[11]Andrew Lipscomb and Albert Bergh, eds., *The Writings of Thomas Jefferson*, 20 vols. (Washington, D.C., 1903–4), 16:8–13.

uing imperial unity probably would have hastened the international suppression of the African slave trade, slowed down the westward expansion of slavery, strengthened pressures for amelioration in accordance with standards prescribed in London, and delayed slave emancipation especially in such colonies as New York and New Jersey, where there was significant resistance to even gradual emancipation.

On the other hand, it is also indisputable that the American Revolution opened the way for Britain's emancipation of 780,000 colonial slaves. This worthy achievement, celebrated as the dawning of a millennial era of universal emancipation, confirmed Britain's self-image as the world's altruistic champion of liberty and civilization. It cast shame upon the United States, inspiring both abolitionists and their opponents to vindicate in different ways the revolutionary mission of the founding fathers. If imperial unity would have precluded legislative emancipation in 1833, it also would have muted sectional rivalries and blurred sectional boundaries; there would have been no Northwest Ordinance and no truly "free soil," even if there were imperial experiments with contract or indentured labor in the West. Assuming that British administrators would have been flexible enough to avoid revolution—and we must remember that the ideology of the American Revolution would now lack the radiance of success—the alliance between manufacturers and planters would have given politics a more conservative cast on both sides of the Atlantic. This is not to deny a probably inevitable conflict between capitalism and slavery. Emancipation would no doubt have come eventually—but perhaps as slowly and as ambiguously as it did in British Africa.

I V

Epilogue

BENJAMIN QUARLES

The Revolutionary War as a Black Declaration of Independence

DURING THE SUMMER of 1777 Capt. William Whipple, a soldier from Portsmouth, New Hampshire, noted that his slave,
Prince, was quite dejected. Asked by Whipple to account for
his moodiness, Prince explained, "Master, *you* are going to
fight for your *liberty*, but I have none to fight for." Struck by
the essential truth of Prince's complaint, Whipple lost no time
in freeing him.[1]

Before his emancipation Prince had been one of the oars-
men who rowed George Washington and his party across the
ice-choked Delaware River in a blinding snow and sleet storm
Christmas night 1776. But even had Prince Whipple not taken
part in one of the most significant battles of the Revolutionary War, there was nothing unusual about his longing to be
free. This yearning for freedom was common among those
in bondage and its roots ran deep. The contagion of liberty
had long infected blacks, reaching epidemic proportions with
the outbreak of the war against England. As was the case for
other Americans, regional differences characterized Afro-
American culture, and within each regional group status de-
terminants such as occupation and skin color further divided
both slave and free blacks. Moreover, in ever-changing early
America the patterns of black life were not static from one
generation to another.[2] But regardless of these distinctions,

[1]Charles W. Brewster, *Rambles about Portsmouth: Sketches of Persons, Local-
ities, and Incidents of Two Centuries: Principally from Tradition and Unpublished
Sources* (Portsmouth, N.H., 1859), p. 153.

[2]On this point see Ira Berlin, "Time, Space, and the Evolution of Afro-
American Society in British Mainland North America," *American Historical*

all blacks during the Revolutionary era shared a common goal—the pursuit of freedom and equality.

The exchange between Captain Whipple and his slave illustrated another major characteristic of Revolutionary War blacks, their tendency to differ with whites in interpreting the rhetoric and the meaning of the war itself. When whites, for example, accused England of trying to enslave them, they had in mind such measures as stamp acts and trade restrictions, royal decrees and Parliamentary legislation. To white Americans the war meant freedom and liberty in a politico-economic sense rather than in the sense of personal bondage. Admittedly, the Revolutionary War did have its social overtones, as J. Franklin Jameson reminded us half a century ago.[3] And, as Jesse Lemisch, Alfred F. Young, and others have pointed out more recently, various underprivileged white groups, including women, had distinctive reactions to the war, each of them viewing it as an opportunity for advancement.[4]

With all due credit for its pivotal role in the history of human freedom, the American Revolution fell considerably short of the egalitarian goals it proclaimed. Like many subsequent armed outbreaks, it was essentially a colonial war of liberation; it was waged, however, against a country not unlike America itself. White Americans claimed that they were fighting for the rights of Englishmen—rights that they had long enjoyed but that the Crown had tried to abrogate; they struggled to retain freedom rather than to acquire it.

Although white patriots might not have cared to acknowledge it, the American Revolution bore the overtones of a civil war; indeed, it was more a war of independence than one of revolution. Moreover, unlike other colonial wars of liberation, as Moses Coit Tyler pointed out, it was "directed not against tyranny inflicted, but only against tyranny antici-

Review 85 (1980):44–78, and idem, "The Revolution in Black Life," in Alfred F. Young, ed., *The American Revolution: Explorations in the History of American Radicalism* (DeKalb, Ill., 1976), pp. 351–82.

[3] *The American Revolution Considered as a Social Movement* (Princeton, 1926).

[4] Jesse Lemisch, "The American Revolution Seen from the Bottom Up," in Barton J. Bernstein, ed., *Towards a New Past: Dissenting Essays in American History* (New York, 1968), pp. 3–29; Young, *American Revolution*.

pated."[5] Its inherent conservatism limited the revolutionary potential of the American War for Independence.

Slaves saw the matter differently. In its impact on them the war was truly revolutionary. Seizing the opportunity, they gave a personal interpretation to the theory of natural rights and to the slogans of liberty and independence. Such a patriotic exhortation as "Give me liberty or give me death" carried special meaning to people in bondage.

The desire of blacks for freedom did not, of course, originate with the American Revolution. In one of his midweek lectures to Boston slaves, delivered on May 21, 1721, Cotton Mather denounced the "*Fondness* for *Freedom* in many of you, who lived Comfortably in a very easy Servitude." Obviously not alluding to religious freedom, Mather had in mind a freedom of the person which, in his opinion, was not the state God had ordained for the assembled bondspeople.[6] Half a century later, on the eve of the Revolutionary War, this fondness for freedom had become even more prevalent. The number of blacks had multiplied, and they had become more at home in provincial America and more responsive to its ways of life, particularly those tinged with egalitarianism of substance, tone, or spirit.

The special circumstances of Afro-American life sharpened the desire to be free. In sheer numbers blacks composed in 1774 a larger proportion of the total population than they ever would again, 500,000 out of 2,600,000, nearly 20 percent. These half-million blacks had become Afro-Americans in the true sense of the hyphenated word. Reinforced by more recent arrivals from overseas, they retained strong spiritual and aesthetic ties with their ancestral homelands, their rich cultural heritage already working its way into

[5]*The Literary History of the American Revolution, 1763–1783*, 2 vols. (1897; reprint ed., New York, 1957), 1:8.

[6]*Tremenda: The Dreadful Sound with Which the Wicked Are to Be Thunderstruck* . . . (Boston, 1721), quoted in Lawrence W. Towner, "'A Fondness for Freedom': Servant Protest in Puritan Society," *William and Mary Quarterly*, 3d ser. 19 (1962):201. For a penetrating analysis of Mather's views on slavery, see Daniel K. Richter, "'It Is God Who Has Caused Them To Be Servants': Cotton Mather and Afro-American Slavery in New England," *Bulletin of the Congregational Library* 15 (1979):3–13.

American music, dance, folk literature, and art. Indeed, in reference to Americans from Africa the term *acculturation* lacks precision; it would be better to use *transculturation*, a process of exchange and not a one-way street. Despite the persistence of their African heritage, however, most blacks by 1774 had undergone a transition from Africans to Afro-Americans and were no longer the "outlandish" blacks slave traders had deposited in the New World.

Their Americanization had resulted from a complex of influences, economic, socioreligious, and genetic. They certainly had been integrated economically, as a vital source of labor. Slaves in the southern colonies, numbering 90 percent of the total slave population, produced the agricultural staples of the late colonial period, tobacco, rice, and sugar. A plantation required skilled laborers as well as field hands, and these too were black. As Marcus W. Jernegan pointed out, "It is hard to see how the eighteenth-century plantation could have survived if the Negro slave had not made his important contribution as an artisan."[7] In South Carolina, Peter H. Wood has noted, slaves not only engaged in the full range of plantation activities "but were also thoroughly involved wherever experiments were made with new products," such as the development of silk culture.[8] North Carolina's blacks likewise performed complex and essential tasks. "If their status often forced them into menial labor," observed Jeffrey J. Crow, "they still contributed skills and know-how to the colony's agriculture and crafts."[9]

The northern provinces also had their component of slaves with industrial skills. Slave workers in New York, as described by Edgar J. McManus, "showed proficiency in every field of human endeavor."[10] Lorenzo J. Greene, another authority on

[7]*Laboring and Dependent Classes in Colonial America, 1607–1783* (Chicago, 1931), p. 23.

[8]*Black Majority: Negroes in Colonial South Carolina from 1670 through the Stono Rebellion* (New York, 1974), p. 199.

[9]*The Black Experience in Revolutionary North Carolina* (Raleigh, N.C., 1977), p. 12.

[10]*A History of Negro Slavery in New York* (Syracuse, N.Y., 1966), p. 47.

blacks in the colonial North, painted a similar picture of the slave in New England who might be called upon "not only to care for stock, to act as a servant, repair a fence, serve on board ship, shoe a horse, print a newspaper, but even to manage his master's business."[11] And in New England, as elsewhere, slave women were proficient spinners, knitters, and weavers.

Daily contacts between black worker and white owner inevitably led to a sociocultural interaction between the parties, with the slaves becoming familiar with and sometimes adopting the beliefs and behavior patterns of their owners. Such personal contacts were most frequent when a master owned only one or two slaves. The pattern of person-to-person association between the races was less pervasive on the larger plantations, but even there one would find a corps of domestic slaves, whose children, it may be added, tended to play with the children of the master.

In the absence of a slave row with its separate quarters, the slaves in New England and the middle colonies were in close and constant contact with their owners. In the cities above the Potomac, Ira Berlin has argued, the acculturation of blacks "was a matter of years, not generations."[12] If somewhat slower, the process also went on in the northern countryside. Traveling in rural Connecticut in 1704, Sarah Kemble Knight took note of white masters who permitted what she termed a "too great familiarity" vis-à-vis their slaves, dining at the same table with them. A terse entry in Madame Knight's diary bespoke her displeasure: "Into the dish goes the black hoof as freely as the white hand."[13]

Out of such white-black proximity, North and South, emerged another force in the Americanization of blacks—their conversion to Christianity. Although many masters considered it imprudent, the idea of bringing slaves to Christ gained momentum throughout the eighteenth century. The

[11]*The Negro in Colonial New England* (New York, 1942), p. 101.

[12]"Time, Space, and the Evolution of Afro-American Society," p. 49.

[13]*The Private Journal of Sarah Kemble Knight: Being the Record of a Journey from Boston to New York in the Year 1704* (1825; reprint ed., Norwich, Conn., 1901), p. 52.

movement was led by the London-based Society for the Propagation of the Gospel in Foreign Parts (S.P.G.), an Episcopal organization that operated mainly in the southern colonies. A handful of Puritans and Quakers, more often laboring individually than in organized groups, also took up evangelical work across the color line. In 1740 the conversion of blacks assumed major proportions with the religious revival known as the Great Awakening, with its central theme of equality before God. Negroes entered the churches in unprecedented numbers, imbibing the "New Light" ideas that characterized the crusade. Writing in 1743, Charles Chauncy, a cleric critical of the Great Awakening, complained that it permitted "women and girls; yea Negroes . . . to do the business of preachers."[14]

A significant by-product of this eighteenth-century evangelistic impulse was the emergence of a small but steadily increasing contingent of blacks who could read and write, a case of religion with letters. The S.P.G. established several schools for blacks, one of which, in Goose Creek Parish, South Carolina, employed two black teachers, the first of their race in colonial America.[15] The Quakers were especially notable for their efforts to provide education for blacks, their zeal spurred by Anthony Benezet, the leading abolitionist of his day. In 1750 Benezet established in Philadelphia a night school for blacks that was still in operation, and with an enrollment of forty-six, when the Revolutionary War broke out.[16] In New England many slaves received training in the "three R's," not only so they could read the Bible but also because literate slaves brought a higher price on the market.

The close relationship between religion and literacy among blacks was reflected in the two best-known poetic publications of the period, one by Jupiter Hammon and the other

[14]*Seasonable Thoughts on the State of Religion in New England* (Boston, 1743), quoted in Eldon J. Eisenbach, "Cultural Politics and Political Thought: The American Revolution Made and Remembered," *American Studies* 20 (1979):74.

[15]Frank J. Klingberg, *An Appraisal of the Negro in Colonial South Carolina* (Washington, D.C., 1941), pp. 111 and 114–15.

[16]George S. Brookes, *Friend Anthony Benezet* (Philadelphia, 1937), p. 45.

by Phillis Wheatley. Hammon's work, a broadside of eighty-eight lines, bore the revealing title "An Evening Thought. Salvation by Christ, with Penetential Cries: Composed by Jupiter Hammon, a Negro belonging to Mr. Lloyd, of Queen's Village, on Long Island, the 25th of December, 1760." Far more celebrated than her predecessor, Phillis Wheatley at the age of twenty-three became in 1773 only the second woman in colonial America to publish a volume of poetry. The title of her path-breaking work, *Poems on Various Subjects, Religious and Moral,* conveys the basic outlook and orientation of a writer who had in 1771 been baptized in Boston's Old South Meeting House.

If Hammon and Wheatley personified the religious acculturation of Afro-Americans, the scientist Benjamin Banneker personified another characteristic of white-black proximity, the mixing of bloodlines. Banneker's white English grandmother had freed and married one of her slaves, Bannaky, a former African chief. As Banneker's ancestry illustrates, blacks in the thirteen colonies were by no means of exclusively African stock. Early Virginia permitted white-black marriages, but even after all the southern colonies, as well as Pennsylvania and Massachusetts, outlawed racial intermixing, miscegenation remained extensive, as evidenced by the large numbers of mulattoes, some of them blue-eyed and red-haired. "It is impossible," Winthrop D. Jordan has argued, "to ascertain how much intermixture there actually was, though it seems likely that there was more during the eighteenth century than at any time since."[17] It is hardly necessary to add that blacks, like whites, also mingled their blood with that of Indians.

As a result of the white-black contacts previously mentioned—economic, socioreligious, and sexual—the half million Afro-Americans of 1774 had begun to experience a sense of distinct identity, a race-conscious identity if you will, but one that reflected the essential values of the Revolutionary era. Watered by the Revolutionary War, this sense of self-identity would flower into a collective sense of community,

---

[17]*White over Black: American Attitudes toward the Negro, 1550–1812* (Chapel Hill, N.C., 1968), p. 137.

the latter too an affirmation of the most cherished values of the early republic.

The Revolution, with its slogans of liberty and equality, inevitably appealed to a group such as the blacks. If this were the credo of the new America, they would joyfully make the most of it. As a class black Americans were not strong on theory and would hardly have been prepared to discuss the ideological origins of the war. But they could readily understand propositions to the effect that all men were created equal and that everyone was entitled to personal freedom. Themselves short on worldly goods, most blacks did not consider private property, particularly the ownership of slaves, a basic natural right.

Like other Americans, blacks viewed the war in terms of their own interests and concerns. Perceiving what they regarded as an inescapable inconsistency between the ideals of the Revolution and the institution of slavery, they redoubled their efforts for emancipation, their methods including freedom suits, petitions to state legislatures, and military service. In states like Massachusetts that considered them not only property but also persons before the law, slaves instituted suits for freedom. Such actions cast the master in the role of defendant, obliged either to defend the validity of his title or to answer the charge that slavery itself was illegal or unconstitutional.

The effect of a judicial decree extended only to the litigants immediately involved in the case. Hence blacks seeking freedom collectively rather than individually drafted petitions to their state legislatures. Typical of such pleas was that sent in November 1779 to the New Hampshire assembly by nineteen slaves from Portsmouth. Contending that "the God of nature gave them life and freedom," the petitioners asserted that freedom "is an inherent right of the human species, not to be surrendered but by consent."[18]

Slaves in the Revolutionary War South, denied recourse to the courts or the legislatures, expressed their protests more directly. Exhibiting an insubordinate disposition, they be-

[18]Petition reproduced in Isaac W. Hammond, "Slavery in New Hampshire in Olden Time," *Granite Monthly* 4 (1880):108–10.

came harder to handle. Ronald Hoffman concluded in his study of Revolutionary Maryland that the Eastern Shore centers of black population "were severe sources of strain and worry during the Anglo-American conflict."[19] By way of example, Hoffman cited a late 1775 dispatch from the Dorchester County Committee of Inspection reporting that "the insolence of the Negroes in this country is come to such a height that we are under a necessity of disarming them. We took about eighty guns, some bayonets, swords, etc."[20]

Slave discontent was further evidenced in the marked increase of runaways. To escape-minded blacks the war was a godsend; the number of fugitive slaves reached flood proportions during the conflict. Thomas Jefferson estimated that during the war more than 30,000 Virginia slaves took to their heels.[21] Attesting to their numerical strength, runaway slaves in Revolutionary Georgia established communities of their own.

Blacks' desire for freedom found its greatest fulfillment in wartime service as arms-bearers. British overtures and American military necessity enabled slaves to join the armed forces and thereby win freedom with their muskets. The invitation to blacks to join the British ranks was first offered in the early months of the war by Lord Dunmore, Virginia's last royal governor. In June 1779 Commander in Chief Sir Henry Clinton issued the most sweeping of the slave-freeing proclamations by the British command. It promised blacks their freedom and stipulated that they would be given their choice of any occupation within the British lines. Blacks welcomed such overtures, their motivation being more pro-freedom than pro-British.

By 1779 the Americans too were welcoming blacks to their armies. In the early stages of the war American military and civilian authorities had adopted a policy of excluding Ne-

[19]"The 'Disaffected' in the Revolutionary South," in Young, *American Revolution*, p. 281.

[20]*A Spirit of Dissension: Economics, Politics, and the Revolution in Maryland* (Baltimore, 1973), p. 148.

[21]John Chester Miller, *The Wolf by the Ears: Thomas Jefferson and Slavery* (New York, 1977), p. 26.

groes, a policy based on the mistaken supposition that the war would be over quickly. By the summer of 1777, with the war dragging into its third year, a policy reversal began when the northern colonies and Maryland decided to enlist blacks whatever the risks.

Slaves needed no second invitation. Recruiting agents had only to mention or hint at that magic word *freedom* to bring them into the fighting forces. It is striking, for example, that of the 289 identifiable blacks in the Connecticut army, five reported "Liberty" as their surname when they signed on, and eighteen reported "Freedom" or "Freeman."[22]

Free blacks also welcomed the coming of the Revolutionary War. Just as their lot was akin to that of the slaves, so was their response. Like the slaves, the free blacks drafted petitions and joined the army. Prince Hall, for example, did both. Led by the Cuffe brothers, blacks in Massachusetts lodged an official protest against the denial of their right to vote even though they paid taxes. In a 1780 petition to the state legislature they invoked the patriotic slogan "No taxation without representation."[23]

Free blacks who joined the army were variously motivated. They shared the common hope, however, that the high-sounding affirmations of the Revolution were more than hollow rhetoric. With a touch of the wishful thinking not uncommon to those who are reform-minded, black Americans tended to take seriously the proclaimed goals of the patriots.

Hence in assessing the temper and spirit of the Revolutionary War blacks, one finds that, slave and free alike, their loyalty was not to a locality in which they were propertyless, not to an assembly in which they could not sit, and not to a social order that denied their worth. They reserved allegiance for whoever made them the best and most concrete

[22]David O. White, *Connecticut's Black Soldiers, 1775–1783* (Chester, Conn., 1973), pp. 57–64.

[23]Petition reproduced in Roger Bruns, ed., *Am I Not a Man and a Brother: The Antislavery Crusade of Revolutionary America, 1688–1788* (New York, 1977), pp. 454–56.

offer in terms of man's inalienable rights, which is only to say that the loyalty of black Americans centered on the fundamental credos upon which the new nation was founded.

The hope of black Americans for a new day of equality was not realized; it was a dream deferred. True, the Revolutionary War had its positive side. It was imbued with a strong moral overtone, leading some whites to question an institution such as slavery, no matter how time-honored. To whites of a reformist turn of mind the war had exposed the inconsistencies and contradictions in American thought about the rights of man, particularly those of the black man. But if heightened sensitivity to the presence of an underprivileged black group characterized some whites, they were far outnumbered by those who detected no ideological inconsistency. These white Americans, not considering themselves counterrevolutionary, would never have dreamed of repudiating the theory of natural rights. Instead they skirted the dilemma by maintaining that blacks were an outgroup rather than members of the body politic. They subscribed to an equation of equality that excluded nonwhites, regarding them as outside the sociopolitical community encompassed by the Revolutionary War tenets of freedom and equality.

Black Americans, not unexpectedly, gave an entirely different reading to these war-spawned concepts. To them freedom was everyone's birthright; everyone had certain inalienable rights. In black circles the feeling of independence that these beliefs had fostered outlasted the roar of the guns. Still unspent, the spirit of '76 found new outlets among blacks. The Revolutionary War as a black Declaration of Independence took on a power of its own, fueled by residual Revolutionary rhetoric and sustained by the memory of fallen heroes and the cloud of living black witnesses. To black Americans the theory of natural rights did not lose its relevance with the departure of the British troops. Blacks were left no choice other than to oppose all efforts to de-revolutionize the Revolution.

However complacent and self-congratulatory their white countrymen may have been after expelling the British, the less euphoric black Americans turned their thoughts to the

unfinished business of democracy. Their sense of self-identity, forged in the colonial period and honed by the Revolutionary War, now gave way to a sense of community, of
cooperative effort in a cause that was no less true-blue Amer-
icanism simply because its advocates were dark-skinned. Their
problems pressing, their resources meager, black Americans
took heed of the Revolutionary War slogan "Unite or die."
They were brought together not so much by a blood knot or
a common Old World heritage as by a shared experience,
particularly during the war, and by a shared pursuit of the
goals articulated by Jefferson in 1776.

Free blacks assumed the leadership roles as keepers of the
flame; in 1790 they numbered nearly 60,000. The 700,000
slaves were hardly in a position to become spokesmen for the
new freedom, although a growing number of skilled and literate slaves were more likely to resort to extreme measures
as they recalled wartime slogans of liberty. As Gerald W. Mullin pointed out, it was just such a freedom-inspired, literate,
skilled slave, the blacksmith Gabriel Prosser of Richmond,
who planned one of the most ambitious slave conspiracies in
United States history.[24] St. George Tucker, a Virginian and a
contemporary of Prosser's, observed that there was a difference between the slaves who responded to Lord Dunmore's
proclamation in 1775 and those who took part in Gabriel's plot
in 1800. The slaves of 1775 fought for freedom as a good,
said Tucker, whereas those of 1800 claimed freedom as a
right.[25]

The dwindling component of slaves in the post-Revolutionary War North, however, found it unnecessary to resort
to overt rebellion; time was on their side and gradual emancipation the vogue, especially with the increased availability
of white workers. But, like those to the south, northern slaves
were not the same after the war. Even the pacifist-minded
bondsman Jupiter Hammon was affected. In February 1787
he published "An Address to the Negroes in the State of New
York," a poignantly worded leaflet. "That liberty is a great

[24]*Flight and Rebellion: Slave Resistance in Eighteenth-Century Virginia* (New
York, 1972), pp. 140–63.

[25]Ibid., p. 157.

thing," wrote Hammon, "we may know from our own feelings, and we may likewise judge from the conduct of the white
people in the late war. How much money has been spent, and
how many lives have been lost to defend their liberty. I must
say that I have hoped that God would open their eyes, when
they were so much engaged for liberty, to think of the state
of the poor blacks, and to pity us."[26]

With northern slaves quiescent in their expectation of
emancipation and southern slaves under surveillance, free
blacks led the movement for racial unification and solidarity.
As might be expected, such leadership fell largely to those
living above the Mason-Dixon line. Their counterparts in the
South were not entirely stripped of citizenship rights, but their
limited opportunity for independent reformist action is suggested by the title of Ira Berlin's perceptive study of their
marginal status, *Slaves without Masters*.[27]

Out of this impulse toward organized independence in the
North came the mighty fortress of the independent black
church, a church that preached the equality of all human
beings before God and had its own interpretation of the
Christian theme of the apocalypse. It was a church whose
mission of reconciliation was not only between God and man
but also between man and his own noblest ideals, a church
that envisioned a new earth as logically ancillary to a new
heaven. By the end of the century the pattern of racially
separate churches had been firmly fixed.

In the South small independent black Baptist churches first
appeared during the Revolutionary War years. Many of these
churches were offshoots of white congregations which, for a
time, exercised a nominal "watch-care" over them. As in the
religious services held by slaves, a characteristic feature of
these black churches was the singing of spirituals. If these
Negro spirituals had their escapist, otherworldly overtones,
they also abounded in code words and double meanings, many
of them striking a note of social protest and carrying a barely

---

[26]Oscar Wegelin, *Jupiter Hammon, A Negro Poet: Selections from His Writings and a Bibliography* (Miami, Fla., 1969), p. 27.

[27]*Slaves without Masters: The Free Negro in the Antebellum South* (New York,
1974).

concealed freedom ring. It was during the late eighteenth century that blacks began to sing one of the greatest of these spirituals with a hidden or double meaning:

> *Go down, Moses,*
> *Way down in Egypt land.*
> *Tell ole Pharoh*
> *Let my people go.*[28]

In the North, Richard Allen, a former slave who had purchased his freedom, led the movement for the independent black church. In 1786 Allen attempted to establish a separate congregation of Negro Methodists in Philadelphia. Rebuffed in this effort by an official of St. George's Methodist Episcopal Church, Allen withdrew his membership a year later when, at a Sunday morning worship service, a white trustee ordered him and two other black communicants to hie themselves to the gallery. They would never return to St. George's.[29]

By then Allen who, in the words of biographer Carol V. R. George, had "imbibed the philosophical preferences of Revolutionary America" had come to the conclusion that an independent black church and a gospel of social deliverance would be mutually supportive.[30] Deeply religious, he would never lose sight of "that city called Heaven." But to him, to his co-workers who founded Bethel Church in 1794, and to succeeding generations of black churchgoers, the theology to which they subscribed was a theology of liberation in which God spoke out in thunder tones against chattel slavery and sharply condemned other forms of injustice inflicted upon any of His children. Thus the black church was not only a spiritual fellowship; it was also a social unit, and for this reason represented a fusion of redemptions, religious and racial.

[28]Miles Mark Fisher, *Negro Slave Songs in the United States* (Ithaca, N.Y., 1953), p. 40.

[29]Charles H. Wesley, *Richard Allen: Apostle of Freedom* (Washington, D.C., 1935), pp. 52–53.

[30]*Segregated Sabbaths: Richard Allen and the Rise of Independent Black Churches, 1760–1840* (New York, 1973), p. 9.

In whatever sphere it operated, however, a given church tended to confine its immediate services to members of its own congregation, its own denomination. Hence the movement toward black independence also led to the establishment of organizations that cut across denominational ties, even while retaining a broadly Christian orientation. During the early years of the republic a number of societies and organizations emerged to promote black solidarity, self-help, and self-improvement. Blacks certainly played their part in making post–Revolutionary War America a nation of joiners.

The earliest of these black secular organizations was the African Union Society of Newport, Rhode Island, founded in November 1780; it was followed seven years later by the Free African Society of Philadelphia. The 1790s witnessed the birth of the Brown Fellowship Society, located in Charleston (1790),[31] the African Society of Providence, Rhode Island (1793), the African Society of Boston (1796), and the Friendly Society of St. Thomas, in Philadelphia (1797).[32] A sense of racial identity and pride accounts for the frequent use of the word *African* in the naming of these groups.

As might be expected, the major emphases of these organizations were mutual aid programs, such as supporting one another in sickness and in want, and requirements that their members lead upright lives, minding their morals and their manners. If these goals appeared to be limited exclusively to the welfare of their own participants, however, such was not their overall design. The societies were bent on demonstrating that blacks as a class were, if given the opportunity, prepared to assume the full responsibilities of freedom and citizenship, thus disputing the argument that blacks had never amounted to anything except as slaves, and never would. In a 1794 public letter Richard Allen, founder (with slaveborn Absalom Jones) of the Free African Society, urged his fellow blacks to fulfill "the obligations we lie under to help forward the cause of freedom." A special obligation, Allen insisted,

[31]E. Horace Fitchett, "The Traditions of the Free Negro in Charleston, South Carolina," *Journal of Negro History* 25 (1940):144.

[32]Floyd J. Miller, *The Search for a Black Nationality: Black Emigration and Colonization, 1787–1863* (Urbana, Ill., 1975), pp. 8, 16, and 34.

fell upon those who themselves had tasted the cup "of which the slave has to drink."[33]

The wider concerns of these early societies are revealed by their interest in Africa, particularly in establishing a black Christian presence among their brethren abroad. This missionary impulse to uplift the Africans and at the same time strike an indirect blow against slavery, was particularly strong in the Rhode Island societies. In Newport the movement was led by Newport Gardner, in Providence by Bristol Yamma, both literate former slaves born in Africa.[34] The efforts of these eighteenth-century black emigrationists were unsuccessful, but later blacks would echo their call, although with additional reasons, including disillusionment with the American dream.

In company with church and secular groups, the roster of late eighteenth-century Afro-American organizations included the first black secret fraternal order in this country, the Masons. If black Masonry can be said to have had a single founder, it was Prince Hall of Boston, a Revolutionary War veteran and, to use a present-day term, a civil rights activist. Determined to establish a black Masonic lodge and rebuffed by white Masonic authorities in America, he succeeded after a ten-year struggle in obtaining a charter from the British Grand Lodge. On May 6, 1787, African Lodge No. 459 (its charter number) was formally organized with Prince Hall as Master. Ten years later Hall, now bearing the title of Grand Master, established lodges in Providence and Philadelphia, in the latter instance installing Absalom Jones as Worshipful Master.[35]

In common with other black self-help and self-improvement organizations, the Masons placed great emphasis on formal education, especially reading and writing. If blacks of the colonial period deemed such education a privilege, blacks of the Revolutionary War era thought of it as an American

---

[33]Dorothy Porter, ed., *Negro Protest Pamphlets* (New York, 1969), p. 23.

[34]Miller, *Search for a Black Nationality*, pp. 7–9, and 15–20.

[35]Charles H. Wesley, *Prince Hall: Life and Legacy* (Washington, D.C., 1977), pp. 124 and 142. For a facsimile of the charter from the British Grand Lodge, see p. 49.

entitlement, if not an inherent right of man. "Let us lay by our recreations, and all superfluities, so that we may . . . educate our rising generation," Prince Hall urged in an address to the African Lodge on June 25, 1792. And in the same breath Hall berated the selectmen of Boston for taxing blacks while not permitting them to attend the public schools.[36]

In Philadelphia, Absalom Jones established a school for blacks in 1799. "It is with pleasure that I now inform you that the school was opened on the 4th day of March," Jones wrote to the Pennsylvania Abolition Society, expressing "unfeigned thanks for the encouragement you were pleas[ed] to give me."[37] As a result of the sacrificial efforts of such black leaders as Hall and Jones and the extensive educational operations of white-membered abolitionist societies, the pursuit of formal education became a mainspring in black life during the formative years of the new nation.

Blacks of the Revolutionary War era could work independently, as in their churches, or cooperatively with whites, as in providing schools. But neither by independent nor cooperative action could they make any headway in winning suffrage, a right so vital to the "created equal" concept in the Declaration of Independence. In the New England colonies during the colonial period, slaves had been permitted to establish mock Negro governments, electing their own "governors." Primarily a form of diversion, these slave "elections" were occasions for feasting and merriment, but as Lorenzo Greene has argued, the "governments" they set up "acted as a sort of political school wherein slaves received the rudiments of political education which could be drawn upon once they were enfranchised."[38]

Five of the thirteen states forming the new nation—New

---

[36]"A Charge Delivered to the Brethren of the African Lodge . . .," in Dorothy Porter, ed., *Early Negro Writing, 1760–1837* (Boston, 1971), p. 67.

[37]Jones to Pennsylvania Abolition Society, Mar. 11, 1799, Papers of the Pennsylvania Society for Promoting the Abolition of Slavery, and for the Relief of Free Negroes Unlawfully Held in Bondage, and for Improving the Condition of the African Race, Pennsylvania Historical Society, Philadelphia.

[38]Greene, *Negro in Colonial New England*, p. 255.

York, Pennsylvania, Delaware, Maryland, and North Carolina—did not exclude blacks from voting. Indeed, in one of
these states, Maryland, a black candidate ran for public office
in 1792, very likely the first of his color ever to take this bold
step. Thomas Brown, a horse doctor, sought one of the two
seats allotted to Baltimore in the House of Delegates. In a
September 24, 1792, public letter addressed "To the virtuous, free and independent electors of Baltimore-Town,"
Brown asserted that he had "been a zealous patriot in the
cause of liberty during the late struggle for freedom and independence, not fearing prison or death for my country's
cause." Brown closed his somewhat lengthy letter with a pledge
that "the corpulency of my body shall be no clog to the exercise of my genius, and agility of my limbs, which shall be
kept in perpetual motion for the good of the state."[39] His
vote so minuscule as not to have been recorded, Brown was
defeated in his bid for office, a circumstance reflecting the
times. In but a few scattered instances were blacks a political
factor during the eighteenth century, and black enfranchise-
ment in post-Revolutionary America was generally short-lived.
In fact after 1810 Thomas Brown himself could not even
have voted, Maryland having barred blacks from the polls as
of that year. Politically minded blacks could hope for little
when propertyless whites were subject to disfranchisement.[40]

Postwar blacks resorted to another form of political participation, the right to petition for redress of grievances. On
December 30, 1799, as the Revolutionary War era was drawing to a close, a group of seventy-four blacks from the Philadelphia area addressed a petition "To the President, Senate,
and House of Representatives," requesting abolition of the
overseas slave trade and modification of the fugitive slave law
so as to prevent the kidnapping of free blacks. The docu-

[39]*Baltimore Daily Repository*, Sept. 26, 1792.

[40]Indeed, down to the Civil War era blacks wielded little power as voters
except for a twenty-year span, 1800–1820, when the Federalist party wooed
their vote. See Dixon Ryan Fox, "The Negro Vote in Old New York," *Political Science Quarterly* 32 (1917):252–75. No black would hold elective office until 1854, when the voters of Oberlin, Ohio, chose John Mercer
Langston as township clerk.

ment concluded with a plea that blacks might "be admitted to partake of the liberties and unalienable rights" to which they were entitled.[41] Although invoking the language and the spirit of the Declaration of Independence and the Constitution, the appeal was couched in the most respectful and conciliatory of tones, and it issued from a city in which the Liberty Bell once had rung, heralding the birth of the new nation. But the House of Representatives did not prove to be liberation-minded; the Congressmen rejected the petition by a chilling vote of eighty-five to one.[42]

This rejection of Revolutionary principles, like others, did not deter blacks from pressing for the Revolution's goals of freedom and equality. Determined and patient, they would hardly have heeded J. R. Pole's observations that "revolutions by the nature of the historical process are always incomplete" and that a revolution tends to raise hopes that it cannot satisfy.[43] Blacks of the Revolutionary War era would have been more receptive to the contention of jurist Benjamin N. Cardozo that a principle has a tendency "to expand itself to the limit of its logic."[44] For them the war and the freedom concepts it sprouted bore their own seeds of regeneration.

In fine, the Revolutionary War can be termed a black Declaration of Independence in the sense it spurred black Americans to seek freedom and equality. The Afro-Americans of that era stood wholeheartedly among those who viewed the war as an ongoing revolution in freedom's cause. To a degree approaching unanimity, they clothed the War for Independence with a meaning and a significance transcending their own day and time and not confined to the shores of the new republic. To them the full worth of the American Revolution lay ahead.

[41]Petition in Porter, *Early Negro Writing*, pp. 330–32.

[42]U.S., Congress, House, *Congressional Record*, 6th Cong., Jan. 3, 1800, pp. 244–45.

[43]*The Pursuit of Equality in American History* (Berkeley, Calif., 1978), p. 325.

[44]*The Nature of the Judicial Process* (New Haven, 1932), p. 51, quoted in A. Leon Higginbotham, Jr., *In the Matter of Color: Race and the American Legal Process* (New York, 1978), pp. 383–84.

Contributors
Index

Contributors

IRA BERLIN teaches at the University of Maryland and directs the Freedmen and Southern Society Project, a documentary history of Civil War emancipation. He has written extensively on the antebellum South and on black life during slavery. In 1975 the National Historical Society awarded his study of southern free-men, *Slaves without Masters: The Free Negro in the Antebellum South*, its best-book award. In addition to his work on emancipation, he is currently completing a study of the southern urban working class.

DAVID BRION DAVIS is Sterling Professor of History at Yale University and was recently the first incumbent of the French-American Foundation Chair at the Ecole des Hautes Etudes en Sciences Sociales, Paris. His publications include *The Problem of Slavery in Western Culture* and *The Problem of Slavery in the Age of Revolution, 1770–1823*. He is currently completing a book, *Slavery and Human Progress*, and has received NEH research grants for *The Problem of Slavery in the Age of Emancipation*.

RICHARD S. DUNN is Professor of History at the University of Pennsylvania. His works include *Puritans and Yankees* (1962), *The Age of Religious Wars* (1971), and *Sugar and Slaves* (1972). He is currently engaged in two quite different projects: a four-volume edition of *The Papers of William Penn*, with Mary Maples Dunn, and a comparative study of slave life on a Virginia plantation and a Jamaica plantation between 1760 and 1860.

HERBERT G. GUTMAN is Distinguished Professor of History at the Graduate School and University Center of the City University of New York. Author of *The Black Family in Slavery and Freedom, 1750–1925*, Gutman is now examining the intersection between race, class, and "ethnicity" in the formation of nineteenth-century American class structure.

FRANKLIN W. KNIGHT is Professor of History at the Johns Hopkins

University. He has written extensively on the Caribbean and Latin America. His books include *Slave Society in Cuba during the Nineteenth Century* (1970), *The African Dimension in Latin American Societies* (1974), and *The Caribbean: The Genesis of a Fragmented Nationalism* (1978). He edits the Caribbean section of the Handbook of Latin American Studies and is currently preparing a study on Spanish-American creole society in Cuba during the late eighteenth century.

ALLAN KULIKOFF is Assistant Professor of History at Princeton University. He has published articles on slavery and on the economy and society of the eighteenth-century Chesapeake colonies, and his book on that topic, *Tobacco and Slaves: The Development of Southern Cultures in the Chesapeake Colonies, 1680–1780*, is forthcoming. His current research concerns the migration and transplanting of white and Afro-American cultures from the upper to the lower South between the Revolution and the Civil War.

DUNCAN J. MACLEOD is University Lecturer in American History at the University of Oxford and a Fellow of St. Catherine's College. His book *Slavery, Race and the American Revolution* was published in 1974.

PHILIP D. MORGAN is a Fellow at the Institute of Early American History and Culture, Williamsburg. He is completing a comparative study of slave life in eighteenth-century Virginia and South Carolina. His current research concerns the black experience in the late eighteenth- and early nineteenth-century Chesapeake.

GARY B. NASH is Professor of History at the University of California, Los Angeles. Among the books he has published are *Quakers and Politics: Pennsylvania, 1681–1726* (1968); *The Great Fear: Race in the Mind of America* (1970), edited with Richard Weiss; *Red, White and Black: The Peoples of Early America* (1974; 2d ed., 1982); *The Urban Crucible: Social Change, Political Consciousness, and the Origins of the American Revolution* (1979); and *Struggle and Survival in Colonial America* (1981), edited with David Sweet. He is currently working on a book on free black life in the northern cities after the American Revolution.

MARY BETH NORTON is Professor of American History at Cornell University. She is the author of *The British-Americans: The Loyalist Exiles in England, 1774–1789* (1972) and *Liberty's Daughters: The Revolutionary Experience of American Women, 1750–1800* (1980), the coauthor of *A People and a Nation* (1982), and is the coeditor of *Women of America: A History* (1979). Her current research interest is the history of women—black, white, and Indian—in colonial America.

BENJAMIN QUARLES is Professor of History, emeritus, at Morgan State University. His articles and books focus on the role of Afro-Americans in United States history. Included among these are *The Negro in the American Revolution* (1961), *Black Abolitionists* (1969), *The Negro in the Civil War* (1953), and the more popular *The Negro in the Making of America* (1964).

ALBERT J. RABOTEAU is Associate Professor of History and Afro-American Studies at the University of California, Berkeley. His first book was *Slave Religion: The "Invisible Institution" in the Antebellum South*. He is currently writing a general history of Afro-American religion.

Index

Abby (slave), 179
Abner (slave), 137
Ackee, 250
Adams, John, 225, 242–43
African Baptist Church (Williamsburg), 206–7
African culture, in the lowcountry, 129, 132–33
African Lodge No. 459, 298–99
African Methodist Episcopal Church, 212
African Society (Boston), 297
African Society (Providence), 297
African Union Society (Newport, R.I.), 297
Allen, Richard, 41, 211–12, 296–98
Allison, James, 140
All Saints Parish, S.C., 93
Amelia County, Va., 58, 62, 66, 67, 69
Amherst County, Va., 66–67, 70–71
Anderson (slave), 183
Andrew (driver), 109, 110, 120
Anstey, Roger, 249
Anthony (slave), 181
Anthony, Old, 181
Antigua, 243, 246
Antislavery, 50, 52, 77, 275–77
Armistead (slave), 182
Asbury, Francis, 198–99, 211
Augusta County, Va., 62
Austin (slave), 183

Bahamas, 246
Ball, Charles, 98, 157–59
Baltimore, 75
Bannaky, 289
Banneker, Benjamin, 289
Baptists, 195–98, 200–203, 277
Barbados, 243, 245, 247
Barnaby (slave), 177
Barrow, David, 197
Bear Creek Quarter, 182

Beck (slave), 187
Bell, Graham, 189
Benedict, David, 195–96
Benevolent societies, black, 44–47, 297–98
Benezet, Anthony, 276, 288
Bennehan, Richard, 177, 188
Berlin, Ira, 20, 235–36, 287, 295
Bermuda, 246
Bess, Old, 181
Bet (runaway), 190
Bethel African Methodist Church (Philadelphia), 212, 296
Betty (slave), 185
Bishop, Jacob, 204
Black culture: in the lowcountry, 133–38; in the lower South, 162–67
Black population: in British North American mainland colonies, 217–18; in the Chesapeake, 54, 56, 58–59, 61–63, 65–66; in northern cities, 4, 6, 8, 11–12, 220
Blacks: acculturation of, 285–89; military service, 291–92
Bligh, William, Comdr., 250–51
Bob (slave), 187
Boston: black population in, 4, 6, 11–12; free black family in, 31, 34–35, 38–39; slave family in, 28
Bray, Henry, 9
Breadfruit, 251
Brown, Thomas, 300
Brown Fellowship Society (Charleston), 297
Bryan, Andrew, 210–11
Bull, William, 110
Butler, Eleanor, 190–91
Butler, Mary, 190–91
Butler, William, 190–91

Calvert, Charles, 190–91
Cardozo, Benjamin N., 301

INDEX

Caribbean colonies: economic dependence on North American mainland, 242–45; food production in, 243–44, 250–51; impact of the American Revolution upon, 237–40, 246–57, 259–61, 264–65; slave population in, 263; sugar production in, 243

Carroll, Charles, of Annapolis, 175–76

Carroll, Charles, of Carrollton, 176

Carter, Farish, 153

Carter, Robert, 74, 176, 185

Cary (slave), 184

Cate (slave), 179, 182

Census returns, for information on Chesapeake slavery, 52–54

Charles County, Md., 61, 65

Chesapeake: antislavery movement in the, 50, 52, 77; black population in the, 54, 56, 58–59, 61–63, 65–66; economy of the, 51; first families in the, 71–74; free black population in the, 62, 74–75, 77–80; manumission in the, 74–75, 80; slaveholding in the, 66–74; slave population in the, 62–63, 65–66

Churches, black, 43–47, 206–13, 295–96

Clinton, Henry, Sir, 271, 291

Coke, Thomas, 198–99

Colonies, types of, 240–42

Constituent Assembly, 257

Conucos, 243, 250

Cotton, 271–72, 275; cultivation of, 106–7

Covington, Alexander, 155–56

Covington, Leonard, 151, 155–56

Cretia (slave), 183

Crow, Jeffrey J., 286

Cuba, 243, 255

Curtin, Philip D., 169

Daniel (slave), 183

Davidson County, Tenn., 161

Davis, David Brion, 259

Degler, Carl, 234

Demerara, 271–72

Dick (slave), 113

Dislocation, slave, during the Revolution, 144–45; in the lowcountry, 110–13

Dominica, 246

Doohoregan Manor, 182

Dover Baptist Association, 200

Drayton, John, 98

Drescher, Seymour, 249, 268

Drivers, black, 118–20

Du Bois, W. E. B., 14, 43

Dunmore, Lord, 233, 291

Edwards, Bryan, 243–44

Elizabeth City County, Va., 77–78

Emancipation, 277–80; in Massachusetts, 11; in New York, 11; in Pennsylvania, 11

Emancipation Act, 279

Engerman, Stanley L., 264, 277

Evangelicals, 194–97; and black churches, 206–7; and black preachers, 203–6; and slave discipline, 200–201; and slave marriage, 201–2; and slavery, 197–200

Evans, Henry, 205

Eve (slave), 182

Family, free black, in northern cities, 27, 31–35, 38–40

Family, slave, 177–89; in the lowcountry, 124–25, 127, 129; in northern cities, 27–28, 30–31

Fauquier County, Va., 66, 67, 70–71

Federalists, 270

First African Church (Augusta, Ga.), 210

Fitzpatrick, John, 163

Flora (slave), 183

Flora, Old, 181

Florida, 264

Fogel, Robert W., 277

Foner, Eric, 275

Foster, Thomas, 164

Frederick County, Md., 58

Frederick County, Va., 59, 62, 66, 67, 70–71

Free African Society (Philadelphia), 297

Free black migration, to northern cities, 4, 6, 8–12, 14–15

INDEX

Books published by the University of Illinois Press
in the series *Blacks in the New World*

Before the Ghetto: Black Detroit in the Nineteenth Century
David M. Katzman

Black Business in the New South: A Social History of the North Carolina
Mutual Life Insurance Company *Walter B. Weare*

The Search for a Black Nationality: Black Colonization and Emigration,
1787–1863 *Floyd J. Miller*

Black Americans and the White Man's Burden, 1898–1903
Willard B. Gatewood, Jr.

Slavery and the Numbers Game: A Critique of *Time on the Cross*
Herbert G. Gutman

A Ghetto Takes Shape: Black Cleveland, 1870–1930
Kenneth L. Kusmer

Freedmen, Philanthropy, and Fraud: A History of the Freedman's Savings
Bank *Carl R. Osthaus*

The Democratic Party and the Negro: Northern and National Politics,
1868–92 *Lawrence Grossman*

Black Ohio and the Color Line, 1860–1915 *David A. Gerber*

Along the Color Line: Explorations in the Black Experience
August Meier and Elliott Rudwick

Black over White: Negro Political Leadership in South Carolina during
Reconstruction *Thomas Holt*

Keeping the Faith: A. Philip Randolph, Milton P. Webster, and the
Brotherhood of Sleeping Car Porters, 1925–37 *William H. Harris*

Abolitionism: The Brazilian Antislavery Struggle
Joaquim Nabuco, translated and edited by Robert Conrad

Black Georgia in the Progressive Era, 1900–1920
John Dittmer

Medicine and Slavery: Health Care of Blacks in Antebellum
Virginia *Todd L. Savitt*

Alley Life in Washington: Family, Community, Religion, and Folklife in
the City, 1850–1970 *James Borchert*

Human Cargoes: The British Slave Trade to Spanish America,
1700–1739 *Colin A. Palmer*

Southern Black Leaders of the Reconstruction Era
Edited by Howard N. Rabinowitz

Black Leaders of the Twentieth Century
Edited by John Hope Franklin and August Meier

Slaves and Missionaries: The Disintegration of Jamaican Slave Society,
1787–1834 *Mary Turner*

Father Divine and the Struggle for Racial Equality
Robert Weisbrot

Communists in Harlem during the Depression
Mark Naison

Down from Equality: Black Chicagoans and the Public Schools,
1920–41 *Michael W. Homel*

Race and Kinship in a Midwestern Town: The Black Experience in
Monroe, Michigan, 1900–1915 *James E. DeVries*

Down by the Riverside: A South Carolina Slave Community
Charles Joyner

Black Milwaukee: The Making of an Industrial Proletariat, 1915–45
Joe William Trotter, Jr.

Religious Philanthropy and Colonial Slavery: The American
Correspondence of the Associates of Dr. Bray, 1717–1777
John C. Van Horne

Black History and the Historical Profession, 1915–80
August Meier and Elliott Rudwick

Rise to Be a People: A Biography of Paul Cuffe
Lamont D. Thomas

Making Their Own Way: Southern Blacks' Migration to Pittsburgh,
1916–30 *Peter Gottlieb*

Reprint Editions

King: A Biography
David Levering Lewis Second Edition

The Death and Life of Malcolm X
Peter Goldman Second Edition

Race Relations in the Urban South, 1865–1890
Howard N. Rabinowitz, with a Foreword by C. Vann Woodward

Race Riot at East St. Louis, July 2, 1917
Elliott Rudwick

W. E. B. Du Bois: Voice of the Black Protest Movement
Elliott Rudwick

The Negro's Civil War: How American Negroes Felt and Acted during
the War for the Union *James M. McPherson*   .

Lincoln and Black Freedom: A Study in Presidential Leadership
LaWanda Cox

Slavery and Freedom in the Age of the American Revolution
Edited by Ira Berlin and Ronald Hoffman